HOW THERA

HOW THERAPISTS ACT

Cases Combining Major Approaches to Psychotherapy and the Adaptive Counseling and Therapy Model

Don W. Nance and Associates

ACCELERATED DEVELOPMENT
A member of the Taylor & Francis Group

USA	Publishing Office:	ACCELERATED DEVELOPMENT
		A member of the Taylor & Francis Group
		1101 Vermont Ave., N.W., Suite 200
		Washington, DC 20005
		Tel: (202) 289-2174
		Fax: (202) 289-3665
	Distribution Center:	ACCELERATED DEVELOPMENT
		A member of the Taylor & Francis Group
		1900 Frost Road, Suite 101
		Bristol, PA 19007-1598
		Tel: (215) 785-5800
		Fax: (215) 785-5515
UK		Taylor & Francis, Ltd.
		4 John Street
		London WC1N 2ET
		Tel: 071 405 2237
		Fax: 071 831 2035

HOW THERAPISTS ACT: Cases Combining Major Approaches to Psychotherapy and the Adaptive Counseling and Therapy Model

Copyright © 1995 Taylor & Francis. All rights reserved. Printed in the United States of America. Except as permitted under the United States Copyright Act of 1976, no part of this publication may be reproduced or distributed in any form or by any means, or stored in a database or retrieval system, without prior written permission from the publisher.

1 2 3 4 5 6 7 8 9 0 BRBR 0 9 8 7 6 5

This book was set in Times Roman by Princeton Editorial Associates. Technical development and editing by Cynthia Long. Prepress supervisor was Miriam Gonzalez. Cover design by Douglas Pickarts. Printing and binding by Braun-Brumfield, Inc.

A CIP catalog record for this book is available from the British Library.
♾ The paper in this publication meets the requirements of the ANSI Standard Z39.48-1984 (Permanence of Paper)

Library of Congress Cataloging-in-Publication Data

How therapists ACT : cases combining major approaches to psychotherapy and the
    adaptive counseling and therapy model / [edited by] Don W. Nance and associates.
       p. cm.
    Includes bibliographical references and index.

    1. Psychotherapy. 2. Psychotherapy—Case studies. I. Nance, Don.
    [DNLM: 1. Counseling—methods. 2. Psychotherapy—methods. 3. Models,
Psychological. WM 55 H847 1995]
RC480.5.H687 1995
616.89'14—dc20
DNLM/DLC
for Library of Congress   94-49231
                                                      CIP

ISBN 1-56032-410-4 (case)
ISBN 1-56032-390-6 (paper)

TABLE OF CONTENTS

LIST OF FIGURES	ix
PREFACE	xi

CHAPTER 1
GETTING READY: INTRODUCTION AND OVERVIEW   1
Don W. Nance

Key Concepts of ACT	3
Selection Process for Orientations and Authors	7
Limitations/Restrictions in Range	12
Recommendations for Reading	14
References	17

CHAPTER 2
COGNITIVE-BEHAVIOR THERAPY AND ACT   19
Jerry L. Deffenbacher

Cognitive-Behavioral Approaches to Counseling	19
Relationship of ACT to CBT	22
Bill: A Case of High Anger	26
Summary and Reflection	47
References	49
Comments	51
Questions	53

vi *Table of Contents*

CHAPTER 3
HUMANISTIC PSYCHOTHERAPY AND ACT 55
Willis D. Poland

Personal Statement	55
Elements of a Humanistic Orientation	57
Perspective on Readiness	59
Therapeutic Interventions	61
Kevin: A Case of Internal Conflict	62
Closing Reflections	76
Bibliography	78
Comments	79
Questions	82

CHAPTER 4
TIME-LIMITED PSYCHODYNAMIC COUNSELING
AND ACT 83
Steven B. Robbins and Karen P. Lese

Mann's Three Stage Model	84
Commonalities Between Mann and ACT	87
Curtis: A Case of Measuring Up	87
Conclusion	98
References	100
Comments	101
Questions	103

CHAPTER 5
SYSTEMS THEORY AND ACT 105
Pennie Myers

Systems Theory and ACT: A Successful Marriage	106
The Schools of Family Therapy	107
The Process of Family Therapy	109
Greg and Suzanne: A Case of Public Commitment	110
Commitment to an Integrative Systemic Approach	122
References	123
Comments	126
Questions	128

Table of Contents **vii**

CHAPTER 6
AN ECLECTIC APPROACH TO COUNSELING WOMEN 129
Eileen T. Nickerson

Theoretical Perspectives	129
Selection of Clients	131
Marie: Movement out from a Cloistered Life	131
Lily: Movement out of the Past	140
Marie and Lily: Some Comparisons	146
Reflections on ACT	147
Bibliography	151
Comments	153
Questions	155

CHAPTER 7
DEVELOPMENTAL ECLECTIC COUNSELING
WITH MEN 157
Gordon M. Hart

Developmental Issues for Men	159
David: A Case of High Expectations	162
Conclusions and Reflections	180
References	182
Comments	185
Questions	187

CHAPTER 8
UPDATING ACT 189
Don W. Nance

Organizing vs. Integrating	189
ACT—A Compatible Additive	190
Style 1—In the Structure vs. the Interaction	190
Style 2—Teach Them to Fish	191
Style 3—Home Base for the Outpatient Therapist	192
Style 4—What Doesn't Need Attention	192
Assessing Client Readiness—Just Ask	193
Redefining the Tasks, Reassessing Readiness	193
Therapist Readiness	194

viii *Table of Contents*

Range in Style/Range in Content: Generalist vs. Specialist and
    Individual vs. Team   196

INDEX   199
ABOUT THE AUTHOR   207

LIST OF FIGURES

Figure 1.   Therapist dimensions and styles.   4

Figure 2.   Client readiness.   6

Figure 3.   Matching therapist style and client readiness.   8

PREFACE

Let's be honest. The preface is in the front of the book, but it's written last. Anyone who has completed a book can identify with the mixture of relief and grief present at this point in the process. The need to polish just once more competes with the need to get it to the publisher until the balance tips to the completion side. To be able to say it is finished brings a sense of a vacuum left by completing a project that literally has been years in the making.

To the chapter contributors who agreed to work with me on this endeavor, I owe a debt of gratitude-for their willingness, for their abilities, and for their patience. I hope they and you will agree that the revisions and reworking involved in bringing this book to press were worth it. Certainly my sense of community and colleagueship was enriched in the process. The chapter contributors are the essential ingredient in a unique book. The approach to developing the tone and content of *How Therapists ACT* was guided by a vision of what was wanted and a sense of what to avoid.

A primary, overarching goal was to develop a book that is realistic in claims, in content, and in tone. ACT is a very useful model and a limited one. Organizing the book to demonstrate compatibility with major approaches validates a spirit of cooperation rather than competition. Little to no time, energy, or space is spent knocking other models or theories. The cases presented are not unusual, bizarre, or headline making. The clients were all struggling with some issues in their lives and sought counseling services. Similarly, the therapists are not flashy; rather, solidly competent. The single brilliant intervention that changed the client forever is missing from these pages. A desired outcome from reading the book is that you feel more competent, more confident, and thus more ready as a therapist as

xii *Preface*

opposed to feeling more inadequate in the face of such brilliant moves described by the author/therapists.

As soon as I was free to seek a publisher for the manuscript, I wrote one letter—to Joe Hollis, publisher at Accelerated Development. My impression, since confirmed, was that realistic, practical books held a special place in Accelerated Development's publishing priorities. I was impressed by Joe's willingness to operate informally and in an atmosphere of mutual trust and respect. His insights regarding structure and emphasis were freely given and warmly received. I have felt like a valued member of the publication team.

The goals and purpose in developing *How Therapists ACT* suggest the intended readerships of students in the helping professions and those professionals already applying their professional skills. Graduate education, in any of the helping professions, involves selecting texts to inform and promote the student's professional development. The organizing use of ACT, the major approaches, the cases, and the questions provide important perspectives when considering theories or techniques on how all the information fits together. Ours is/are professions in which the degree is truly a license to learn, as well as to practice. The hope is that colleagues in practical, service delivery settings will find the book interesting and informative. ACT, with its emphases on tasks, readiness, and matching treatments with clients, may become increasingly useful in the emerging changes in mental health delivery systems. As another step in the development and refinement of ACT, I'm proud to present *How Therapists ACT.*

Don W. Nance
March 1995

Chapter 1

GETTING READY: INTRODUCTION AND OVERVIEW

Don W. Nance
Wichita State University

What am I going to do?
How should I behave?
How am I supposed to act?

These questions could be voiced by a beginning practicum student in anticipation of meeting with a "real live" client for the first time. The questions also could be asked by a master therapist with years of successful experience. The questions and the issues reflected by the questions are fundamental constants for therapists. The basic questions have a myriad of variations. The experienced therapist, for example, may not share the practicum student's concern for "What do I do if the client doesn't talk?" and "How do I explain the tape recorder?" Questions about how to behave in therapy take a variety of forms:

Do I listen attentively and offer support?
Do I confront?
Do I inform, educate, instruct, or teach?
Do I self-disclose?
Should I initiate a topic?
Should I shift the focus?

2 *Don W. Nance*

Should I follow the client's lead?
If I am able to do all these behaviors, when do I do what?

The Adaptive Counseling and Therapy model offers a systematic way of answering questions about what behaviors are likely to be therapeutic in a clinical situation. More easily identified by its acronym, ACT, the model is aptly named since it focuses on how therapists *act* or behave in therapy. The central tenet of ACT is that to be effective with a range of clients and problems the therapist needs to adapt his/her behavior to fit the client.

ACT is a relative newcomer among the models and theories used by mental health professionals. As such, some relevant issues need to be explored. One issue concerns exclusivity. You may ask questions such as, "Do I have to give up my preferred theoretical orientation(s) to use ACT?" and "Can I integrate ACT concepts into my existing framework and methods?" From its initial published presentation, ACT has been presented as an integrative metatheoretical model (Howard, Nance, & Myers, 1986). Fundamental to such a claim is the ability of ACT both to integrate or organize a variety of theoretical perspectives and to demonstrate its utility to those practitioners operating from within a particular theoretical perspective. In terms common to research design, the question becomes, "Can the utility of the model be demonstrated both *between* theoretical perspectives and *within* a given theoretical orientation?"

The organizing theme of this book is to illustrate how practitioners utilized the ACT model in clinical practice while operating from *within* a generally recognized theoretical perspective. The use of cases enables the reader to experience vicariously the myriad of choice points in the process of counseling. The chapters demonstrate how the ACT model is used to identify the most appropriate therapist behaviors in particular situations. In each chapter, the contributing author brings to the surface important aspects of processes that frequently are internal. How does the therapist conceptualize the client, the issues, and the goals of treatment? How does the therapist develop a plan for the course of therapy? Through the use of verbatim transcripts and summarized dialogue, the reader has an opportunity to gain insight into how the plans are carried out.

The purposes of this initial chapter are to provide an orientation to the organization of the book, a brief overview of the ACT model, the rationale for the selection of orientations and authors, and an acknowledgement of limitations and restrictions. The accomplishment of these tasks will increase your readiness to read each of the remaining chapters. Each chapter illustrates the use of a major theoretical approach with particular aspects of ACT and identifies how ACT assists in the treatment process. Each chapter is unique in tone and style reflective of both the contributing author and the orientation being presented. No attempt was made to homogenize the various approaches or to remove the differences in writing style and emphasis.

KEY CONCEPTS OF ACT

Therapist behaviors can be organized into two dimensions. The *direction* dimension deals with task definition and accomplishment. What's the problem? What needs to change? What is involved in the process of change? How is the progress determined? Other terms sometimes associated with this dimension are "task" and "structure." *Support* is the second dimension. Support behaviors of a therapist include all the "core conditions" of caring, empathy, positive regard, and nonverbal attending behaviors. Positive and negative reinforcement also are elements of this dimension. Other terms sometimes include "relationship," "social-emotional support," and "caring."

Both dimensions are continuums. Effective counseling situations require 100% of *direction* (answering the task/structure questions of What? How? Who? When? Where? and Why?) and 100% of *support* (providing attention, concern, empathy, feedback, and reinforcement). Treatment decisions are based on the answers to the questions: How much direction and how much support are supplied by the client? How much by the counselor? Over the course of therapy, what changes is the source(s) of the direction and support/reinforcement. Fundamental to the process is allowing the client to utilize his or her own resources as much as possible. The counselor need only provide as much direction and support as is required to assist the client in his or her progress toward internalized, independent functioning with regard to particular counseling goals. In Figure 1 the two dimensions, direction and support are divided at each midpoint creating four quadrants of styles. This categorization of these continuous dimensions is intended to aid understanding, application, and research. The four quadrants are labeled by the styles associated with each: *Style 1—Telling,* when the therapist's behavior is very directive with little support; *Style 2—Teaching,* when the therapist offers high amounts of both direction and support; *Style 3—Supporting,* when the supportive behaviors of the therapists predominate over any directive elements; and *Style 4— Delegating,* when the therapist provides little support and little direction, thereby delegating the direction and support responsibilities to the client.

The various options for actions available to a therapist can be characterized as having varying degrees of direction and support. The behavior of the psychoanalyst during free association is low in both direction and support (S 4). Prototypic

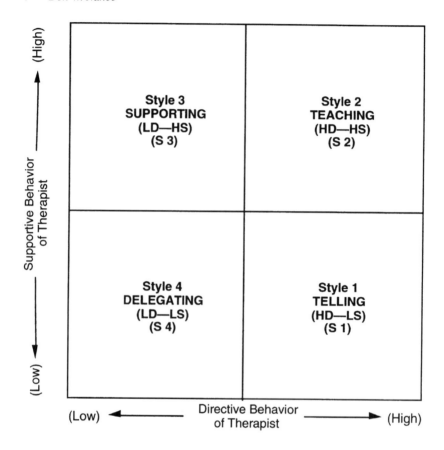

Figure 1. Therapist dimensions and styles.

client-centered behavior is high on support and low on direction (S 3). The instructive teaching of various cognitive behavioral methods is high on direction and also may be high on support and positive reinforcement (S 2). The clear contingencies of a behavioral modification program or the confrontation of denial in chemical dependency treatment is likely to be high on therapist direction and low on therapist support (S 1).

Thus far, the two dimensions of therapist behavior, direction and support, have been identified, and the four styles of therapist behavior have been described and illustrated briefly. Now let's turn the focus to the client. **Client readiness** is another of the key concepts in ACT. The therapist adapts his/her style based on the assessment of how ready the client is to accomplish the counseling task at hand.

The therapeutic goal may be to get a job, choose a major, differentiate from enmeshed family of origin, be less anxious or less depressed, or be more responsible. Client readiness is likely to vary depending on the task.

The three components of readiness are willingness, ability and confidence. These components are not independent of each other. A client's confidence may impact willingness. Increases in ability may build confidence and increase willingness.

Willingness is the client's current motivation for working on the therapeutic task. Is the client eager to change? Ambivalent? Resisting? Coerced? *Ability* is the client's current ability level on the task. Information, knowledge, and skills are aspects of ability. If the task is to get a job, one client (by experience, training, and connections) may be quite able to accomplish the job search task, while another hasn't got a clue about where to start and what to do. One client may be eager to engage in the job search, while another may be resistant to the search process. The amounts of direction and support from the therapist need to be different depending on each client's level of current ability and willingness. If the task requires abilities or skills the client is incapable of developing, then the task/goal and/or the path to the goal need to be reevaluated.

The client's own view of his or her ability to be successful at the task is one way to view the third component of readiness—*confidence.* How does the client's view match the therapist's impressions? Does the client's confidence match with ability? Is confidence unrealistically high or too low? How does confidence impact the client's willingness?

The three components of client readiness are displayed in Figure 2 in various combinations. The readiness dimension ranges from willing, able, and confident at the high end (R 4) to unable, unwilling, and unconfident at the low end (R 1). Also presented in Figure 2 are the *developmental cycle* and the *regressive cycle.* If the client is becoming more willing, able, and/or confident, the movement is in a developmental direction toward R 4. The regressive cycle represents those instances when the client's readiness is decreasing or moving backwards. Decreases in readiness most often are tied to changes in confidence or motivation. If ability seems to have decreased, it may be that the task has changed.

The basic therapeutic mechanisms for the therapist are

1. to increase ability, provide direction, and support while teaching skills.
2. to address unwillingness on critical, essential tasks, use direction, power, and contingencies. If lacking power or contingencies, the thera-

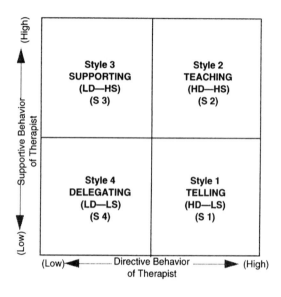

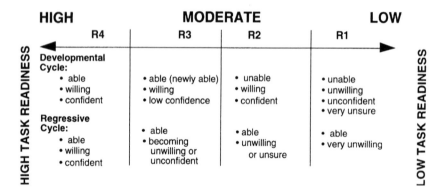

Figure 2. Client readiness.

pist should choose not to work on those tasks for which the client is unmotivated.
3. to develop confidence, use support, feedback, and increased ability.

The ACT concept of ***match and move*** is illustrated in Figure 3 by the vertical arrows that go from readiness level to a corresponding therapist style. If the client's readiness for the task is R 2, willing but unable, the therapist style of choice is to teach using high direction and high support. That's the *match*. The *move* takes place by systematically altering the amounts of direction and support as the client's readiness increases. The bell shaped curved line in Figure 3 represents this process. Movement in a developmental direction is actually a step-wise process of reducing direction while increasing support through Styles 1 and 2 and reducing both direction and support through Styles 3 and 4. The movement is forward or backward *one* step or style at a time. The client who is regressing from functioning independently, R 4, with the therapist providing little attention, direction, or support to the topic or task (S 4) is likely to need an increase in support (S 3) rather than lots of direction (S 1).

SELECTION PROCESS FOR
ORIENTATIONS AND AUTHORS

The major theoretical orientations within the helping professions are included here—cognitive behavioral, humanistic, and psychodynamic. Those selections are supported by surveys reported in the literature (Zook & Walton, 1989). The systems orientation also is included. This orientation is central to marriage and family therapy work and increasingly employed by mental health practitioners across academic disciplines. Additionally, much of mental health, particularly counseling psychology, is rooted in the developmental perspective and two chapters are included using a developmental conceptual framework. Thus, the orientations and authors to be presented are

Cognitive Behavioral—Jerry Deffenbacher
Psychodynamic—Steve Robbins and Karen Lese
Humanistic—Willis Poland
Developmental Issues: Women—Eileen Nickerson
Systems—Pennie Myers
Developmental Issues: Men—Gordon Hart

The two chapters on the developmental issues for women and for men represent another major theoretical perspective—eclectic. The question of whether eclectic can be considered a "theory" and the debate over conceptual purity vs. eclecticism (Nance & Myers, 1991) do not alter the fact that many practitioners apply the eclectic label to identify their theoretical orientation. The psychodynamic and humanistic threads in Eileen Nickerson's chapter (Chapter 6) are apparent and acknowledged. Similarly, Gordon Hart uses an awareness of the developmental issues for men to conceptualize the client (Chapter 7). He then employs concepts and interventions associated with a systems orientation and

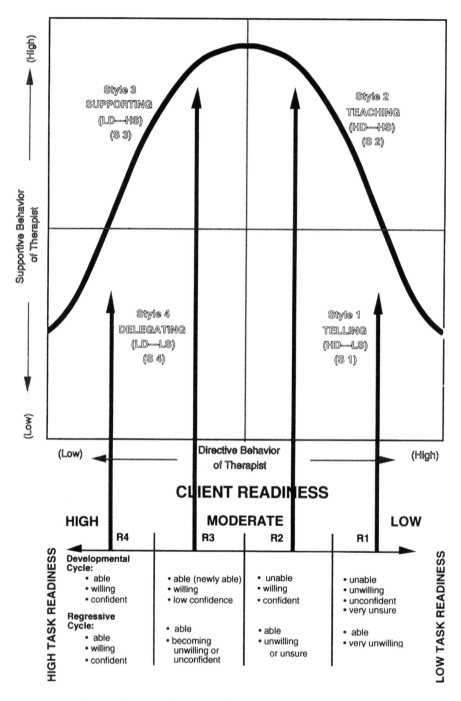

Figure 3. Matching therapist style and client readiness.

with humanistic/existential approaches. Aspects of behavioral/environmental modification are evident also in the course of treatment.

Having gained a brief exposure to the ACT model and to the orientations included, a discussion of the process for selecting contributing authors offers an opportunity to use concepts central to the model. Consistent with the ACT concept of readiness, contributing authors were selected based on a mutual assessment of their readiness to accomplish the task of illustrating the use of ACT within their identified theoretical orientation. Examining the role of each component of readiness will provide an opportunity to apply ACT concepts to this critical task in developing this book.

Ability Component of Readiness

The initial conceptualization of the task was the organizing author's. Identification of the *ability* components essential to the task is a critical element in assessing readiness. As is frequently found using ACT, many of those readiness components are apparent or obvious once the task is clearly identified. If the task is integrating the use of a particular theoretical orientation with ACT and illustrating that integration with a clinical case example, then all contributing authors need (1) to be actively practicing therapists, (2) to have expertise in a particular theoretical perspective, and (3) to have integrated the ACT model into their counseling. Each element of the task became a selection criteria.

Criteria 1: Actively practicing counselors/therapists. Establishing this criteria ensured that all contributors would have access to recent/current client case material. The cases would not be a rehash of old or previously published materials but would be fresh in the author's awareness. In most instances, access to recordings for transcription was possible. All the authors have academic affiliations, thus none are full-time therapists. The organizing author made no attempt to systematically vary the setting in which the contributing authors practice by seeking out private practitioners or full-time agency therapists. The restriction in setting probably is related to the other criteria.

Criteria 2: Experts in their chosen theoretical perspective. Each author was very able to operate within his/her identified theoretical perspective. Jerry Deffenbacher (1988) and Steve Robbins (1989) have both written extensively in the literature on cognitive-behavioral and psychodynamic approaches, respectively. Eileen Nickerson was instrumental in founding the counseling women's emphasis within the graduate program at Boston University. She has written extensively on developmental and women's issues and action therapies, as well as

10   *Don W. Nance*

mentored many women entering the field (Nickerson & O'Laughlin, 1982). Gordon Hart's (1982) ability to present on the developmental issues for men arises from both his clinical practice and his professional study on the topic. Willis Poland has taught, practiced, supervised, modeled, and lived from a humanistic perspective. He shares a bit of that history with readers in his chapter. Pennie Myers (1984, 1991) operates from a systemic orientation, particularly in her work with couples and families. As one of the developers of ACT, she is very able as well on the third criteria.

Criteria 3: Knowledge and use of ACT.   All the contributing authors were aware of ACT from the initial publication regarding the model, if not before. In the years between 1986 and the writing of his or her chapter, each author integrated the concepts of ACT into his or her clinical work with clients. In one critique of ACT, Kelly (1988) stated "The best feature about ACT is that it makes sense and seems to represent how counselors work" (p. 212). Many of the authors echo that ACT helped describe or conceptualize what each had been doing clinically for many years. Authors also used the model to predict or select intervention strategies for use with clients to stimulate movement toward therapeutic goals. Obviously all the authors find the model helpful and are willing to associate themselves professionally with the use of ACT. Each author offers an individual assessment of ACT as a part of his or her contribution. Potential contributing authors could meet all the ability criteria and still not write a word. Another component of readiness was also critically important—Were they willing?

Willingness Component of Readiness

A second component of readiness is *willingness.* A person's willingness to engage in a task, whether therapeutic or professional, is tied to some source of motivation. The client may be motivated to change by psychological discomfort or pain. When the pain is relieved the motivation may disappear with a subsequent disappearance of the client from treatment. A client may be motivated to avoid some external consequence. "Go to alcohol treatment or lose your job" may initially have a client more motivated by the threat than the treatment. The client may be motivated to develop increased skills and competencies, gain understanding, or receive support, attention, and approval from the counselor.

Each contributing author had to be willing to write his or her chapter. No significant external rewards or sanctions were available to be dispensed. Promises of great wealth or fame were not made. Threats such as not receiving tenure without this publication are not relevant to already tenured professionals. Some professional recognition may be anticipated from their participation, since most authors are in settings where writing and publishing is valued. All the authors expressed internal motives for their involvement. Most were attracted to the organizing theme of the book. The potential usefulness of the book for both practicing professionals and students was a motivator. It is likely some authors were influenced by a positive relationship with me, while for others no significant professional relationship or friendship existed prior to the project.

The willingness component is not static. It is impacted by the success or the lack of progress, by the motivation level of the other person (e.g., the high degree of professional burnout among counselors treating unwilling clients such as in court-referred, mandated situations), and by the nature of the counselor/client relationship. My initial motivation for the book was significantly increased by the clear willingness expressed by contributing authors to participate.

Confidence Component of Readiness

Confidence, the third component of readiness, was a bit more variable among the authors than willingness or ability. Certainly the range was only from moderate to very high. To have sold or cajoled a potential author with low confidence into participating in the project would have meant I was agreeing to assume an active, high support/high direction involvement, a role I was unwilling to assume. High confidence is evident when an author says

> I'm very familiar with the ACT model and excited about the project. The case I have in mind has just been completed, and the tapes are still available to select portions for transcription. Looking at my schedule, I can complete a draft by the scheduled date. Usually the initial draft I send is in pretty good shape. We'll touch base after you review it.

The author then proceeded to do precisely what was promised, thereby validating the high level of confidence.

When confidence issues were involved for contributing authors, it often was related to a characteristic of their task that may or may not be present in a counseling context. The need to clarify and understand what I wanted may have some parallel to the client wanting to perform to the therapist's expectations. A proposed outline gave initial direction. Those directions were modified in the process of the project by both the contributing authors and me. Each contributing author needed to have feedback to questions. Is this what you had in mind? How does my chapter fit or compare to the others? I occasionally was in the awkward position of saying, "You did exactly what I asked. Now these changes need to be made."

12 *Don W. Nance*

The authors sometimes initiated changes. The messages were as follows:

"I tried following the outline, and this part just didn't work." This resulted in various requests of me.

On some occasions, little or no direction or support was requested (Style 4). "So I wrote it another way that seems to work better."

At other times, the request was for support (with direction optional) (Style 3). "I added a section. Let me read it to you. Hope you like it."

A request for direction and support (Style 2) took the form of "I'm having trouble with this. Give me some ideas about how to proceed."

A request for Style 1 would be "I have no idea what to do here and don't want to spend a lot of energy figuring it out. Tell me what to do, and I'll do it."

The exact form of support varied for each author. Supporting one author came in the form of encouragement for "coloring outside the lines," i.e., modifying the structure of the chapter. Support for another was affirming how the case was conceptualized using ACT, while for a third, support addressed writing clarity and style.

Varying therapist direction and or support is a central concept of ACT. If the therapist is providing various amounts of direction and support, how does he or she know whether the amounts of direction and/or support provided are appropriate? As discussed in more detail in Howard, Nance, and Myers (1987), signs of receiving too little support are discouragement, loss of enthusiasm, and feeling neglected and not attended to. Too much support can result in dependency and a transfer of responsibility for the task. Too little direction results in floundering, frustration, and false starts. The fact that initial drafts of these chapters were all "in the ball park" suggested that initial direction was adequate. The signs of providing too much direction include resistance to direction and suggestions, and control conflicts. Although authors may have "questioned my parentage" immediately upon receiving editorial comments, an appropriate match was indicated by the consistently positive and thoughtful responses these authors gave to editorial suggestions.

LIMITATIONS/RESTRICTIONS IN RANGE

Experimental design provides an analogy for interpreting several limitations and restrictions in range evident in this book. The independent variable for the book was to systematically vary the theoretical orientations of the chapters. Therefore, a few dimensions, such as form or setting of treatment, were held

Introduction and Overview **13**

constant, while the variability of other dimensions, such as length of treatment and client demographic characteristics, were not systematically controlled.

All counseling was conducted on an outpatient basis. In ACT terms, outpatient treatment is characterized at the form level of treatment as more supportive (F 3) than consultation (F 4) and less directive/structured than either programmatic treatments (F 2), such as programs for chemical dependency, eating disorders, sexual offenders, or institutional treatments (F 1) frequently involving hospitalization of some kind. ACT concepts and principles are very applicable in these other forms of treatment but are simply beyond the scope of this book. Restricting the form of treatment presented to outpatients matches the most frequent type of treatment conducted by counselors, social workers, and psychologists.

Several restrictions in range flow from the decision to limit the form of treatment to outpatient psychotherapy. All the clients described in the chapters were appropriate for outpatient treatment. None were psychotic. All were employed or readily employable. All were essentially self-referred for counseling. None were court ordered or remanded for treatment. The overall willingness of the clients to be in counseling means that Style 1—Telling, appropriate for unwilling and unable clients, is least frequently demonstrated directly in the transcripts.

In voluntary, outpatient treatment, S 1 is more likely to occur as the therapist defines for the client *how* the counseling will take place even while agreeing to the client's view of what initial topics receive attention. In the process of reading the cases, take note of how the time-limited psychodynamic approach, used by Robbins and Lese, communicates to the client: "As therapist, I will (1) decide if you are an appropriate candidate for this treatment; (2) limit the number of sessions; and (3) identify the central therapeutic issue around which therapy will focus." Note also how Gordon Hart accepts the client's initial definition of the problem while telling the client the path of counseling will not be smooth or solely rational. If those parameters are not agreeable to the client, treatment does not proceed. If the client agrees to those basic conditions, then the treatment process itself may contain very little Style 1.

The demographic characteristics of those clients presented are essentially random (not controlled) variation. These clients, in aggregate, seem to represent a range on some typical demographic dimensions. The clients presented range in age from 20s to 50s, and in family socioeconomic background from working class to upper middle class. Ethnic roots were important and attended to in some instances and not in others. Career interests, if measured, would likely range through most of Holland's types (Holland, 1966). Marital/relationship status includes single, engaged, married, divorced, and in significant other relationships.

14 *Don W. Nance*

Values orientations included "hippie" and "yuppie." Clients are "currently," "formerly," and "never" religious.

The cases are certainly not all-inclusive. Each reader may wish that a particular set of demographic and cultural descriptions was represented. Such a wish is easily understandable. From an ACT perspective and within the context of the book, perceived omissions can be formed into questions such as: What would be different if the client were _____? What differences would exist in tasks? In readiness? In counselor style?

Variations in length, tone, and amount of dialogue are found among the chapters. The sources of variation are several. Foremost, from an ACT perspective, is that less direction was given about these elements of the process. The differences in length reflect writing style variations, differences in clients, and amount of dialogue presented. For example, Eileen Nickerson's writing about two cases with whom she has had long-term therapy relationships has more length and complexity than some other chapters. The variations in tone enrich the book and match the approaches being presented. The self-disclosures of Will Poland are reflective of his humanistic approach. In turn, the clearly enumerated goals in Jerry Deffenbacher's cognitive-behavioral chapter are congruent with the theoretical orientation being presented.

RECOMMENDATIONS FOR READING

We suggest you form additional questions while reading each case. One question is, "How are you, the reader, going to *approach* the task of reading, studying, and evaluating each chapter?" Clearly you have some choices about the approach taken toward the task. In this section, some suggestions (direction) are offered regarding how to approach a task. Many of the suggestions have a parallel in how clients and counselors approach the counseling process. In the context of a book, it is impossible to interact individually with each reader in order to provide direction only when necessary . Recognizing the possibility for overdirection, here are several recommendations for what to do and what not to do.

1. **Approach the task with a goal of understanding the author's perspective and the use of ACT.** The book offers an opportunity to adopt, in turn, the perspectives of both the counselor and the client in each case. Avoid approaching the process with a goal of reinforcing your current preferences and perspectives while discounting the value or

contribution of other approaches. As a reader, and as a counselor, you are in a much better position to evaluate, to agree or disagree, after you can adopt and understand the perspective being offered. This recommended approach is consistent with a frequent first task in counseling. A client may enter counseling for the purpose, implicitly or explicitly, to gain support for his or her current perspective on a situation or about other people, or to buttress a current self-image. If the process were overt, clients might say the following:

Client: *My goal is to present my situation in such a way that you will agree with my current view of myself, my situation, my options.*

Therapist: *My first goal is to understand your current view of the situation. In the process some relationship will be built. I probably won't agree fully with your view. After I understand your perspective, I am likely to ask you to reexamine some aspects of your current view. I may suggest alternative perspectives and new ways of behaving.*

2. **Avoid using personal "litmus tests" that must be passed in order to be acceptable.** In therapy, a particular criteria (e.g., Style 1) may be a requirement for either the client or the therapist. If such a criteria is not met, therapy does not proceed. The client does not seek our services in the first place, does not come back, or is referred to a therapist who meets the required characteristic. In response to such a situation, most therapists are likely to respond in the same vain as I have here:

Reader 1: *"You did not include_____* (classic behaviorist, traditional psychoanalysis, existential, etc.) *orientation."*

Reader 2: *"There is not a case included in which the client is_____* (black, gay, a recovering addict, Hispanic, codependent, etc.)."

Author: *"You're right. It might have been helpful if such a case had been included. My hope would be that you can still benefit from reading the orientations and cases that are presented. Ways of dealing with the omissions have been offered. How do those seem to you? What other ways can you see to approach the readings given that changes and additions are not possible?"*

3. **Use questions to actively explore the concepts and cases presented.** Develop a set of questions to consider as you read each chapter. Some of the questions might be developed from an initial understanding of

ACT and the theoretical orientation under consideration. Examples of such questions related just to the concept of tasks might include

How are the tasks of counseling conceptualized in the chapter?
How is task readiness determined?
How are the tasks sequenced?
Does readiness influence the sequence of tasks?

Another source of questions to consider arises from the issues you have faced or anticipate facing as a practicing professional. The overall question might take the form of, "What aspects of the case, the conceptualization, and the treatment can be applied in my professional work with clients?" More specific questions might deal with different aspects of the counseling process such as

How is the counseling contract developed?
How is resistance approached?
How does the counseling process evolve over time?

Whatever the content of your questions, the process of being an active reader is likely to increase both the motivation for reading and the ability to understand, analyze, and apply the information presented. The major purpose of this initial chapter has been accomplished if your readiness has increased for the task of reading the chapters that follow.

REFERENCES

Deffenbacher, J.L. (1988). Cognitive-behavioral treatments of anxiety. *The Counseling Psychologist, 16,* 3–95.

Hart, G.M. (1982). *The process of clinical supervision.* Baltimore, MD: University Park Press.

Holland, J.L. (1966). *The psychology of vocational choice: A theory of personality and model environments.* Waltham, MA: Blaisdell Publishing.

Howard, G.S., Nance, D.W., & Myers, P. (1986). Adaptive counseling and therapy: An integrative metatheoretical approach. *The Counseling Psychologist, 14,* 363–442.

Howard, G.S., Nance, D.W., & Myers, P. (1987). *Adaptive counseling and therapy: A systematic approach to selecting effective treatments.* San Francisco: Jossey-Bass.

Kelly, K.R. (1988). Defending eclecticism: The utility of informed choice. *Journal of Mental Health Counseling, 10,* 210–213.

Myers (Cohen), P. (1984). Violence in the family—an act of loyalty? *Psychotherapy: Theory, Research and Practice, 21,* 249–253.

Myers, P. (1991). Using adaptive counseling and therapy to tailor treatments to couples and families. *Topics in Family Psychology and Counseling, 1,* 56–70.

Nance, D.W., & Myers, P. (1991). Continuing the eclectic journey. *Journal of Mental Health Counseling, 13,* 119–130.

Nickerson, E.T., & O'Laughlin, K. (1982). *Helping though action: Action-oriented therapies.* Amherst, MA: Human Resource Development Press.

Robbins, S.B. (1989). Role of contemporary psychoanalysis in counseling psychology. *Journal of Counseling Psychology, 36,* 267–278.

Zook, A., II, & Walton, J.M. (1989). Theoretical orientations and work settings of clinical and counseling psychologists: A current perspective. *Professional Psychology: Research and Practice, 20,* 23–31.

Chapter 2

COGNITIVE-BEHAVIOR THERAPY AND ACT: A CASE OF HIGH ANGER

Jerry L. Deffenbacher
Colorado State University

This chapter will explore the interface and contribution of Adaptive Counseling and Therapy (ACT) to a cognitive-behavioral orientation (Howard, Nance, & Myers, 1986, 1987). The general characteristics of cognitive-behavior therapy (CBT) will be described and related to ACT. This general discussion will be amplified by case demonstration of the interface of ACT with CBT interventions for anger reduction.

COGNITIVE-BEHAVIORAL APPROACHES TO COUNSELING

Although CBT (e.g., Beck & Emery, 1985; Burns, 1980; Kanfer & Goldstein, 1991; Meichenbaum, 1977, 1985) encompasses many different strategies and interventions, CBT approaches share several characteristics or emphases in common.

1. **Psychological problems can be broadly conceptualized within a learning framework.** Many human concerns can be viewed as a product of excessive, insufficient, and/or inappropriate learning experiences.

For example, an angry individual may have learned excessive emotional arousal and distorted appraisals and may have been reinforced for intimidating behavior in response to provocation. However, unlike some early behavioral positions, CBT emphasizes both overt and covert processes. Overt behavior and its relationship to the environment continue to play an extremely important part in CBT, but consideration also is given to covert processes such as images, memories, feelings, self-dialogue, information processing, and schema. These internal dimensions are considered to be important parts of the client's problem complex, often to be in need of change, and to follow the same general principles of change as do more overt behavioral processes.

2. **A positive therapeutic relationship is critical.** CBT counselors form warm, supportive, collaborative relationships with their clients. Often through the medium of the therapeutic relationship, change is initiated. For example, trusting the therapist may lead the client to try a new behavior or empower the therapist to confront a defensively held belief. The therapeutic relationship may provide the therapist with reinforcement value or make him or her a credible model. CBT is not a cold set of techniques brought to bear, but a warm, collaborative emergent process that is actively shared by client and therapist. The therapeutic relationship is essential and vital. In general, CBT tends to be moderate to high on the support dimension of ACT.

3. **There is an active attitude of personal science.** CBT counselors encourage a collaborative empiricism in which the client and therapist work together to understand the nature of problems, to determine jointly the goals of treatment, and to design and implement change strategies, all of which are framed in client language, examples, and metaphors. Clients are encouraged to conceptualize problems as hypotheses to be tested, rather than factual, victimizing conditions beyond their control. Alternative hypotheses are explored through inductive and experimental processes. For example, Socratic questions often are employed to help clients identify and explore dysfunctional beliefs and images, and to consider alternative thoughts, feelings, and ways of dealing with problem situations. This style of questioning tends to be a series of open-ended questions that facilitate an exploration of issues. For example, the counselor might ask a series of "And then what would happen?" questions to explore catastrophic predictions, questions like "And, what is another way of looking at that?" to elicit alternative explanations and attributions, or questions like "What is your evidence for that?" to push the logical limits of conclusions. Self-explorations via the Socratic process are extended through behavioral experiments developed by the

counselor and client to assess predictions and/or change perspectives and coping skills.

Also an emphasis is on data collection. Client and therapist work together to develop monitoring strategies, to collect information about the successes and failures of the personal experiments, and to be able to answer the question "And how will we know?" Thus, in the pursuit of personal science, CBT attempts to provide just enough structure, which at times may be quite high, to help the developing scientist (client) in further exploration, hypothesis testing, and critical experiments. However, a bias is toward introducing the minimum structure needed and removing it over time, such that the client becomes his or her own independent personal scientist.

4. **Detailed, situation-specific assessments are undertaken.** Since learning histories are unique and problems occur in specific parts of the client's world, client and counselor work together to develop a shared understanding of the client's problems in the context in which they occur. This understanding develops primarily out of the collaborative, Socratic explorations and jointly developed assessment strategies. For example, self-monitoring of anger might be developed as a way of "getting a better handle on what torches me off." However, even when the therapist introduces specific assessment strategies, effort is made for these to emerge as a natural extension of client exploration. For example, the MMPI might be introduced as a way of helping an angry client gain a better understanding of the mix of anger, anxiety, and depression, or interviews with significant others as a way of "getting a different perspective on my anger."

5. **Intervention strategies are targeted to specific components of the problem complex.** Interventions are linked conceptually to the emergent understanding of the client's problems. Since not all parts of the problem are assumed to respond equally well to the same intervention, interventions are tailored to facilitate maximal change in each element. For example, with an angry client, relaxation interventions might be targeted to heightened emotional and physiological arousal, assertion and communication skills training to reduce abrasive, coercive communication patterns, and cognitive restructuring to change hostile attitudes and interpretations. Again, every effort is made for interventions to emerge relatively naturally as an extension of client exploration (e.g., relaxation as a way of "calming myself down").

6. **Attention is given to rehearsal and transfer.** Rehearsal is an outgrowth of the general learning assumption. CBT does not assume that self-exploration and understanding are sufficient. They may be, and

they may not. It is often necessary to define alternative coping processes, shape their components, and then assure their integration and accessibility through practice. Rehearsal formats vary widely (e.g., practice in response to imagery, simulations, role-plays, and graded *in vivo* experiences). However, attention is given to making initial rehearsals "safe" and to maximizing success. CBT also does not assume that change will transfer automatically from the safe, therapeutically controlled environment to naturalistic environments. Effort, therefore, is directed to training for and assessing transfer. As change is demonstrated within therapy, it is transferred to the external environment by *in vivo* practice fading therapist's contact, by rehearsal in increasingly more difficult simulations, and by homework and graded assignments.

7. **Attention is given to maintenance and relapse prevention.** Maintenance over time also is not assumed. Environments and reinforcements may shift, new stresses and problems may emerge, and once effective insights and skills may be ignored. Any or all of these may lead to the return of old patterns. Maintenance and relapse prevention, therefore, receive attention as part of the termination process. For example, an angry client may be told to expect anger in the future, at times quite high, but to view it as an opportunity to continue to cope. Relapse may be simulated directly or drawn from naturally occurring examples with the therapist assisting the client in ways of conceptualizing it and employing problem-solving strategies. Time and therapy structure may be altered to facilitate relapse prevention. For example, later sessions may be spaced more infrequently to give the client greater opportunity for external application and possible relapse, which can be worked as part of therapy. Booster sessions can be scheduled at say 1-, 3-, 6-, and 12-month intervals. Written contracts, correspondence, and phone contact may be used to keep the focus on continued coping and troubleshooting difficulties.

RELATIONSHIP OF ACT TO CBT

ACT and CBT have different historical and conceptual roots. ACT adapts situational leadership theory (Hersey & Blanchard, 1977) from organizational behavior and is a general scheme to enhance a better fit of client's needs to intervention style. CBT is an emerging orientation to conceptualizing and intervening with human concerns, and has its roots in both experimental and applied cognitive and behavioral research. Although their histories differ, many of the basic tenets and principles of ACT fit well with CBT. For example, although ACT is more atheoretical and does not explicitly endorse a general learning orientation to conceptualizing therapeutic change as does CBT, it subsumes learning based interventions. Many of the examples and strategies discussed in the low support-high structure, high support-high structure, and high support-low structure intervention styles fit well with a learning model. Likewise, attention to rehearsal, transfer, maintenance, and relapse prevention, which are central to CBT, are congruent with assessment of competence, motivation, and confidence regarding implementation and maintenance of therapeutic gain in ACT.

Other basic concepts are also parallel. For example, client readiness dimensions of willingness, competence (ability), and self-confidence of ACT are similar to motivational, competency/coping capacity, and self-efficacy/self-schema concepts (e.g., Bandura, 1977; Beck, 1976; Beck & Emery, 1985; Meichenbaum, 1977, 1985) of CBT. ACT, however, emphasizes these concepts and provides specific guidelines for the assessment and use of these dimensions in treatment selection and deployment, guidelines that can guide use and timing in CBT.

The developmental processes and general principle of match and move inherent in ACT are also consistent with CBT. Specifically, ACT suggests that successful counseling is a developmental process in which the counselor assesses client's readiness, matches his or her intervention style to the client's readiness, and moves toward conditions of low structure-low support, a condition of maximal the client's responsibility within therapy and for movement toward termination. That is, within ACT, assessing the client's readiness as low on willingness, competence, and confidence requires a low support-high structure intervention style. The therapist takes over and "tells" the client what to do because the client is least able to do so for himself or herself. As the client's resources increase or readiness is assessed higher from the start, the therapist shifts his or her style toward greater support and structure, from these to greater support but less structure, to lower support and structure. In this way, he or she matches intervention style to the client's readiness level and moves developmentally toward the client's greater independence in the low structure-low support condition. This emphasis on the client's readiness assessment and matching and moving is very similar to CBT tactics of assessing and entering counseling where the client is and moving from high external control of reinforcement and behavior to greater internal control of both. That is, CBT starts with the least intrusive, yet effective intervention and works toward greater client self-control (low support and structure). Clients are assessed in terms of the degree of external control needed to modify thoughts, feelings, and behaviors, and effort is made to make as much change as possible toward the development of maximal client self-direction and self-efficacy.

24   *Jerry L. Deffenbacher*

Both ACT and CBT deal explicitly with the importance of the counseling relationship. ACT suggests that relationship (support) characteristics are one of two fundamental dimensions along which interventions can be organized. Further, ACT suggests that although high support interventions may not be most appropriate in every case, they are rarely totally incompatible with the client's readiness, especially at the beginning of therapy. CBT, on the other hand, specifies a particular type of therapeutic relationship. CBT is based in a high quality (high support), collaborative relationship. The therapeutic relationship and alliance are fundamental cornerstones of CBT. Thus, in general, CBT would fit heavily in the high support dimension of ACT with the amount of structure varying depending on the nature of the intervention (e.g., from relatively low structure in some Socratic explorations to relatively high structure in some structured learning experiences). Finally, some of the "telling" activities (e.g., a therapist-directed assignment or referral directive such as seeing a specific physician or social service agency), which would be considered part of high structure-low support in ACT, could be done within the context of a supportive relationship in CBT. Thus, both ACT and CBT place importance on quality therapeutic relationships. ACT, however, provides additional principles and suggestions for matching the degree of support to the nature of the client's readiness.

Perhaps in the area of assessment and treatment, matching is where ACT and CBT share their greatest convergence. Both suggest the need for detailed, situation-specific, therapeutic task assessments. Careful assessment leads to a careful matching of treatment strategies or styles to characteristics of the client and his or her problems. Although both ACT and CBT place great emphasis on careful assessment and treatment matching, they do so in somewhat divergent, yet complementary ways. CBT generally focuses more on the specific content of therapeutic interventions that are matched to characteristics of the presenting problem complex, whereas ACT focuses assessment more on the client's readiness and matching general therapy style (support and structure) to readiness level. That is, in a very general sense, CBT assesses and matches on the strategies of therapy, whereas ACT assesses and matches on the style of therapy processes. CBT focuses more on the nature of the intervention and ACT on whether the client is ready for this style of intervention (i.e., is there a good fit for this client at this time). Thus, both ACT and CBT stress similar assessment and matching principles, but assess and match on somewhat different dimensions, dimensions that are complementary and have a positive interface.

Although ACT is generally described as a means of assessing and matching more general therapeutic styles to the client's readiness, a major thesis of this chapter is that ACT principles can be very useful *within* a therapeutic orientation. Within an orientation such as CBT, a wide range of therapeutic strategies are available that differ significantly in structure and support needed for successful implementation. Assessment of readiness both across and within presenting problems can aid the CBT counselor in making a number of important therapeutic decisions.

First, readiness assessment and matching can be helpful in selecting which therapeutic targets have the greatest probability of being addressed successfully with strategies requiring different levels of structure and support. For example, the same dysfunctional cognitions may be explored through gentle, Socratic questioning (at least moderate support and moderate to minimal structure) or through directive confrontation and persuasion techniques (high structure and varying support). The decision of style could depend on the readiness level of the client. Alternatively, two equally phobic and avoidant clients might be dealt with differently depending on competence and confidence assessment. The low confidence, low competence client may require more highly structured and supportive teaching activities to increase confidence and competence, whereas the low confidence, but somewhat competent individual might engage in self-directed exposure with the therapist acting as an encouraging consultant (high support and low-moderate structure).

Second, readiness information may assist in choice of timing of an intervention. An intervention strategy may be highly appropriate but poorly timed if readiness issues are ignored. For example, self-directed, *in vivo* exposure can be very appropriate when motivation and efficacy are high, and competence is at least moderately high some time into therapy, but be inappropriate early on when at least competence and efficacy are low. Ongoing readiness assessment also may help the therapist choose when to begin with a strategy of a certain style and when to shift toward interventions requiring more or less structure and support. For example, reports of increased competence and self-efficacy (competence and confidence) may lead to a shift toward less structure and support.

Third, readiness information may assist in resolving therapeutic impasses. Certainly, the therapist must consider whether he or she has an appropriate working conceptualization and intervention plan. Readiness assessment, however, may suggest that the strategy is sound, but that he or she has entered inappropriately into or moved too rapidly in the match and move process with that strategy. Resolution of the impasse may require more a modification of structure and support parameters (e.g., dropping back and providing more practice and support to enhance confidence) within an intervention than a new intervention plan.

Finally, readiness information may suggest that readiness factors be the target of intervention (i.e., competence, confidence, and motivation should be the focus

26 *Jerry L. Deffenbacher*

of discussion and intervention). CBT interventions are well designed to increase competence and confidence or self-efficacy (e.g., learning of social skills to enhance competence and use of response induction aids to enhance self-efficacy). However, motivation may sometimes be overlooked, and the counselor may move ahead without a clear assessment of motivation. Accurate assessment of motivation may minimize premature intervention and wasted effort that would lead to an impasse. In fact, it may suggest that motivation (e.g., reasons for being in therapy, resistance, etc.) become the focus of intervention. For example, therapist and client may collaboratively explore the consequences of not becoming fully involved in therapy, and employ problem-solving and decision-making strategies that lead either to termination or enhanced motivation.

In summary, it is suggested that ACT can assist the CBT therapist in selecting and timing his or her interventions effectively and in assessing and resolving therapeutic impasses. The remainder of this chapter will attempt to demonstrate this interface between ACT and CBT in a case of inappropriate anger. Intervention will be conceptualized within CBT principles and strategies. The case and transcript material will be presented to show how the readiness assessment of ACT influenced my therapeutic choices.

BILL: A CASE OF HIGH ANGER

Demographics and Background

Bill is a 36-year-old, divorced, white male. He is self-referred having learned of the therapist through a neighbor. He is verbal, cooperative, moderately introspective, autonomous, demanding of self and others, and generally motivated to explore issues in counseling. No evidence of substance abuse, physical abuse, suicidal ideation, delusional thinking, psychosis, or severe pathology was evident.

He is the father of two children—a daughter, Sharon, age 8, and a son, Dan, age 10—both of whom live with him in a single family dwelling in the local community. His wife left the family abruptly and divorced him three years earlier after being diagnosed as having a major degenerative disease. She lives approximately 400 miles away and sees the children on major holidays. Bill reported that he had been shocked and saddened by the divorce, but while he felt sorry for his ex-wife and her condition, he was no longer angry with her. He reported that up until the time of her illness and sudden departure, his wife had worked part-time as a substitute teacher and had the major parenting role with the children. His parenting skills appeared generally good, evidenced in an adequate knowledge of child development, typical use of positive behavioral control strategies, and general nurturing and caring behavior toward his children. He reported enjoying his children, taking many satisfying family excursions, spending considerable time with them in school and non-school activities, and the like. These impressions were confirmed in half-hour interviews with each child.

He has a bachelor's degree in electrical engineering and a master's degree in computer science and works as a project manager for a national computer firm. He is well respected in the work environment, possessing both good interpersonal and technical skills. He earns $47,000, sufficient to provide well for himself and his children.

Psychosocial history reveals relatively normal educational, social, and sexual development. He was the eldest of five children in a Roman Catholic family. He reported his father as a capable businessman who was successful as a sales representative and later regional manager for a national company. He described his father as a gentle and supportive man who was reasonable and fair. Discipline and rearing of the family were left primarily to his mother as his father was often away on business. He described his mother as a warm person who was somewhat overwhelmed by rearing five children. He reports feeling cared about by her, but that she placed considerable "parental" responsibility on him. In this arena, he indicated that she was very demanding of him and that she controlled him and the other children by quiet coaxing followed by angry, verbal demands, and threats. By the time that he was 10 or so, she would often leave much of the discipline of the younger children to him, especially after becoming angry with them. Occasional swats were used as part of discipline, but there was no evidence of physical abuse in his family of origin.

Conceptualization of the Problem

Client conceptualization. He did not want to be angry with and yell at his son. He was tired of and embarrassed by the angry outbursts between Dan and himself. He felt guilty about his anger and found it alien to his identity of himself as a caring, loving father. His overall description was as follows:

> Dan is a really neat kid, but he can drive me crazy. One of the worst things is when I try to make a deal with him. We'll agree to something. I do my part, like, take him to the store or let him go to his friends, and then its like he has a big memory problem. When it comes his turn to do his part, it's like we never had a deal. He

disagrees and says we didn't agree or simply ignores his part of the bargain. I get really pissed and that is when we fight. Other times, I'll ask him to do something, and he'll ignore it or do it half way. I'll ask him calmly a time or two and then pretty soon I am furious and screaming at him. God, I thought I'd never say this, but I sound just like my mother used to. I just gotta change this. I don't want him growing up like that . . . you know, being yelled at. I don't want to feel this way . . . all angry and crazy. Sometimes I get all angry, even when I don't yell at him.

Therapist conceptualization. The presenting concern was inappropriate anger in interactions with his son and, to a lesser degree, in some meetings and interactions at work. Self-monitored anger over a 3-week assessment interval ranged from 0 to 7 times daily (average 2+) and ranged from 30 to 90 (average 60+) on a 100-point severity scale. Anger and negative verbal exchanges appeared provoked by Dan's inattention to requests, lack of follow-through on chores, leaving messes, talking back, and noncooperation and follow-through on commitments, especially when Dan had already received his part of an agreement or bargain. Anger incidents were more frequent on the weekends and when Bill was tired, stressed, or feeling ill. Anger was marked by (1) high emotional and physiological arousal; (2) demanding, overgeneralized, catas-trophized, inflammatory, and misattribution cognitions; and (3) negative verbal exchanges ranging from mild badgering to yelling at his son. Angry verbal interactions did not escalate to physical interactions as he reported that, in the past six months, he had "swatted" (described as giving two open hand swats to the buttocks) his son once and had taken him firmly by the arm to his room on another occasion.

High levels of cognitive, emotional, and physiological arousal (anger is conceptualized as an internal state that is separate from the behavior it prompts or is associated with) appeared to prompt negative verbal behavior and to interfere with other competencies for dealing with provocative situations. That is, problem-solving and parenting competencies were generally good (see exception below), but they were not employed when in a highly angry state. The one parenting problem evident was too frequent use of agreements where his son received rewards and privileges prior to executing his part of the agreement (one of the prime provocations). Reversing contingencies (i.e., clearly stating expectations for son's behavior and having son engage in behavior prior to receiving reinforce-ment) needed attention but was viewed as being easily done, given overall child management skill base and positive relationship with children. Thus, cognitive-emotional-physiological involvement was seen as a primary area in need of change with parenting strategies and alternative verbal behavior as a secondary area (i.e., with lowered anger the client would be able to access competencies in his repertoire, competencies that needed only minor modification).

The above pattern of behavior appeared to be a learned pattern of responding to provocations. As a youngster, Bill's father had modeled patience and reasonable negotiation with the children. However, his mother, who was the primary parental model, responded to frustrating interactions with the children in a pattern of interaction parallel to Bill's. She would make a few reasonable requests and then explode angrily, making threats and accusations and withdrawing shortly afterwards. As the oldest child, Bill was often left to settle issues with his siblings and tended to manage them by angry, demanding, but more supportive interactions. He was rewarded and supported in this behavior by his mother and by the reduction of stress as the siblings generally complied with his requests. Early in his marital history, Bill's wife had primary child rearing responsibilities. Bill had positive interactions with his children and was involved in discipline, but the developmental level of the children and the amount of time spent as a primary disciplinarian did not lead to change in his latent emotional and behavioral patterns. When he was thrust rapidly into the role of single, working parent, he generally did well. However, when patience, calm requests, and negotiation failed, or when his personal resources were low, his developmental vulnerability was laid bare. He then reverted to the pattern of emotion and behavior modeled and reinforced in childhood and not offset by subsequent experience.

General Readiness Assessment

Generally, the client was a good candidate for therapy. Motivation was generally high. He was frustrated by his emotions and behaviors and found them ego alien. He was self-referred through a neighbor who knew the author. The therapist also had significant sources of positive power entering into therapy. He possessed connective power through his association with the university, which was valued by the client, expert power through the author's background in anger and stress reduction as well as his friend's recommendation, and personal power through the rapid development of a positive relationship. Thus, the client was personally motivated, and the therapist had several positive power bases to encourage and support therapeutic activities. General competence was moderately high. He functioned well in many roles and had generally good parenting and problem-solving skills. He had a positive history of learning new skills and making major changes vocationally, interpersonally, and as a single parent. Confidence was also moderately high. He possessed a positive self-image

30   *Jerry L. Deffenbacher*

and generally felt good about his interaction with his children. He stated that at an abstract level he was sure that he could learn to manage his anger, but he was not sure how.

As his general readiness was high, therapy focused on increasing anger management skills. However, as will be seen in the next section, readiness factors varied significantly across specific therapeutic tasks.

Therapeutic Tasks, CBT Interventions, and ACT

Six, roughly sequential therapeutic tasks were addressed in this case. First, a warm, collaborative relationship was developed (Task 1) as a basis from which to develop a shared assessment and conceptualization (Task 2) and to intervene (Tasks 3 through 6). The assessment suggested that high levels of emotional and physiological arousal were prominent, led the client to feel out of control, and interfered with deployment of other coping skills in the client's repertoire. Reducing emotional and physiological arousal, therefore, became the first target of intervention (Task 3). Anger engendering interpretations, attributions, and images also needed attention (Task 4) in order to reduce their impact on anger arousal and prompting of negative interactions. Finally, angry, demanding behavior needed to be replaced by calm, negotiating, assertive, and problem-solving behaviors (Task 5) and by employment of clear behavioral contingencies with follow-up consequences (Task 6). Each therapeutic task was targeted by multiple CBT interventions and interfaced with readiness assessment and match and move principles of ACT. This interface of CBT and ACT is summarized in sections labeled "ACT interface" and exemplified by transcript segments depicting the interface. Additionally, transcript segments noted by "T:" and "C:" reflect therapist and client comments, respectively. Therapist thoughts have been added within parentheses to reflect some of the logic of the moment for specific interventions.

Task 1: Develop a positive, collaborative relationship.   A positive relationship is necessary in order to engage the client in assessment and intervention tasks.

CBT intervention. From the start, the therapist attempted to establish good rapport and a relationship high in factors such as a warmth, empathy, and genuineness. These efforts began in an initial, 25-minute interview in which the counselor briefly clarified the nature of the presenting problem and negotiated self-monitoring of anger and completion of an intake form since the initial session could not be held for nearly two weeks.

ACT interface. Since the relationship appeared to be developing well, support was kept high, and structure was increased somewhat by using a series of directing, but open-ended questions to assist the client in developing a self-monitoring system prior to the initial session. Readiness appeared high as he was motivated to talk, demonstrated competence in tracking questions and giving detail, and seemed confident enough to handle the task.

A transcribed segment related to this initial task shows the use of both support and direction by the therapist. The material in parentheses makes explicit the therapist's internal decisional processes.

Therapist: (This interaction is going well. He's been highly cooperative and giving rich detail. Let me see if I can get him to come up with a self-monitoring strategy to track anger since it will be almost 2 weeks before we get together.) *You've been doing a great job of describing anger with Dan generally. Is there a way that we could have you monitor your anger on a daily basis in the next week or so? So we could get a more detailed, day-to-day picture of your anger.*

Client: *I guess I could keep track of it.*

T: (Good. Let me see if I can't get him to come up with the specific means of monitoring anger. He'll be more invested if it's his idea.) *And how might you do that?*

C: *I guess I could get a notebook and write things down . . . like what happened, how I felt, and stuff like that.*

T: (This is a good start. Let me just clarify the task and make arrangements for him to drop it off. I want him to get the idea that I will do my homework too. Since self-monitoring is a fairly unusual behavior, I will ask him to paraphrase our agreement so we are clear.) *That's a great idea. You will get a notebook, and when you get angry, you will write down the incident or what triggered the anger and how you felt and what you did. Is that what we are agreeing to?*

C: *Yeah. That's fine. You want me to write down at the time?*

T: *Yes, as close afterwards as you can. That way we will get as much detail as we can while it is still fresh in your mind. Otherwise, things can fade on you. Also, would you be willing to rate how strong your reaction was*

32   *Jerry L. Deffenbacher*

on that 100-point scale we spoke about? (Earlier an analogy had been made to a centigrade thermometer measuring his boiling point.) *You know where 0 = calm and 100 = furious, boiling mad?*

C: *Sure.*

T: *Good. Maybe you could just write it down as part of your reaction, just put a number between 0 and 100 in that part of the description. Also, I would like to make arrangements for you to drop off your notebook a day or so before we get together. That will give me time to look it over and get a feel for the day-to-day interactions. . . . (Therapist makes arrangements for it to be dropped off and asks client to paraphrase the collaboratively developed task.)*

Task 2: Develop collaborative assessment and conceptualization.   A shared working definition of the presenting problem was needed in order to enhance the working alliance and to develop a tailored treatment plan.

CBT intervention. Much of the initial assessment was addressed concurrently with developing the therapeutic relationship in the first two sessions. Assessment activities included (a) detailed, but open-ended questioning regarding the presenting problem, current life status, and psychosocial history; (b) review of self-monitoring; (c) half-hour interviews with each child (see below for how this developed); and (d) completion of the Trait Anger Scale and Anger Expression Scale (Spielberger, 1988), the Anger Situation and Symptom measures (Deffenbacher, Story, Brandon, Hogg, & Hazaleus, 1988), the Anger Inventory (Novaco, 1975), and the MMPI (see below for how these were introduced).

ACT interface. All readiness parameters were relatively high as he talked easily and provided detailed descriptions, even when describing negative feelings of anger, embarrassment, and guilt. Therefore, a high support-relatively low structure style was employed with the therapist primarily using open-ended questions, paraphrasing, and summaries to acquire problem descriptions and history. An example of this style from late in the second interview and a shift in style to greater structure are given below.

T: (OK, we are getting a pretty well developed picture. Let me see if the client can come up with anything we may have missed, and I'll try to bridge off of this to administering the paper-pencil questionnaires.) *Bill, it seems like we are getting a pretty good picture of what happens when you are angry and how it may have developed.*

Cognitive-Behavior Therapy and ACT **33**

C: *Seems that way to me too.*

T: *Are there any other ways you can think of that we might better understand your anger?*

C: *I don't know. Well, I guess we could ask the kids. Maybe they could tell you something we've missed.*

T: (Terrific! We were both missing the obvious. Let me follow up on that.) *That's a great idea. Can we make arrangements for me to talk to them for half-hour or so each?*

C: *Sure.* . . . (Details are then made for after school appointments.)

T: (Let me follow up further and introduce the questionnaires.) *That was a really good idea about talking to the kids. Are there any other ways we can get a perspective on your anger?*

C: *I don't think so . . . no . . . can't think of any.*

T: *Bill, I have one other idea I would like to share that I think will help us check out anger and other areas. I have four or five questionnaires that I would like you to fill out. Most of them are short, but one will take about an hour or so to complete. They will help us look at anger primarily, but will help us check out some other things like anxiety and depression as well. Would you be willing to complete these and return them prior to the next session so I can go over them and have them ready for our next session?*

C: *Sure, happy to.* . . . (Questionnaires were given to him and arrangements made for their completion and return when he brought the children in.)

Task 3: Reduce heightened emotional-physiological arousal. Emotional and physiological arousal appeared to be prime sources of interference with cognitive processes and behavioral competencies. Marked tension in hands, arms, and shoulders; tight jaw; and drawn facial features were prominent elements of physiological arousal. Reported emotions included anger, fury, "pissed off," "mad as hell," and extreme frustration.

CBT intervention. Emotional and physiological arousal were targeted with a number of interventions.

1. Self-monitoring was included not only for assessment, but also as part of intervention because the client seemed relatively insensitive to internal cues of anger arousal and to internal and external cues that precipitated anger. Over the first five sessions, self-monitoring was made more complex and included monitoring situational, cognitive, emotional, physiological and behavioral elements of anger. Awareness of increases in these factors was to serve as a cue for application of various interventions.

2. A self-controlled relaxation training program (Deffenbacher, Demm, & Brandon, 1986; Deffenbacher & Stark, 1992; Hazaleus & Deffenbacher, 1986) was employed to develop applied relaxation coping skills for control of emotional and physiological arousal. This program involved progressive relaxation training and development of specific relaxation coping skills of (a) relaxation without tension (focusing on muscle groups and letting them go); (b) breathing-cued relaxation (taking 3 to 5 slow deep breaths relaxing on each exhalation); (c) imagery-cued relaxation (visualizing a personally relaxing experience); (d) cue-controlled relaxation (relaxing to the slow repetition of the word "relax"); and (e) unobtrusive adaptations of tension-release exercises (e.g., sucking stomach in firmly and releasing tension with release of muscles). After being developed over three sessions, relaxation coping skills were employed to reduce anger generated by visualizing images of anger incidents. Over sessions, the anger level of scenes was increased, and therapist assistance in retrieving relaxation faded based on increased client competence and confidence. Skills were transferred through client-directed homework assignments for application in angering and other stressful situations and through two sessions in which angry interactions were role-played in the client's home. Applied relaxation also was combined with time-out to decrease ongoing provocation and increase probability of successful application. Additionally, the client noted on his own that he could use relaxation coping skills as a preventive measure to reduce feelings of hassle, being hurried, tiredness, and the like which were associated with greater probabilities of anger. That is, the client began employing brief self-directed relaxation periods (self-proclaimed "meditation" periods) when he felt tired, ill, or hassled. In turn, this practice broke up negative affective cycles and increased his tolerance for frustration.

3. A portion of self-instructional training included palliative, affect control elements. For example, self-instructions included self-dialogue like "Chill out and calm down. Getting all pissed doesn't help." or "Calm down. That's it, just take those three big deep breaths and relax. . . ." Such self-instructions were designed to initiate a calming mental perspective as well as specific relaxation skills.

4. Time-out (i.e., removing self from the provocation) was integrated with relaxation coping skills. This was done to decrease building arousal and to enhance the probability of coping skill application. Self-instructions included elements such as "Wait a minute. You can do better than this. Just go in the other room, initiate your relaxation, and get your head together." or "Just calm down, Bill. Go upstairs to your room and relax. Things will probably look different then."

ACT interface. Readiness assessment revealed a high motivation to lower emotional and physical elements of anger ("I really want to control being so damned pissed."), but very low competence and confidence (the client indicated he could walk away but even this did not usually help). Intervention, therefore, started with a high support-high structure teaching style that involved some elements of "telling" the client what to do early on. However, with increased competence and confidence, shifts were made to high support-lower structure and finally to self-controlled interventions with lessened therapist support and structure. Examples of these changes are given below.

T: (Demonstrating relatively low support-high structure in relaxation training.) *OK, now clench your hands into tight fists. . . . Hold it. . . . That's it, now release the tension and focus on the feelings in your hands . . . noticing the feelings around the fingers and knuckles . . . perhaps noticing warmth or how your fingers may twitch or jump as those little muscles in the hands relax. . . .*

T: (Demonstrating relatively low support-high structure in early relaxation homework.) *I would like you to practice the relaxation daily if you can, but let's say at least five of the next seven days. Is that reasonable?*

T: (Demonstrating high support-high structure in scene visualization and relaxation retrieval.) *In a moment, I am going to ask you to switch on that anger scene involving your coming into the family room with Dan watching TV and his backpack and stuff all over the floor. When I do, I want you to really get into that scene, get mad all over again, and signal by raising your finger. Then stay with that anger, let it build and pay attention to how you feel. Then I will have you switch off the scene and will help you relax again. So, right now switch on that scene. . . .*

T: (Demonstrating high support-lower structure in scene visualization and relaxation retrieval.) *In a moment, I am going to ask you to switch on that situation from a couple of weeks ago* (higher anger than scene above) *where you were getting ready to yell at Dan about the mess before dinner.*

36   Jerry L. Deffenbacher

> *When I do that, I want you to really get into that scene and get mad as we've done before and signal me when you are angry. However, when I shut the scene off, I want you to initiate relaxation and relax away the anger, perhaps saying "relax" as you breath out deeply like you were successful with this past week. Since I will need to know when you have relaxed away anger, why don't we change our signal system. Put your finger up when you are angry, keep it up while your are angry, then lower it when you have brought anger under control. . . .*

Later in this session a switch was made to even lower structure with greater client self-control based on feedback of greater competence and, by implication, confidence.

T: (I think he is getting the hang of this. Relaxation retrieval time has come down from 2 minutes in prior sessions to about 15 to 20 seconds, he doesn't show the physical tension of past sessions, and he reported success in applying relaxation this past week. Normally, I would wait until next session to make a shift to greater self-control, but he appears ready.) *Bill, I would like to change our procedure slightly. Instead of relaxing away the tension after I shut off the scene, I would like to have your stay in the scene and initiate the relaxation; that is, relax away the anger right while you are confronting it in the scene. So, when I ask you to switch on the scene, get right into the scene, feel the anger, and signal me. Then, when you are ready, initiate the relaxation, signaling me by lowering your finger when you are once again calm. So right now . . .*

The next excerpt demonstrates a low support-low structure interaction regarding relaxation coping skills two sessions later. Also the therapist consciously shifts to reflecting the client's sense of satisfaction and gain, rather than a more externally reinforcing style, which is consistent with match and move toward lower support and structure.

T: *I noticed* (pointing to the log) *some interesting entries this week. The first one here on Tuesday looks like Dan left one of his messes in the family room, but you didn't get very angry. What happened?*

C: *I did something different. You know, you and I noticed that I seemed to lose my cool more on days when I was tired, hurried, and things like that. Well, Tuesday was one of those days. You know, we have been trying to get this project done, and we're behind some. It was one of those days. Damn meetings all day long with everyone asking us when we were going to be done, rather than giving us the time to get it done. Well, by 5:15 I* *was whipped. I literally ran into my office to grab my coat and head off to pick up the kids. Then, I thought about what we had been talking about. I thought, "This is crazy. I am going to run out of here half crazy and be ready to jump all over them." So, I thought to myself, "Get a hold of yourself. Just sit down here and get your act together." So, I sat down and took about 5 minutes and did the relaxation stuff. You know, let that wave run through my body and took my mental trip to the beach in Mexico* (reference to his relaxation scene). *I opened my eyes and felt great. After my little "meditation," I focused on staying calm on the way home. I walked in and saw Dan's mess. I just went into the other room, took 3 to 4 deep breaths, and went in and calmly ask him to pick up his stuff before watching more TV. It was great. The "meditation" really worked.*

T: (Great. He's put it together on his own. I'm going to try to reflect his sense of accomplishment as well as clarifying the steps of his process. Then, I'll see if there are other examples I can clarify and nurture. We appear to be at a stage where he is ready to take more responsibility.) *Uh-huh, and you're feeling really pleased with yourself for noticing that hurried, harassed feeling, consciously stopping and relaxing, and carrying that calmness home to the kids.*

C: *Yeah, it feels good.*

T: *Feeling really good about figuring it out and managing it on your own. Were there any other examples of using your "meditation" this last week?*

C: *Yeah, I did it again on Thursday. Thursday was not at all like Tuesday. It was a great day. We finished the project, and my boss took us out to lunch. However, by time I got home, I felt really lousy. I don't know, must have been coming down with something. I came in feeling rotten and irritable. I tuned into that and went upstairs and relaxed on my bed for about 10 minutes. Almost went to sleep. Then I came downstairs and calmly told the kids that I wasn't feeling good and asked them for their cooperation. I still felt lousy, but it felt good not to let that spill over.*

T: *And your feeling proud of your ability to read your lousy feelings and relax so that they don't spill over. . . .*

Task 4: Alteration of dysfunctional cognitions. Three different dysfunctional cognitive patterns were consistent parts of anger and angry verbal behavior:

38   *Jerry L. Deffenbacher*

(a) demands (e.g., "He should/shouldn't have [typically things not attended to]. . . ." "I shouldn't have to put up with [whining, inattention, etc.]. . . ."); (b) inflammatory labels and implied catastrophes (e.g., crap, shit, awful, fucking mess, pig sty, reference to son as "little shit," etc.); and (c) overgeneralization (e.g., "He always/never. . . .").

CBT intervention. As with emotional-physiological arousal, different strategies were targeted to cognitive elements.

1. Self-monitoring was tailored to monitoring use of obscenities and demands (e.g., having coined a verb "to should," the client monitored "shoulding") as these were highly correlated with anger arousal and escalation of other dysfunctional cognitions. Over time, monitoring obscenities and demands came to cue cognitive restructuring as well as other interventions.
2. Cognitive restructuring included a combination of Socratic and confrontive exploration of the meaning and function of cognitions (see examples below). Early in cognitive restructuring, the therapist modeled alternative cognitive dialogue as a way of increasing the saliency of alternative ways to construe situations. As part of homework, the client wrote out new, functional counter responses to dysfunctional cognitions revealed within sessions and self-monitoring activities. As new counter responses were developed, these were rehearsed via anger imagery (Deffenbacher, Story, Stark, Hogg & Brandon, 1987; Deffenbacher et al., 1988; Deffenbacher & Stark, 1992). Then they were incorporated in *in vivo* application assignments and rehearsed in simulations during the two sessions in his home.
3. Silly humor (i.e., nonhostile but funny shifts in perspective or reconceptualizations of events) can provide a brief cognitive distance, allow alternative cognitions to be employed, and produce an anger-incompatible emotional response of laughter. Humor in some of the client's cognitions (e.g., referring to his son as a "little shit," his son's room as a "pig sty" or "fucking mess") was explored. Typically, this was done by raising rhetorical questions and requests for definitions and descriptions (e.g., description of his son as a "little shit," an operational definition of a "fucking mess," etc.). Once raised, the silliness of these labels and interpretations was explored along with any other cognitive distortions embedded in them (e.g., "God damn little shit" incorporates an implicit demanding position, as well as humorous godlike and fecal elements). As with other cognitive distortions, the client developed alternative verbal counter responses (e.g., replacing "little shit" with "frustrating kid") and, wherever possible, drew a picture of humorous items (e.g., a

Cognitive-Behavior Therapy and ACT **39**

picture of himself as a "god" complete with long gray beard and flowing robes who had the right to command others, a "pig sty" complete with pigs in his son's room, a pellet of manure for his son as a "little shit," etc.). Humorous images and dialogues were rehearsed as part of cognitive restructuring and self-instructional rehearsal.

4. Self-instructional training included not only rehearsal of cognitively restructured dialogue, but also task-oriented self-instructions to focus on the situation at hand and to develop a plan for dealing with it. For example, parent-child difficulties were reframed from "power struggles" and "driving me crazy" to "natural difficulties in getting along" and "problems in communication." A problem-solving attitude and approach was emphasized, and problem-solving steps and questions (Meichenbaum & Deffenbacher, 1988) were integrated into and rehearsed in self-instruction to initiate improved verbal behavior (see Task 5 below). The following is an example of one of these complex self-instructional sets:

> OK, he's not a little shit. He is just a kid who has left his backpack out, not put away the laundry, and not made his bed (cognitive restructuring of label with reality description and humorous image value). That's frustrating, but hardly lethal (cognitive restructuring of catastrophe and palliative relabeling). I want him to take care of these, but nobody appointed me God (cognitive restructuring with humorous image value and reframing in terms of personal wants). OK, take 3 to 4 deep breaths and relax (palliative self-instruction to initiate relaxation), and ask him calmly to take care of them (task-oriented self-instruction for calm assertive requests). If he ignores you, set clear contingencies. So what will I do if he doesn't follow through (task-oriented self-instruction and preplanning alternative coping strategies)?

5. Time-out was integrated with cognitive restructuring and task-oriented self-instruction (i.e., the client was to rethink and problem-solve, as well as relax, when he removed himself from provocation). Self-instructions for time-out were rehearsed in the anger imagery, the self-directed homework, and the two simulations in the home environment.

ACT interface. Readiness factors were mixed. The client was generally cognitively competent and possessed problem-solving strategies. However, motivation and skill for this specific therapeutic task were initially low. He demanded that things be his way, saw little reason why he should have to put up with his son's behavior or change his own behavior, and resisted explorations and alternative interpretations. Confidence parameters were hard to assess. Initially, confidence was high, but for dysfunctional cognitions. Confidence for alternative ways

40 *Jerry L. Deffenbacher*

of thinking was irrelevant as he initially saw no need to change. A low support-high structure intervention style might have been chosen. However, given his overall motivated, cooperative style, a high support-variable structure style was chosen. This style generally matched and moved from greater structure and support to lower structure and support consistent with client change evidenced between sessions. Additionally, it is the author's experience that motivational issues (resistance and avoidance due to misinterpretation of therapist intent) may develop from the use of humor. Therefore, humor interventions were delayed until the relationship and trust were well developed (six sessions). Excerpts below demonstrate this relatively high support-structure combination and lessening of structure when possible.

T: (He has considerable control over relaxation now. I thought this might impact some of his cognitions, but he continues with many examples of demands and obscenities. He resisted cognitive probes and reinterpretation before, but the relationship is solid, and we have a little time left. I think I will push on this again.) *I've noticed that a lot of your anger with Dan* (nodding toward the self-monitoring homework) *stems from his not doing what he is told.*

C: *Does it ever.*

T: (He nibbled. Let me see if I can't get him to explore his demandingness, trying to model alternative thoughts framed as personal desires wherever I can as I think he will need these to see the difference. He's pretty locked into his way of thinking right now.) *But, why should* (voice emphasis) *he do what he is told?*

C: *Huh?*

T: (I'm not sure he is with me, but let's continue. I may have to press pretty hard, but he is ready to handle it.) *Well, I can understand that you want him to do things when you ask, but why should he?*

C: *I don't understand. He should do it just because I'm his dad and asked, because it's the family's rules.*

T: (Good, he's in the ballpark. Let's continue exploring this, tightening the pressure as needed.) *So, he should just because you say so. Is that right?*

C: *You got it!*

Cognitive-Behavior Therapy and ACT **41**

T: *You are his father by birth, but who appointed you God?*

C: *Huh? I don't understand what you mean.*

T: *Well, people get to desire and want, but gods get to dictate and tell other people what to do and how they should behave. Since you are demanding and dictating how Dan should be, you sounded more like a god than a person.*

C: *I guess I never thought about it that way. But do I have to hassle him about everything? Can't he do what he's told some of the time?*

T: (He appears to have part of it, but I am not convinced. He seems to want to compromise and slip off. Let me try for a specific example and see if that helps. I am going to use the one with the "damn it" reference because it has God built in and may make a contrast with personal preference easier.) *Maybe we could take a specific example, like the other evening* (pointing to the self-monitoring log) *when you got mad at him when he didn't put away his books, coat, and backpack after school. Your thoughts were* (reading from the log), *"God damn it! Here we go again. Crap all over the place!" How angry do you suppose you would have felt if you had been thinking to yourself* (modeling alternative self-dialogue), *"Stuff all over the place again. I sure wished he'd pick up after himself. It's really frustrating to have to deal with this as often as we do. While I don't like it, it's not the end of the world. I hear the TV going. I feel strongly enough about this that I am going to ask him to pick it up before watching more TV. I'll calmly turn the TV off until it's done if he hassles about it." How angry would you have been if you'd thought like this?*

C: *I suppose I'd felt frustrated.*

T: (He's made part of the cognitive switch, but let's get even more concrete for contrast.) *How frustrated?*

C: *Pretty frustrated.*

T: *But, how much on our 100-point scale?*

C: *I don't know, maybe 30 to 35, I was pretty tired that night.*

T: (Good, we're getting there. Now pose the contrast and close the session with him thinking on this along with relaxation application.) *So, 30 to 35*

42   *Jerry L. Deffenbacher*

> *if you thought about how you wanted it. And how mad were you on Monday evening* (pointing to the log)?

C: (Client looks.) *70.*

T: *So when you want him to pick up his stuff and he doesn't, you get frustrated say 30, but when you appointed yourself God, and you must have been as a god as you sought fit to damn it* (pointing to the log) *and demanded how Dan should behave, you experienced the wrath of a god at 70.*

C: (Client interrupting.) *Damn it* (said with a big acknowledging grin), *I really do go around demanding a lot of Dan. That's when I sound just like my mother. . . .* (Client goes silent for 15 to 20 seconds and then looks back at the therapist.)

T: *What were you just thinking?*

C: *I was just being sad. I was thinking how mom used to threaten and demand all kinds of things and then blow up at us and how I'm kinda like her.*

T: *And feeling kinda sad for yourself too?*

C: *Uh-huh* (said softly).

T: (Said gently, but firmly.) *That's a pretty heavy price the two of you pay for appointing yourselves gods and demanding how your children should be.*

C: *Yeah . . .* (pausing about 5 seconds). *Boy, I gotta think about that.*

T: (Good. He seems to be processing this meaningfully and emotionally. Let me reduce the structure and see if I can get him to come up with a way to stay focused. I may have to take a shortcut or two as time is up.) *I'd really like to support that. How might you keep yourself focused on thinking about your demandingness?*

C: *I don't know . . .* (pauses about 5 seconds). *I know I'm going to think about it . . . and I could make a note in my book, you know, when I catch myself doing it.*

T: *Those are good ideas, thinking about it more and noting it in your log. I'd like to make one little suggestion since we need to go. Demands are often*

Cognitive-Behavior Therapy and ACT **43**

phrased in certain words like should, have to, gotta, oughta, expect, supposed to, need, and the like (therapist writes these on a slip of paper and hands it to the client). *You may want to listen for when you are using those words* . . . (finishes with a brief review of relaxation assignment).

A similar match of high support-high structure and move to lower support and structure was noted for humor interventions. Initial readiness for humor was hard to gauge. Rapport and motivation were high, the client appeared to have a good sense of humor, and cognitive restructuring in the prior session had gone well.

T: (His self-dialogue is laced with obscenities and inflammatory labels. I'll try to introduce silly humor as an antidote. We have a good relationship, and cognitive restructuring went well last session and during the week. Maybe we are ready for humor.) *Bill, I noticed here on Saturday* (pointing to self-monitoring) *that you labeled Dan a "little shit." I'm not sure I know what you mean. What is a little shit?*

C: (Laughing.) *I don't know. I guess I never thought about it.*

T: (He's interested in what I am getting at. Let's push it.) *Well, it's like other aspects of your thoughts. Maybe calling him a "little shit" makes you madder. So, I want to know what you mean by calling him a "little shit." How was he a "little shit" on Saturday?*

C: (Laughing.) *I guess he was just a kid who left his room in a mess.*

T: (Let's link it to cognitive restructuring and then go back to humor.) *So he didn't do what you wanted, and you were legitimately frustrated. But, how does that make him a "little shit?"*

C: (Looking a little embarrassed.) *I guess it doesn't.*

T: (He's getting it. Now, let's try to give him a concrete humorous image as an alternative response and to start using silly humor and silly humorous images as a coping skill.) *Bill, I'd like to ask you to do something for a few moments. I want you to sit back, close your eyes, and picture clearly what a "little shit" is. When you're ready, open your eyes and tell me what you pictured. OK?*

C: *Sure.* (Client settles back and closes eyes. After about 10 seconds, a grin breaks across his face accompanied by a chuckle. After about another 10

44   *Jerry L. Deffenbacher*

seconds, the grin decreases, and he opens his eyes.) *It was really funny. I saw a small pellet, you know like a rabbit pellet. I guess that is what a "little shit" is. You know what was even funnier was that I thought to myself, if Dan is a "little shit," then I must be a "big shit." Then the image changed. It was like a family portrait. There was the small pellet alongside me, this great big pile of manure* (laughing). *It was really funny. I don't think I will ever be able to call him a "little shit" again without that image coming to mind.*

T: (He really got it. Let's try another while it's working.) *So, it doesn't seem quite as angering when you really think about and picture what a "little shit" is.*

C: *Yeah. I never thought about how my thoughts make me madder. I guess this is like the demand stuff we talked about last time.*

T: (I want to support this linkage and then go back to the humor.) *That's right. If you turn your wants into demands, you move from frustrated to mad. If you call him a "shit," then you respond as if it was "shitty," rather than frustrating. You know, while we are talking about it, I also wondered what a "fucking mess" is. Could you define that for me?*

C: (Laughing.) *Beats the hell out of me.*

T: (This is good. Let's go for the images as this could be really funny.) *Since you can't define it, maybe you can picture it. Close your eyes again* (waits about 5 seconds for client to do so). . . . *Now imagine what a "fucking mess" is, and when you're ready, open your eyes and tell me what you saw.*

C: (About 15 seconds into visualization, client blurts out laughing.) Now I understand why there's always such a mess. All the stuff he drops starts breeding making a bigger mess (opening his eyes). *What a crazy image; it's like something out of Alice in Wonderland. But I guess that is what a "fucking mess" would be, copulating backpacks, and clothes and every-thing* (laughing).

Task 5: Reduction of angry, demanding verbal behavior.   He tended to escalate quickly to angry, verbally demanding behavior (e.g., "Dan, damn it, get up here!" "Stop the damn whining and clean up this mess!"). These tended to increase provocation and noncompliance from Dan, escalating more anger and negative verbal exchanges.

CBT intervention. As with other domains, multiple interventions were employed.

1. Time-out was adapted (i.e., when starting to engage in angry demands, he was to remove himself from the environment and engage in relaxation, cognitive restructuring, and problem- solving/planning self-instruction). Time-out was construed as a behavior for regaining self-control. Time-out was rehearsed as noted before, but also included rehearsal of time-out or exiting statements (e.g., "Dan, I am starting to get angry. I'm going to go in the other room, think things over, and come back to talk to you when I am calm.").
2. Rehearsal of calm, direct requests for alternative behavior were developed and linked to task-oriented self-instruction as the action component of planning. Three types of responses were rehearsed: (a) positive reinforcement of Dan's compliance without request (e.g., "Dan, thanks for putting your stuff away without my asking."); (b) simple requests, which were followed by reinforcement for compliance (e.g., "Dan, I would appreciate you putting away your books, backpack, and coat before watching more TV."); and (c) calmly executing a series of requests and contingent behaviors following noncompliance and resistance (e.g., "Dan, please put your stuff away and come to the table. Dinner is in 2 to 3 minutes." . . . "Dan, you did not put your stuff away. You may not have dinner until you do." . . . "Dan, if you are going to hassle about it, you will have to go to your room without dinner. It's your choice, but you may not stand here and harass your sister and me." . . . Followed by firmly, but calmly removing Dan to his room if needed). These strategies were discussed, modeled, and rehearsed. Not much rehearsal was needed as he could, when he was not angry, generate reasonable requests and follow through appropriately. Escalating noncompliance with the therapist acting Dan's part was a major part of the two simulations in his home.

ACT interface. Readiness was generally high. Motivation, competence, and confidence were generally high. This allowed quicker movement through rehearsal stages. Nonetheless, intervention started at the high support-high structure teaching style in rehearsal activities, but within two sessions style was changed to the lower support-lower structure format (see two excerpts below) which, in turn, prompted the scheduling of the two home simulations for integration and evaluation of transfer to the naturalistic environment.

T: (Demonstrating high support-high structure in imagery rehearsal.) *OK, now stay with that image. You've got your act together* (based on signal

46 *Jerry L. Deffenbacher*

of control in other room). *Now, see yourself walking back into the other room and saying to Dan, "Dan, you know the rules about backpacks, coats, books, and the like and Nintendo playing. Please pause the game and put those things away before you turn the game back on." . . . (5- to 10-second pause) . . . Now, let yourself feel good about asking calmly, thinking, "Good, I did it. I didn't blow up, just got my act together and asked him calmly."*

C: (A segment demonstrating lower support-structure two sessions later, also the therapist's attempts to reflect good feelings about self-control.) *I got some really good news to report.*

T: *Great, tell me about it.*

C: *Well, last weekend, I started to lose it. Then I thought, "Wait a minute." I went into the living room, relaxed, screwed my head on straight, and planned out what I was going to do. I went back in and asked him calmly to clean up his stuff from the table. About 5 minutes later, just about when I was going to phase 2 of my plan, he did it. I didn't yell, and he did it!!*

T: *And, you're feeling really proud of yourself for managing yourself—stopping, relaxing, clearing your head, making a set of plans, and then implementing them calmly.*

C: *Yeah. That's the way I want to be. You know, calm, straightforward, with a good backup plan. I really think I could have gone calmly all the way through, though I was glad that he didn't push it.*

T: *Really savoring that good feeling about being in control of your anger and having a sense of being able to handle it.*

C: *Yeah . . .* (pausing a few seconds). *It really feels good.*

Task 6: Reversing dysfunctional contingencies. One element of angry interactions was reversed contingencies (i.e., Bill would make contracts or exchanges of behaviors and privileges where Dan received his payoffs or rewards prior to executing or following through on his part of the contract). Often, Dan did not follow through on his part, resulting in an argument.

CBT intervention. Interventions were twofold and easily integrated into other interventions.

Cognitive-Behavior Therapy and ACT **47**

1. The therapist and client had a brief developmental discussion. Although the client had skills in using clear logical and natural consequences, a brief discussion of developmental capacities and child rearing was needed to convince him of the inappropriateness of these contracts with a 10-year-old with Dan's tendency to be highly focused. In this discussion, the client noted that his middle brother, for whom he had fond feelings, was like Dan (i.e., very focused and apparently oblivious at times). The client noted that this allowed his brother to be very good at science and computers, but the family too had to be very clear and contingent with him as a youngster. Thinking about Dan like brother Les was a helpful cognitive bridge in this discussion.

2. The various steps of self-instructional training and behavioral rehearsal (see earlier sections) added planning for and stating clear contingency statements that called for the son executing the behavior first (e.g., "When you clean up your room and I have checked it, then you may go to Jimmy's." or "When you've cleared the table, put away your laundry, and finished your math, then you may watch TV." or "If you whine or talk back again, we will not get the movie we discussed."). These self-instructional and verbal statements were anchored in a general ethic of family cooperation and sharing, which the client and both children mentioned as something they wanted.

ACT interface. Readiness assessment paralleled that for Task 5 (see earlier section) as Task 6 could easily be seen as a subtask of Task 5.

SUMMARY AND REFLECTION

Primary intervention lasted 14 weeks. The first two full sessions were devoted to relationship development and collaborative assessment and conceptualization. The next 4 to 5 sessions were devoted heavily to relaxation coping skill training, which was retained throughout. The next several sessions were devoted to cognitive restructuring and self-instructional training with increasing emphases in the later three sessions to rehearsal of calm, assertive requests, reinforcement, and follow-through. The last two sessions were devoted to role-plays in the client's home. Four monthly follow-up sessions were held for support, troubleshooting, and relapse prevention and maintenance activities. During this follow-up period, anger frequency stabilized at .6 per day with average ratings of 30 to 35, which the client rated as minor, reflecting realistic frustration and annoyance. Two "setbacks" were noted during the maintenance period. These were discussed and

48 *Jerry L. Deffenbacher*

strategized over the phone and in the next follow-up session. Phone contact with both children led to reports that Bill was not angry and yelling much anymore, though Dan indicated that his dad still acted like a "dweeb" (a behavioral definition was not forthcoming) at times. Since anger frequency and intensity were down and the client reported success and satisfaction with his children and generalization effects to the work setting, therapy was terminated with an open-end "as needed" contract for "booster sessions" and with the client agreeing to mail or call in a progress report every 2 to 3 months for the next year.

Although CBT principles guided intervention, ACT principles consistently helped guide the style and timing of CBT intervention components. Particularly important were the principles of (1) assessing client readiness on each therapeutic task and (2) matching and moving therapist style to client readiness on each therapeutic task. These two principles helped guide the style and timing of CBT intervention components. The hope is that the general discussion and transcript excerpts and descriptions of ACT interface have shown how ACT may serve the working clinician in making choices about the style and timing of theoretically consistent interventions within an orientation.

REFERENCES

Bandura, A. (1977). *Social learning theory.* Englewood Cliffs, NJ: Prentice Hall.

Beck, A.T. (1976). *Cognitive therapy and the emotional disorders.* New York: International Universities Press.

Beck, A.T., & Emery, G. (1985). *Anxiety disorders and phobias: A cognitive perspective.* New York: Basic Books.

Burns, D.D. (1980). *Feeling good.* New York: Morrow.

Deffenbacher, J.L., Demm, P.M., & Brandon, A.D. (1986). High general anger: Correlates and treatment. *Behaviour Research and Therapy, 24,* 481–489.

Deffenbacher, J.L., & Stark, R.S. (1992). Relaxation and cognitive-relaxation interventions in the treatment of general anger. *Journal of Counseling Psychology, 39,* 158–167.

Deffenbacher, J.L., Story, D.A., Brandon, A.D., Hogg, J.A., & Hazaleus, S.L. (1988). Cognitive and cognitive-relaxation treatments of anger. *Cognitive Therapy and Research, 12,* 167–184.

Deffenbacher, J.L., Story, D.A., Stark, R.S., Hogg, J.A., & Brandon, A.D. (1987). Cognitive-relaxation and social skills interventions in the treatment of general anger. *Journal of Counseling Psychology, 34,* 171–176.

Hazaleus, S.L., & Deffenbacher, J.L. (1986). Relaxation and cognitive treatments of anger. *Journal of Consulting and Clinical Psychology, 54,* 222–226.

Hersey, P., & Blanchard, K.H. (1977). *Management of organizational behavior: Utilizing human resources* (3rd ed.). Englewood Cliffs, NJ: Prentice Hall.

Howard, G.S., Nance, D.W., & Myers, P. (1986). Adaptive counseling and therapy: An integrative, metatheoretical approach. *The Counseling Psychologist, 14,* 363–442.

Howard, G.S., Nance, D.W., & Myers, P. (1987). *Adaptive counseling and therapy.* San Francisco: Jossey-Bass.

Kanfer, F.H., & Goldstein, A.P. (1991). *Helping people change* (4th ed.). New York: Pergamon.

Meichenbaum, D. (1977). *Cognitive-behavior modification: An integrative approach.* New York: Plenum.

Meichenbaum, D. (1985). *Stress inoculation training.* New York: Pergamon.

Meichenbaum, D.H., & Deffenbacher, J.L. (1988). Stress inoculation training. *The Counseling Psychologist, 16,* 69–90.

Novaco, R. (1975). *Anger control: The development and evaluation of an experimental treatment.* Lexington, MA: D. C. Health.

Spielberger, C.D. (1988). *State-Trait Anger Expression Inventory: Professional manual.* Orlando, FL: Psychological Assessment Resources.

COMMENTS

Cognitive Behavior Therapy and ACT

Don W. Nance

What a great beginning! The goodness of fit between ACT and CBT is demonstrated clearly by Dr. Deffenbacher. The identification of the seven common assumptions or principles in cognitive behavioral therapy provides an excellent distillation of the common elements in that approach. One of the major contributions of Cognitive Behavior Therapy is the focus on the internal thoughts or cognitive behaviors of humans as well as their overt actions. Dr. Deffenbacher demonstrated this focus effectively by working with Bill's dysfunctional cognitions. Dr. Deffenbacher also shared with us some of his *internal decisional processes.* By including these pieces of internal dialogue, he helps us better understand how he decided what to verbalize to the client. An entire methodology, **Internal Process Recall (IPR),** is based on reviewing a segment of tape and recalling what was going on internally for each participant. A similar process takes place when the therapist shifts the focus from the content being addressed to what is going on internally for the client. I recommend that you imagine or make up possible internal dialogues while reading the other verbatim samples in the book. What was the therapist saying internally to lead to the response shown on the printed page?

The intentional consideration of how therapeutic tasks should be sequenced is one of the important contributions of ACT. The sequence is based not only on the content of the tasks but also on the readiness of the client to engage each task. The clear delineation of therapeutic tasks, a common activity in CBT, provides an ideal demonstration of how ACT can assist the therapist in deciding on the sequence of tasks and the style to use in approaching each task. As Dr. Deffenbacher demonstrated, attending to client readiness in sequencing tasks builds success, increases confidence and willingness, enhances expert and relationship power, and provides a supportive base for tasks involving lower readiness. In general, ACT principles suggest placing higher readiness tasks earlier in the sequence of therapeutic tasks. Matching the style of treatment to the various levels of readiness is, of course, central to the use of ACT in therapy. The sequencing of tasks based on readiness presupposes that readiness is different depending on the task. In the case of Bill, he was very willing and able to engage in collaborative problem identification (Task 2), willing but unable to reduce his anger (Task 3), and less willing while unable to alter his dysfunctional cognition independently (Task 4).

"Rabbit pellets give perspective." No, it's not a headline from a supermarket tabloid. It is the effective use of humor to make an important therapeutic point. Dr.

52   *Jerry L. Deffenbacher*

Deffenbacher's use of silly humor to impact the client's dysfunctional cognition illustrates a powerful tool that transcends theoretical orientation. The humor tool comes with some instructions for proper use. Notice the humor is intended to provide perspective, not to demean or discount the client or his son. Notice that the therapist directed the client to develop the image, thereby increasing the likelihood of the image and the humor being acceptable and relevant for the client. Notice how the presence of humor and laughter also serve to interrupt the reactive anger previously experienced by the client—almost an alternate form of reciprocal inhibition.

Humor can be a defense against more direct expression of painful affect—"Laughing to keep from crying." Humor can be used as an offense—a way to express anger or other feelings against another person. If cutting "just kidding" remarks find their way into therapy with frequency, then stop and examine what is happening in the relationship. Humor also can be offensive. For some clients, rabbit pellets might be an offensive image. If so, it also would be probable that "little shit" would not be common in their vocabulary. Sexual language, swear words, ethnic references, etc. can be offensive. As a therapist you can follow the lead of the client or not follow. If you lead, do so intentionally and with a readiness to deal with the impact of the humor. As a powerful potential tool in therapy, use humor with skill and care.

Finally, it was powerful to observe that a similar or parallel process was going on in therapy as was transpiring in Bill's relationship with his children. The therapist was consistent, reinforcing, provided clear limits, and gave directions and clear feedback. The process focused on resolving problems and conflicts rather than on blaming or finding fault. Matching the process with the goals is powerful in this example of successful treatment.

QUESTIONS

1. What impacts do you see using readiness to sequence therapeutic tasks? What are drawbacks or cautions?

2. What would you do if a client were unable and/or unwilling to keep appointments? For self-referred counseling? For required counseling?

3. How might the course of therapy have been altered by addressing the dysfunctional cognitions first?
    "Bill, you're just talking yourself into these angry outbursts. The major thing you need to do is change what you say to yourself."

4. How does sharing the internal processes aid in understanding? When is it particularly useful to discuss overtly what is happening internally? What is the impact of sharing internal thoughts with the client?

5. What could be some of the results of the internal processes not matching the external behaviors?

6. What positive processes were involved in the course of this CBT treatment? Any negative processes?

7. How is the client's past treated in the CBT approach?

8. What would have indicated the need for a more historical approach, a more intrapsychic focus, a more psychodynamic approach?

9. How funny are you? What role does humor play in your life? In your therapy?

10. What rules or guidelines do you have about using humor in therapy? What kinds of humor are most effective for you with clients? What doesn't work?

Chapter 3

HUMANISTIC PSYCHOTHERAPY AND ACT: A CASE OF INTERNAL CONFLICT

Willis D. Poland
University of Cincinnati

Within the past few years I have become aware of the Adaptive Counseling and Therapy model developed by Howard, Nance, and Myers (1987). Like many therapists, I have been intuitively in sync with this model for many years. As a clinician with a broad-based humanistic/existential/Gestalt orientation, my inclination was to paint the canvas of therapy with broader strokes. The ACT model brings more precision to the process and does not violate the tenets of therapy that are near and dear to my heart. In the chapter that follows, I outline my humanistic theoretical orientation and demonstrate how the ACT model is compatible with a humanistic approach to therapy using a case study.

PERSONAL STATEMENT

As a psychologist who espouses a humanistic perspective, to begin this chapter without providing background information on myself would be inconsistent with what I believe. My long-time conviction has been that who we are when

56 *Willis D. Poland*

we arrive for professional training in psychology is ultimately as important in determining how we will practice our profession as is any theoretical perspective we might try to interject. Unfortunately, many graduate programs attempt to persuade their students to accept a particular orientation without considering the uniqueness of each person being trained. Some graduates take years to overcome the confining boundaries of their training and to develop a way of working with their clients that feels right for them. The movement is from adhering to what was learned to approaching the task with a much more open view. Increased flexibility can result in utilizing what seems to work for the therapist and the client. In this respect, there is fundamental agreement with the central thesis of ACT. The most effective therapy occurs when the therapist's behavior is flexible and varies systematically with the client.

My evolution as a therapist begins with my parents, who set the tone for the person and professional I would become. My mother and father had been married for 65 years at the time of her death. I was aware that my parents genuinely cared for and respected each other. The traditional roles each played seemed right for each of them. They were both interested in the achievements of their children. A clear sense of right and wrong was instilled through involvement in a conservative Protestant church.

From my parents I learned to value people more than things; to make the most of my potential; to treat others fairly, with respect; and to have a purpose in life larger than myself. My mother modeled acceptance. I learned not to judge others or myself too harshly and to try to find what is good in myself and others. From my father, who presented a tough exterior but who had a gentle streak as wide as the Mississippi, I learned that it is possible to be both tough and gentle. I did not have to choose to be tough in order to be a man. It is clear to me that my grounding in a humanistic view of the world was in place long before I knew about psychology and psychotherapy.

In 1949, during my senior year of undergraduate study, I took a counseling course from Dr. Maurice Woolf, a quiet, gentle man who reflected the values and concepts of Carl Rogers in his teaching. While taking this course I first began to think about counseling as a professional goal. After several years of public school teaching, I decided to pursue a Ph.D. in counseling psychology. Through the graduate education process I was exposed to a wide range of theoretical perspectives. Upon graduation I was still more enamored with the humanistic orientation of Rogers than any other, but I knew that I would have to continue my search for what was right for me.

During the late 60s and early 70s, I became involved with group work and got caught up in the Human Potential movement of the times. Training at the National Training Laboratories, followed by the completion of the Intensive Post-Graduate Training Program at the Gestalt Institute of Cleveland, helped me to feel that my approach to therapy was beginning to be congruent with who I was as a person. My expectation was that the client would be *able* to identify and be *willing* to explore the important issues in his or her life. While the client was accountable for choosing *what* we explored, it was my responsibility to provide the therapeutic process or *how* we went about that exploration. Carrying out my part of the contract required that I be flexible in responding to the multitude of ways my clients would present themselves.

It should be clear to those familiar with the ACT model that my expectations of clients are quite similar to the components of client readiness—willingness, ability, and confidence. As for my therapeutic style, I am most compatible with a teaching, supporting, delegating combination, but rarely would telling be a part of the process. It was not surprising to me when I assessed my style using the *ACT Therapist Style Inventory* that my preference was S 2—Teaching with S 3—Supporting and S 4—Delegating next in order. S 1—Telling was seldom my choice.

ELEMENTS OF A HUMANISTIC ORIENTATION

Beliefs about the Human Experience

The humanistic therapist holds that his or her particular view of the world is not the only one possible and that "reality" is not objectively given but is personalized and individual. Consequently, understanding any human being is achieved through focusing on his or her subjective phenomenological world. Each person has an undeniable right to his or her own unique experience. A holistic view stresses that human beings have an essential core that is indivisible. Humanists do not believe it is useful to divide experience into dichotomies (e.g., mind vs. body, thought vs. feeling, conscious vs. unconscious).

Staying in the present with the emphasis on the "what" rather than the "why" of experience is of critical importance when relating to another's phenomenological world. As the Polsters (1973) pointed out, the search for meaning is a human reflex, but the "compulsion" to meaning frequently drowns out experience itself.

58   *Willis D. Poland*

What is not available to immediate awareness will emerge as the person becomes ready through self-exploration and self-discovery. Awareness is coupled with the experience of choice. Experiencing ourselves as having to make a choice is what gives life shape and meaning. In making choices we create much of our own existence and, therefore, are responsible for it.

Beliefs about Counseling/Psychotherapy

Therapy is an encounter between two human beings, both of whom will be changed by what happens between them. For the therapist to be genuine in this encounter, a congruence between life inside and outside of therapy must exist. Therapists, like clients, are indivisible and viewed from a holistic perspective.

Listening/seeing with undivided attention is the first task of the therapist. In the process of listening/seeing, the therapist enters the phenomenological/experiential world of the client. Critical to the therapeutic process is my respect for the uniqueness of my client and my belief that he or she can become more self-aware and change in positive directions. I also am aware that the client often has a resistance that is equal to or stronger than the desire to change.

The first goal of therapy is to facilitate the enlarged awareness of the client, i.e., awareness of the whole person. From this enhanced awareness will emerge the primary therapeutic tasks facing the client, e.g., the emergence of unfinished business, the realization of stuckness, the fear of the unknown (change), the newness and strangeness of this (therapeutic) relationship. It is the therapist's responsibility to support and to challenge the client in order to facilitate awareness and change. ACT provides a conceptual framework for determining degrees of support and confrontation needed.

Therapeutic Process

When the client arrives, I want to be fully present and ready to listen to his or her story. As the client shares his or her story, I am listening and looking for a focus/theme (the figure that emerges from the ground) that carries the most energy. I may ask questions, reflect, or clarify during this initial part of the session. Perls (1973) argued that if the therapist were limited to the following questions, he or she eventually would achieve success with almost all clients: What are you doing? What do you feel? What do you want? While therapy is not as simplistic as this might suggest, this does indicate the importance of focusing on "what" rather than "why." The important point is not to rush or put words in the mouth of the client. For this initial task, my behaviors are centered in the reflective listening of Style 3.

When a theme emerges, I try to create an experiment that will help the client engage in focused self-exploration in order to enhance awareness. This usually involves more directive Style 2 behavior on my part about *how* to proceed in gaining an enlarged awareness. Thus, the therapy process provides the client with the opportunity to become more fully aware of his/her experience/unfinished business; to facilitate the choosing of life-enhancing instead of life-restricting alternatives; and to achieve a greater sense of closure regarding both the old and the possibility of new beginnings.

The emphasis in humanistic/Gestalt therapy is primarily on the present. The past or future is brought into the present moment and worked with in a present-centered context. For example, when it becomes clear that a client is stuck in the present with an experience from the past, the past is brought into the present through the marvelous avenue of the imagination. The encounter with an aspect of oneself or an imagined other becomes immediate and real in contrast to a less lively experience when "talking about" what happened in the past.

PERSPECTIVE ON READINESS

One of the most important contributions of the ACT model is the emphasis on readiness. Too often we treat readiness as a personality construct and try to assess whether the client is ready for therapy in some global way. Inexperienced therapists often assume that because a client seeks professional help he or she is ready for therapy. Much to the therapist's surprise, the process seems to stall after a few sessions. For a time, both the therapist and the client may assume that the problem lies in the failure of the therapist to come up with the right solution.

ACT addresses this issue by examining the match between the readiness of the client with regard to a particular task and the therapeutic style of the therapist. If an appropriate match occurs, then therapy will proceed and some degree of success will be achieved. The critical part of this equation is the assessment of client readiness assuming, of course, the therapist is both self-aware with regard to therapeutic style preference(s) and flexible in the use of his or her preferred style(s).

When considering the question of readiness, I have found the Gestalt concept of polarities to be quite useful. When a client first comes to my office, I believe he or she has reached a point where one part of that person wants to be in therapy and work on whatever it takes to make life better. At the same time, I am aware that almost always a competing force is equally strong advocating for the status quo. One part advocates for change and the other would like the pain to stop but without venturing into the unknown, which may be more frightening than the status quo. The first part is ready to tackle the particular tasks necessary for change to occur, and the second resists with an equal force. Hence, we have an impasse, and the client experiences himself or herself as being stuck. Upon close examination, what becomes clear is that the resistance is not to the therapist or a particular interpretation made before its time; rather, the resistance is to that part of oneself that has decided change is necessary but hasn't convinced the whole person of the wisdom of that decision. The goal in working with a polarized struggle is to help my client become more fully aware of the competing forces and work toward an integrated sense of self. Subjectively the client may not experience the presence or absence of readiness, but rather feel torn between moving forward and standing still. Rarely is the goal to get rid of one aspect of self, but rather it is to discover a way for competing forces to achieve a different balance and work toward an agreed upon direction.

Looking at resistance from the perspective of the ACT model, what I have been describing can be explained in terms of the three elements of readiness. The part of the person not ready to explore and consider change with regard to a particular task may be lacking in motivation, ability, or the confidence to move forward. The therapist just might be able to tip the balance by bolstering limited motivation, supporting limited ability, or even modeling and encouraging enough self-confidence to give the client an opportunity to do his or her work. The therapist who recognizes this struggle will adapt his or her style to work with this issue. Even with therapist recognition and appropriate style intervention some clients will resolve their conflict in the direction of the status quo and decide to leave therapy. The part of them that was willing and/or able is not strong enough to keep them engaged in the therapeutic process. For them change will have to wait for another time and place.

Therapist Readiness

I believe an important aspect of readiness has been neglected. It is usually assumed that the therapist is ready to work with whatever a client brings to the therapy hour. Consequently, ACT suggests spending considerable time and effort in assessing the client's readiness to work on a particular task and almost no time spent be the therapist on examining his or her own readiness for that work. It is not only necessary to have a good match between therapeutic style and client's readiness, but also a good match between therapist's readiness and client's readiness in order for therapy to proceed smoothly. If therapy stalls or goes astray, it may be because the therapist is not motivated, able, or confident to respond to the client, no matter what the preferred therapeutic style/client readiness match may be. What seems likely is that when the therapist is not ready, his or her therapeutic style will be off target and the necessary match for effective therapy will not occur.

Many factors can interfere with the therapist's readiness for working with a particular client or client's task. The therapist's physical and emotional energies may be so depleted that the client is unable to revive those energies with his or her story. The life-experience gap between therapist and client may be too great to allow for an empathic response. The client may begin to explore an issue that the therapist has not resolved personally. The client may be describing such painful or horrendous material dealing with abuse, rape, or incest that the therapist shuts down. The client may present a task with which the therapist has worked a hundred times before and it simply doesn't capture his or her interest today.

An example of readiness assessment occurred a number of years ago when I was going through separation and divorce from my first wife. After much self-examination, I decided I would not work with female clients for a period of several years because I did not believe that I was ready to listen to and work with some aspects of their lives that I knew they would present in therapy.

THERAPEUTIC INTERVENTIONS

In using the Gestalt approach, which has its ground in a broad based humanistic/existential orientation, relatively few techniques or standard interventions are involved. First of all, the focus is on the present, the here and now awareness of the client. This awareness is enhanced by designing experiments that are related to the task facing the client at a particular point in time. An experiment is not something the therapist pulls out of his or her bag of therapeutic tricks. It is a creatively designed process to help the client explore in more depth the task that is already figural at the moment. It is an experiment precisely because, once in motion, it may go in any one of many directions. If the therapist tries to make the experiment follow some predicted path, then the therapist is working his or her agenda, not the client's. The therapist's task is to "track" with the client, fine tune the process, and make suggestions for the client's consideration. Imperatively the therapist checks frequently with the client to determine if the client is going in the direction that feels right for him or her. If the process goes well, the client will have an enhanced awareness of some important aspect of the task involved. An

62   *Willis D. Poland*

important point is to remind the client that this is not a rehearsal for some future action he or she will take. Awareness comes first, and action will follow only if the client decides that is the next step necessary.

The relevance of the ACT model for my work was not so much in the selection and application of treatment strategies as it was in helping me to be clear about and remain aware of my therapeutic style preferences. Perls (1973) indicated that the goal of therapy is to help the client move from environmental support to self-support. This is accomplished using an experiential therapy in which both challenge and support are used by the therapist. It is my belief that Gestalt therapy cuts across all of the therapeutic styles but is most compatible with the teaching, supporting, and delegating styles. In my opinion, it is not as clearly and singularly identified with the S 4 Style as the ACT model authors suggest (Howard, et al., 1987).

Clients tend to be naive about therapy when they first enter into a therapeutic relationship. Regardless of how the therapist goes about beginning the process, he or she is teaching the client the norms and boundaries of therapy. There are, of course, different teaching styles but, whatever occurs, teaching is part of the process. A Gestalt approach tends to be more directive at the beginning in order to help the client learn how the therapist understands and practices the process. The therapist will challenge the client's attempts to make the therapist responsible for the client's life. At the same time, the therapist will support the efforts of the client to become more self-aware and to take charge of his or her life. As a client becomes more and more aware and able to move toward self-support, the therapist will use delegation as a therapeutic style. This movement on the part of the therapist can be seen in a single experiment as well as over the course of therapy.

I am aware that I have provided the reader with a very condensed version of a humanistic perspective. The references at the end of this chapter have been used many times over the years in my teaching and have been invaluable in my work with clients. They contain the flesh for the skeleton presented here, and I highly recommend them to you.

KEVIN: A CASE OF INTERNAL CONFLICT

Kevin was one of those clients who caught my interest almost from the moment he sat opposite me in my office. He was tall, with an athletic build, handsome features, and reddish brown hair. He was articulate, seemed self-confident, and had a nice easy laugh that suggested he enjoyed life. When I first met him, I imagined he would be envied by other young men and sought after by young women.

His pain was not immediately apparent since he told his story in a rather casual manner. A few weeks before seeking help, a young woman with whom he had been involved for approximately five years had decided to end their relationship. From his perspective, Cathy's decision was based on her desire for a greater commitment from him, which he was unable/unwilling to give. He had had other sexual relationships during the course of their relationship that she had known about. She was both hurt and angry but had forgiven him in the past and had continued their relationship. When she told him she was ending their relationship, he said he felt a mixture of sadness and relief. He could not believe their relationship was over. On the one hand, he wanted to pursue her and have their relationship continue. On the other hand, he thought this might be his last opportunity to be free and pursue any woman who might attract his interest. At age 24, he believed he should be ready to "settle down" but couldn't bring himself to make a long-range commitment to Cathy. At the end of the first session, I gave Kevin a "Life History Questionnaire" to complete by the next session. This instrument is quite comprehensive and provides a lot of biographical data and self-impressions of the client. Much of the following information was provided by Kevin's responses to the questionnaire.

Kevin was a graduate student in the second year of a master's degree in social work program at the University. He grew up in a large Irish-Catholic family that he described as "very close." Kevin's father owned a tool rental business that his two older brothers joined after graduating from college. Kevin had been expected to join the family business when he finished his undergraduate degree but, after much agonizing, had decided to pursue his interest in social work. He continues to experience pressure from both his father and brothers to follow their career path. Kevin's mother supports his career choice. He described her as extremely caring and sees her as devoting all of her time and energy to her family. Kevin believes she cares too much for others and not enough for herself. Kevin said he is much closer to his mother than to his father and acknowledges he is sometimes sad and angry that his father was not very available or interested in him when he was growing up. He attended Catholic schools. His fondest memories centered on his participation in sports.

When asked what words or phrases apply to him, he checked the following: angry, feel tense, financial problems, depressed, sexual problems, lonely, anxious, can't make decisions, feeling guilty, confused, misunderstood, worthwhile, intel-

64   Willis D. Poland

ligent, attractive, and considerate. Among his sentence completions were the following: I am too focused on presenting the right image—having it all together. I feel angry, devastated, when I think of Cathy having sex with another man. I think too much. I wish people would really listen to each other. In responding to the question, "What personal characteristics do you think the ideal therapist should possess?" Kevin listed the following: honest, empathic listener, being real and genuine.

Initial Perceptions

When Kevin first sought help he was talking about feeling devastated by the ending of his relationship with Cathy. He was aware that the loss of this relationship was related to his inability to make a clear and monogamous commitment to her. He was torn between trying to make that commitment in order to resume their relationship, if possible, or to accept the end in order to enjoy his freedom while he could. It was obvious to him that neither alternative was to his liking and he felt stuck.

From my perspective, I was quite aware of his stuckness and the dilemma he faced in such a choice. It was apparent that Cathy had been an extremely important part of his life for several years. It also was clear that making the necessary commitment to her was a frightening prospect to him. In the past he had tried to make a commitment to her , then an attractive woman with an inviting look would cross his path, and he would be off and running like the male dog who sniffs the air and finds an interesting female scent down the block. If he could convince Cathy to resume their relationship without having to make a commitment, that would alleviate the pain connected with the loss without his feeling trapped. But that would simply reinstate the status quo, which wouldn't work for long. It would not address the issue of commitment that he knew he would inevitably have to face. Although coping with the grief associated with his loss was an important therapeutic task, it was my belief that a larger and more significant task was deciding how, when, and/or whether to make a long-term commitment in a particular relationship. The latter was his personal struggle, which only incidentally involved Cathy, and had to be fought out and resolved.

From our initial session and the "Life History Questionnaire," another significant issue would affect the course of therapy unless addressed early. Kevin was likely to have difficulty allowing himself to be vulnerable. Having had the opportunity to be a therapeutic guide for a number of mental health professionals, I know how difficult it is for them to be vulnerable in the process. They want to explore the issues that are so troubling to them, but they would like to do it in such a way as to appear strong, capable, and together. As a graduate student in social work, already doing clinical work, Kevin faced a dilemma. Does he tell his story in an open and honest way including all the associated feelings? If so, what does he do with his need to present himself as "having it all together"? It didn't help the dilemma that I was a faculty member of the psychology department, that I was an experienced therapist involved in training clinical psychology graduate students, and that I was sitting across from him with gray hair.

Although he did not present it as a problem, the pressure to join the family business was always in the "ground" of his life. When he was with his family, the issue would become "figural" and he would feel the need to justify his current career choice once again. It was not clear at the beginning of our work together as to whether he would choose to use therapy to address this issue. Since I knew this therapy would be relatively brief because of time constraints (his graduation), it was critical to stay focused and "bracket off" those issues to be considered later, if time allowed. As is true of almost all clients, other issues would emerge as Kevin's therapy progressed.

Readiness

Kevin's readiness. Several facets are involved in assessing Kevin's readiness for therapy. He was bright, articulate, and psychologically minded, and, on the surface, he exhibited a lot of self-confidence. He seemed motivated by the pain of losing an important relationship. At the same time the choice before him was noxious. If he could find a way to temporarily resolve it, I imagined he would do so. Then therapy would not be necessary. So his motivation for that task of dealing with commitment was moderate and mixed. He also would have to confront the dilemma of vulnerability in therapy and coping with the imagined loss of self-esteem that doing so would involve. It was not clear whether he had the personal security (confidence) to take that risk even though he was motivated.

Therapist readiness. As for my readiness to work with him, I liked him and thought he would be an engaging person to get to know. My own struggle regarding commitment was an issue I had to consider. For example, it was five years after separating from my first wife that I became seriously involved in another relationship and another five years before I got married again. I knew the commitment struggle well. I felt resolved enough that I didn't believe it would interfere in my work with him. If anything, I thought I could be very empathic with his struggle without getting personally caught up in it.

66   *Willis D. Poland*

The Course of Counseling

In the first session, while listening to Kevin's initial telling of his story, I became aware of the distance between the words used and the feelings expressed. It was as if he were saying the words to a song but the music was missing. I understood the words and believed that inside him there was a tune that would give fullness of meaning to the words. I did not know why he used powerful words to express what was happening in his life but did so in a very casual and/or controlled manner.

Early in the second session he had been talking about the history of his relationship with Cathy and how he had always felt in control. Now he was having to wait for her to make up her mind as to whether she wanted the relationship. He always had wanted her to be more assertive but not to the point of ending their relationship. He was reluctant to look at what he could do to influence her decision in his direction. In a gentle attempt to get him to share his feelings, I made the following intervention:

Will: *How does it feel to you to be on the other side? What's it like for you?*

Kevin: *Scary. A little bit of jealousy, which I'm trying to avoid. It's altering to my self-image or whatever. Never thought of myself like this—that I couldn't handle it. Almost embarrassing in a way.*

W: *Could you say more about that?*

K: *Yeah. Don't want to say this wrong. It's embarrassing or humiliating to be crumbling like this when I've always been so together or I've tried to be that way. To think that something or someone could make me—devastate me this much and that I could truly lose control of myself or think I'm losing control over them. I realize there are people worse off than me but to me this is pretty low.*

W: *So you feel devastated and like you're losing control.*

K: *Yeah! Not being me at all. This isn't me going around whimpering all the time to people.*

W: *Are you doing that?*

K: *Not really. But when someone comes up to me or calls me and asks how I am, I'm not going to say great. I don't give them a sob story either, but people who know me pick it up. I'm usually high energy and happy.*

W: *So you're not presenting yourself as devastated.*

K: *To a few people. To a few close friends I'm presenting myself as devastated.*

W: *Letting them see how you really are.*

K: *Yeah. It's embarrassing to let Cathy see me like this. I don't want her to think of me as a wimp or something. The thing is the other part of me says, "Hey like, that's the way it is, you're human and you're allowed to lose it once in the while and you're allowed to feel sad or devastated. It's OK. It's almost like a right that I have and don't deny yourself that."*

As hard as I tried, I still could not pick up that Kevin was feeling devastated. Yet I believe that is exactly what he was feeling. Based on this segment it was my guess that his need to present himself as together was the way he stopped himself from fully expressing his devastation. My approach was to listen, to try to understand what he was experiencing, and to be supportive. My therapeutic style had been primarily supportive (S 3). It was my judgment that a teaching moment was now possible and an S 2 therapeutic style would be more effective. This was based on my assessment that Kevin was at least unable to fully express his feelings and perhaps unwilling as well. The following brief segment illustrates this change in therapeutic style and his response:

W: *I hear a struggle going on in you. Let me tell you what I hear and see if you hear the same thing. There is one part of you that is into having it together, presenting yourself as a together person, really being on top of things, really being in charge of your life, presenting an image of a strong, outgoing person. That's the one side. The other part of you is feeling scared, feeling hurt, feeling embarrassed, and not in control. This is the part you don't want Cathy and others to see. The side that makes you very uncomfortable.*

K: *Yeah.*

W: *So part of you really wants to be this together person and there's another part of you that doesn't feel together and you are struggling with that. Is that what you're experiencing?*

K: *That's close. I'll make a few addendums to that. The thing with presenting myself to Cathy—what bothers me about that is if I knew we were quote "us," these things wouldn't scare me. I wouldn't be jealous if she*

68   Willis D. Poland

*went out with some guy to a movie or out with a bunch of girls. I would
see these as healthy and good things for her. I want her to have her own
separate life, but now these things become threatening. The part about
presenting myself as together. I've been working through that all my life
or at least ever since I became aware of myself. It is real important to me
to be quote "together." At this point I realize that is just bull. I've tried to
give up portraying images so I'm not trying to throw out an image. I want
me to show.*

In this segment I was trying to capture the essence of his struggle. If he agreed
with my perception, it was my intent to create an experiment involving the two
parts that might lead to a greater awareness. There was also the possibility that it
might lead to a more full expression of the hurt, scared side of him that felt
devastated. I was aware that we were both operating in a cognitive manner and
were not sharply, succinctly focused on the task. I experienced his last response as
a deflection but at the end provided an opening to move therapy into the here and
now of our relationship. Staying with the S 2 therapeutic style, I asked the
following question:

W: *How do you think you are presenting yourself to me?*

K: (Laughs.) *Partly—a little bit—I feel like I'm going back and forth for one
thing. A little confused as I say things. And probably a little uptight. It is
real important that you understand, so I'm probably trying harder to
make myself clear.*

W: *I have been trying to get a sense of how much you are presenting yourself
as together or if you are presenting yourself as devastated and out of
control. The way you come across to me is that you are more in control
and presenting yourself as more together. You tell me about feeling
devastated and out of control, but I don't pick that up here.*

K: *Yeah, I was wondering about that to. I don't know.* (Smiling and moving
about in his chair.)

W: *Am I making you uncomfortable right now?*

K: (Smiles.) *Not really. No, not especially uncomfortable. You're throwing
out something to me that is not real easy to answer. I have a tendency to
smile or laugh when I get something that is hard to answer. It's a defense
of mine.*

Humanistic Psychotherapy and ACT **69**

W: *I'm not trying to make you defensive. I am trying to help you look at what you are doing here, because if you tell me about feeling devastated and out of control but I can't pick that up then I don't really know what you are experiencing.*

K: *Part of it is that three weeks ago was when I was the most desperate or devastated. I'm definitely much better than I was then. The other part is that I'm learning to be a therapist, and sometimes I put myself in your seat instead of staying in mine.*

W: *And that can be a problem.*

K: *Yeah. And I say, "Don't do that to yourself." Sometimes I feel I'm too knowledgeable about therapy.*

W: *So here you are with a struggle you're having and you can't just come in and talk about it without wondering what I'm thinking and doing.*

K: *Yeah. And so I say, "Shit, of all people, I should be able to come in here and really let loose, and I come in here and try to keep it together."*

W: *Yeah.*

K: *Like a good client or something.*

W: *I don't have a requirement that you come in here and keep it all together. What I would like for you is to be able to come in here and talk with me about whatever is going on with you and that you not require yourself to work on your problems in such a way that you will be thought of as a really together person.*

K: *Yeah. There is something about knowing that you're not together that means you're a little bit together.*

W: *Can you use that to give yourself permission to come in here and do what you need to do?*

K: *Yeah.*

During this segment we started to address the critical process of vulnerability in therapy. Until Kevin could comfortably accept himself as a client without

70 *Willis D. Poland*

having to impress me, he would not be able to fully utilize the therapeutic process. I wanted him to know that I didn't have a rule such as, "Since you are training to be a therapist, you must demonstrate that you have your act together when talking with me." I was trying to give him permission to do his work, knowing that he would have to give himself permission if he were to allow himself to become vulnerable. As we talked he seemed more aware of what he was doing and more willing to allow himself the necessary freedom to do his work. In retrospect, Style 2 seemed the right choice for this particular exchange between us. It also was clear that we would need to continue to monitor how able and willing he would be in allowing himself to be vulnerable. This was not something that could be resolved in one brief exchange.

A little later, in the second session, we were exploring his relationship with Cathy, and we began to address the issue of commitment. Our exploration of this issue began in response to the following question:

W: *What are you experiencing now?*

K: *I don't know. I'm confused. There's some fear of getting back together. I guess the closer it gets or seems like that it could happen I start wondering again. Has it been long enough? Did I do enough? That gets scary too. I don't want this to happen again. I don't want it to happen ever again.*

W: *Don't want what to happen ever again?*

K: *This kind of separation to take place. I don't want us to get together and then two weeks later to realize it was a mistake.*

W: *So when you get back together, you have to be ready to get back together too.*

K: *Yeah.*

W: *Say more about have you "done enough."*

K: *Have I dated enough. The sexual thing. My head is so fucked up about that I don't even know. Don't know whether I should check that out now while I have the chance. Don't know whether it is that important to me or not.*

W: *Check it out?*

Humanistic Psychotherapy and ACT   **71**

K: *Have sex with other women. Check it out while I'm allowed to because we're not together right now. It's never that important for me to have sex with other women until Cathy and I are together. That's when I get scared—one woman the rest of my life!*

W: *Yeah.*

K: *Right now one woman the rest of my life sounds good, you know.*

W: *Since Cathy's not available.*

K: *Yeah.*

W: *Is that what you mean by your "head is all fucked up"?*

K: *Yeah. I found myself last night and this morning wanting to promise her that I would never have sex with anyone else.*

W: *Did you?*

K: *No. I couldn't. Not right now because I don't know what is going to happen in the next two weeks or two months.*

In this segment I was trying to be supportive, and my therapeutic style was more S 3 than S 2. My goal was to follow his lead, match his language, and try to understand the nature of his struggle. Although I believed the commitment issue was broader than promising "to never have sex with anyone else," it was important to work within the context that he was ready to use. In order to sharpen the focus of his struggle, I decided to switch back to a teaching style and work with the polarity that I was hearing.

W: *Let's take a few minutes and focus on the issue of whether you want to be monogamous or not. Is that OK with you?*

K: *Yeah.*

W: *I want you to make statements from the two different parts of you that you have been expressing in the last few minutes. One part is the "I would like to be in a monogamous sexual relationship with Cathy for the rest of my life."*

K: (Smiles and moves about in his chair.)

72   *Willis D. Poland*

W: *And the other part would be "I am not ready to be in a monogamous relationship with Cathy for the rest of my life." Do you recognize those two parts in yourself right now?*

K: *Yeah.*

W: *So, just make statements from each of those places and see what you feel like when you do that.*

K: *OK. I would very much like to be monogamous with Cathy for the rest of my life because it would be real good to know that I can say no. Anything else that comes along, at least right now, would basically be physical, and I've never had a good payoff from just a physical relationship. Maybe right at the time, but it never felt good in the long-term sense. I would like to be monogamous because it would make her very happy and I would have control over myself—that I can say no to that. What was the other side? I'm not ready right now?*

W: *Yeah.*

K: *First thing that comes to my mind is I'm not ready because I'm going to be away from Cathy this summer, and I know this will come up and I might get mad at her or myself if I have to say no. Somewhere in the back of my mind I'm thinking I want to wait until I get back and then I'll be ready. But then the other thing is "I'd like to be able to say no while I'm without her."*

W: *That's the other side.*

K: *Yeah. That's the "I'd like to be monogamous with Cathy." The thing is I know all my life it's going to be there. I'm going to be around women, and I'm going to want to have sex with other women.*

W: *And that's the other side again.*

K: *Yeah. I'm not ready. But it just seems real superficial to me to have sex with a lot of women. But I'm still really turned on by other women. But I'd like to say no.*

W: *So opportunities and your desire are always going to be there, but you'd like to be able to say no.*

K: *Yeah. Why not start saying no now.*

Humanistic Psychotherapy and ACT **73**

W: *And what does the other side say?*

K: *More and more the other side is starting to say, "I don't really know—it's up to you." (Laughs.)*

W: *Would you share with me what you are feeling right now?*

K: *Really torn apart. Unhappy with myself. Embarrassed that I can't decide what to do and stick with it. Mostly frustrated. I just wish this whole struggle would go away.*

W: *I can feel your struggle, and I can tell how extremely difficult it is for you.*

K: *Yeah. It helps to know someone understands.*

Kevin was becoming more able and willing to allow himself vulnerability and had assumed responsibility for his struggle by defining it as his inability to say no in the face of opportunity. Although I could sense that Kevin had strong feelings through much of this segment, he did not mention his feelings until asked. He was still not comfortable being that vulnerable but with encouragement (S 3) shared very eloquently and succinctly exactly what he was experiencing inside. I was greatly encouraged by this brief exchange and excited by my work with him. Near the end of the second session I introduced the concept of commitment, but Kevin was not quite ready to see his struggle that broadly.

W: *What we have been exploring is an ongoing struggle you have been having for some time. Your struggle is around making a commitment to one person, sticking with that commitment, and feeling good about doing that in contrast to enjoying whatever the moment brings and taking advantage of opportunities for other relationships when they present themselves to you.*

K: *I'm around people all the time, and people get close to me, and it's always coming up.*

W: *Uh-huh.*

K: *And that's the thing. I would have to say no a lot.*

I believe Kevin was more aware of his competing forces and had an enhanced picture of how they influenced his life. It was much too early to move toward balance or integration but, at least, the groundwork had been laid. I imagine Kevin

74   *Willis D. Poland*

experienced these forces as mutually exclusive and had very little expectation that he could find an acceptable resolution. This would, no doubt, be a continuing theme of our work together.

The remainder of our work together was focused primarily around the issue of commitment. Kevin was eventually able to see that his task was to stay with his internal struggle until he could find a resolution. He vacillated between hope and despair that he could resolve his struggle. A segment from the 14th session illustrates how intense this war within him could be. He had had several dialogues with himself in previous sessions so that my therapeutic style had become one of delegating the work to him. Kevin had identified and labeled two parts of himself as follows:

KC: The part of Kevin that was ready and willing to make a commitment.

KE: The part of Kevin that wanted to escape and experience life more fully.

W: *What are you experiencing now?*

K: *I'm having my usual battle. Actually, I've been fighting with myself for several days. One day I feel really close to Cathy and decide I will ask her to marry me. The next day I feel trapped and want to run. Back and forth. I'm never in the same place for more than a couple of days.*

W: *So the struggle goes on.*

K: *Yeah. And I'm really sick of it!*

W: *Are you ready to continue the dialogue between KC and KE?*

K: *What's the point! I'm stuck.*

W: *Yeah, I know you're stuck. And I can hear your frustration loud and clear. Do you have an alternative?*

K: *No. And that's what pisses me off. I've got to stay with this goddamned thing until I come out someplace I can live with!*

W: *And you feel angry.*

K: *Yeah! Well, I might as well get on with it* (sounding resigned).

W: *Where would you like to start?*

Humanistic Psychotherapy and ACT **75**

K: *I'll start with KE today since that's been my strongest feeling since last night.* (As Kevin had the following dialogue, he moved back and forth between two chairs.)

KE: *I just want to get in my car and go. Every time I get that feeling you* (to KC) *make me feel guilty and I'm sick of it.*

KC: *You should feel guilty! When are you going to grow up! You're going to chase pussy all your life and drag me along with you. What the hell kind of life is that going to be? I want to be with Cathy and you make it impossible.*

KE: *God! There are things I want to do. Cathy is your thing. I'm not ready for that. I want to experience more of life before I settle down.*

KC: *You stupid fuck! Can't you see you aren't really experiencing life. You're just being led around by your cock. You act like some 15-year-old kid. Grow up!*

KE: *Yeah? Well you act like some 40-year-old man who is afraid of adventure. If I let you run Kevin's life, we will all be bored to death in a year!*

KC: *Yeah and if I let you run Kevin's life God only knows where we will end up. You are disgusting! You know Cathy is fantastic sex. What more do you want, for Christ's sake?*

KE: *Well, you've got a point there. But I don't think that's enough for me.*

KC: *You also know she's a really good person and we may never find anyone better.*

KE: *That's your fear, not mine. I'll take the chance.*

KC: *And you're afraid of commitment. And that's a hell of a lot worse than my fear.*

W: *I am really aware of the intensity of your struggle today. Just a moment ago I imagined there was a little softening of the struggle. I would like for each part to take a little time out and see if there is any compromise you are willing to make no matter how little or how brief it might be.* (After a long pause, KE speaks first.)

KE: *If I make any concessions, I'm not sure I could stick with them anyway.*

76   *Willis D. Poland*

KC: *I'm surprised you are even willing to consider it. If you've got anything to offer, I'm willing to work something out. I'm really tired of this struggle.*

KE: *OK. What I was thinking was I'm willing to stop looking around for a little while if you promise you won't make any big commitment to Cathy.*

KC: *What do you mean "stop looking around"?*

KE: *I mean stop taking advantage of the opportunities for sex when they come along.*

KC: *That means you will say no?*

KE: *Yeah. But just for a little while and only if you agree to keep your relationship with Cathy on hold. No big commitment.*

KC: (Pause.) *I don't like it and I don't think Cathy will like it either.* (Pause.) *Right now I don't see that I have any alternative, so I'll agree. But I expect you to keep your part of the bargain. I don't want any hassle.*

W: *How long is this agreement for?*

KC: (Pause.) *I'd like it for six months. No more and no less.*

KE: (Long pause.) *I'll agree to that now. If I don't like what's happening, we may have to change the time or the agreement.*

Frankly, I was surprised that the two parts reached a small agreement so quickly. I thought my intervention was a long shot with little possibility for success. It may be that both parts were equally tired of the battle and ready for at least a temporary truce. It is also quite possible that the fact that we only had two more sessions before therapy would have to end applied pressure on Kevin to achieve some resolution, no matter how small or temporary.

CLOSING REFLECTIONS

Becoming acquainted with the ACT model has led me to a broader perspective regarding the concept of readiness. It was very helpful to consider not only Kevin's readiness for each task but also to look at my own readiness to work with him on that task. Once I was clear that I was ready, then the question remained, "What would be the most relevant and useful therapeutic style" to help Kevin do his work. Interventions then were guided by both my own theoretical framework and the ACT model. I had been doing therapy for many years before the development of ACT and was comfortable with my approach to the process. Therefore, I did not view ACT as a model to replace what was most familiar to me. Rather, it has been helpful to me in looking at what I do, has enhanced my awareness of my work, and has provided me with increased awareness and the possibility of being a more effective therapist.

Therapy with Kevin occurred over a period of five months and included 16 sessions in all. We agreed that termination was premature. Since graduation was a boundary neither of us could change, it was important to address what reasonably could be the focus of our work in the time available. One of the more difficult tasks in therapy is to identify and bracket off issues that are beyond the scope of the present work. Brief therapy can be used both to work on achievable tasks now and to lay the groundwork for longer-term therapy at some point in the future. Approximately six months after termination, I received a request for information from a therapist in Colorado regarding my work with Kevin. Apparently Kevin's commitment to continue his therapeutic work was strong.

78   *Willis D. Poland*

BIBLIOGRAPHY

Bugental, J.F.T. (1978). *Psychotherapy and process.* Reading, MA: Addison-Wesley.

Howard, G.S., Nance, D.W., & Myers, P. (1987). *Adaptive counseling and therapy.* San Francisco: Jossey-Bass.

Kopp, S.B. (1972). *If you meet the Buddha on the road, kill him.* Palo Alto, CA: Science and Behavior Books.

Maslowe, A.H. (1968). *Toward a psychology of being* (2nd ed). New York: D. Van Nostrand.

May, R. (1983). *The discovery of being.* New York: W.W. Norton.

Perls, F. (1973). *The Gestalt approach and eye witness to therapy.* Palo Alto, CA: Science and Behavior Books.

Polster, E., & Polster, M. (1973). *Gestalt therapy integrated.* New York: Brunner/Mazel.

Rogers, C. (1961). *On becoming a person.* Boston: Houghton Mifflin.

Rogers, C. (1980). *A way of being.* Boston: Houghton Mifflin.

Shaffer, J. (1978). *Humanistic psychology.* Englewood Cliffs, NJ: Prentice Hall.

Zinker, J. (1977). *Creative process in Gestalt therapy.* New York: Brunner/Mazel.

COMMENTS

Humanistic Therapy and ACT

Don W. Nance

How can an approach to counseling with Carl Rogers as a central figure integrate well with the ACT model, which has directive behavior as a central concept? Good question. One which Dr. Poland answered in this chapter. The integration of ACT and Humanistic approaches is not the seamless fit found with CBT. The philosophical underpinnings of a humanistic approach proscribe directing the client about what to do or decide. Dr. Poland does not assess the situation with Kevin and then say, "Make a commitment" or "Find someone else." The emphasis is on expanding awareness so the client has access to affective as well as other types of information in reaching a resolution to his problem.

One goal of humanistic therapy, particularly the Gestalt approach utilized by Dr. Poland, is to increase the affective level, to heighten the impasse, so that the conflict is figural. Many of the techniques of Gestalt therapy, such as "empty chair," were developed to achieve that purpose. These methods also reflect the place where direction enters humanistic therapy. The client determines the content, the what, and the therapist directs the process, the how. Even the non-directive, client-centered approach of a classic Rogerian is very decided on how the process ought to proceed and how the therapist ought to behave, i.e., reflective listening. Some humanistically oriented therapist might emphasize ACT Style 3 to the relative exclusion of the more overtly directive ACT styles. Clearly, Dr. Poland ranges more broadly in his work with Kevin. Dr. Poland's clinical work, plus the tone and content of the chapter, raise interesting topics and questions for consideration. As with Chapter 2, I have selected several to share.

Dr. Poland made a significant contribution by articulating the importance of ***therapist readiness*** in the application of ACT. In our original development of the ACT model, the therapist's readiness was ignored. Consistent with the humanistic emphasis on awareness, Dr. Poland has brought an "obvious," but overlooked, piece of ACT to our collective attention. Dr. Poland focused on the therapist's readiness to be present in the moment with the client. He wants his own personal material not to interfere with his ability to perform this task. His willingness has a great deal to do with his sense of choice. Is the therapist motivated to be present and authentic with this client? If not, the therapist is much less likely to be helpful because of the importance placed on genuineness and congruence. From this humanistic perspective, the ability and confidence dimensions of therapist readiness seem to be based on an internal, personal assessment more than an assess-

80 *Willis D. Poland*

ment rooted in the content of the problem. Since the humanistic therapist is not a content expert, the need to assess that type of expertise is moot. I, as a Gestalt therapist, am not teaching content, e.g., anger management and parenting skills, but rather am assisting the client in gaining increased awareness. Therefore, I can confidently assist that process without being an expert about the topic. In other approaches, the therapist is likely to attend to his or her readiness with respect to both the content, i.e., the nature of the problems, and the therapeutic process indicated. How willing am I to become the therapist for a client with a multiple personality diagnosis? How able? How confident? I may be very able to assist another homesick freshman making the initial adjustment to being in a residence hall, but I may be significantly unmotivated if this is overly familiar territory.

Have you ever started a task and kept expanding it until it became overwhelming, resulting in an unfinished mess? I sure have. Such expansion can happen in therapy all too easily. The key question is how much can be done with the resources available? The resources include time, money, and setting as well as readiness—client and therapist. In the current and predicted future climate for mental health care in the United States, this issue of *bracketing* or limiting the scope and duration of therapy is likely to be an increasingly central issue in treatment planning. Already substantial numbers of college counseling centers and Health Maintenance Organizations (HMOs) set limits on therapy visits.

Dr. Poland uses his work with Kevin to illustrate the importance of bracketing or limiting the task. Kevin is graduating and leaving. What can be accomplished in 16 sessions? Dr. Poland shares with us his sense of more fundamental work Kevin will need to address. However, he respects the limits drawn by time and by readiness. The personal, underlying meaning of Kevin's need for multiple sexual partners is viewed as a sequential task to his current struggle. In the preceding chapter, therapy for Bill came to a more natural termination. The content and tasks were clearly defined, and therapy was completed when the tasks were accomplished. Notice as you read the succeeding chapters how brackets/limits are defined.

The distinction between content, the what, and the process, the how, is discussed at several points in the chapter. As previously noted, the humanistic perspective distinguishes directing the content from directing a process. Providing answers is distinguished from providing a process by which the client can gain clarity and the "answer" that is right for the client. When a problem in the process blocks or interferes with the content, another type of *content/process distinction* is operating. Kevin's need to seem "together" was blocking the self-exploration and awareness needed to reach some resolution to his dilemma. When Dr. Poland experienced this problem in the process, he made it the content. This process-to-content shift, or naming the process, had the effect of directly addressing the process issue. Dr. Poland raised the issue, explored it, normalized Kevin's concern with appearing together, and thereby "neutralized" the negative impact on the therapy. Notice how this content to process shift is evident in the remaining chapters.

QUESTIONS

1. What happens when the nature of the problem seems to require knowledge/skills outside your ability and range? How do you feel? What do you do? What are some examples? Are these variations on willingness?

2. How do you respond to a cancellation or a "no show"? Does it vary with who the client is? Time of day? Other commitments or agenda?

3. What are the limits of the old axiom, "The task expands to fill the time available"? How does this axiom apply to the case of Kevin? What role do time limits play in therapy? In your own experience?

4. How does successfully limiting the task impact client readiness for future therapy?

5. What methods, such as empty chair, do you associate with particular theories? Which seem more common property, public domain?

6. Are there methods you have not used because of their roots?

7. How can you practice expanding the ways in which you use familiar techniques?

8. How would the affective focus of Dr. Poland's work fit for Bill (Chapter 2) and the problem he brought to treatment?

9. If the fit is not good, how should it be resolved?
   a. client picks another problem
   b. client picks another therapist
   c. Bill changes his approach
   d. Dr. Poland flexes to meet Bill's more organized cognitive style
   e. Some other option or combination.

10. How would the CBT focus of Dr. Deffenbacher (Chapter 2) have worked with Kevin? What would be the tasks? The levels of readiness? The sequence?

Chapter 4

TIME-LIMITED PSYCHODYNAMIC COUNSELING AND ACT: A CASE OF MEASURING UP

Steven B. Robbins and Karen P. Lese

Virginia Commonwealth University

Psychodynamically oriented counseling and therapy focuses on the uncovering, reexperiencing, and working through of repressed emotional conflict (Patton & Meara, 1993). Traditionally, this "working through" process does not follow a specified length of time, but rather, is the culmination of the steady process of therapist clarification and interpretation of client thoughts and behavior. In recent years, however, we have witnessed a revolution (Robbins, 1989) in our thinking about the time expectations of treatment, with a number of time-limited psychodynamic models (Davanloo, 1980; Mann, 1973; Sifneos, 1979) emerging. These models are still based on psychoanalytic conceptions of human development but radically alter our thinking about the techniques and strategies available to the therapist. While these models vary in goals and strategies, they also share a number of basic principles, which include limits on the number of sessions, the early delineation and maintenance of a focal issue, an emphasis on ego resources rather than deficits, use of the transference relationship, and the delineation of specific client selection criteria. In all approaches, the therapist becomes engaged as an active participant, replacing the traditionally passive stance of the analyst.

84 *Steven B. Robbins and Karen P. Lese*

These new approaches to psychodynamic therapy, then, establish broader views of appropriate therapist behaviors. These new approaches to psychodynamic therapy make two issues especially important. First, the increase in options for therapist in-session behaviors allows a heightened level of therapist activity. In fact, as many new models maintain focus on one central issue, such activity on the part of the therapist is often required. When and how activity is increased is less explicitly stated in such models. Second, the continual focus on the defined central conflict may cause a high level of client anxiety, necessitating careful client selection. The ACT model is a useful aid in addressing these two issues, as it provides specific guidelines regarding both the amount and type of therapist activity and a system for selecting appropriate approaches for a particular client. Specific implementations of ACT within a short-term dynamic treatment orientation will be illustrated through the use of clinical excerpts. Our approach draws primarily upon the work of James Mann (1973, 1982), whose model prescribes the formal presentation of a focal issue and the setting of a 12-session time limit after an initial evaluation session. We will first present Mann's thinking about the stages of treatment before discussing its relationship with ACT and presenting the illustrative case.

MANN'S THREE STAGE MODEL

Mann's model is based on two assumptions. The first is that clients have chronic and enduring pain relating to a negative self-image. The second is that unresolved problems of separation-individuation will unfold during the course of treatment within the client/therapist relationship. Separation-individuation refers to the process by which a person psychologically separates from his or her parents while gaining a sense of identity as a separate person. The task of the therapist in the initial interview is to understand how the client has actively coped to gain recognition of his or her needs and to formally present the central issue. The therapist is then to follow a prescribed set of activities during the course of the 12-session treatment that follows three phases: initial (sessions 1 through 4), middle (sessions 5 through 8), and termination (sessions 9 through 12).

Assessment and Formulation of the Central Issue

An initial evaluation focuses on client developmental information, including repetitive conflict situations and the client's usual mode of managing conflict. The central issue must recognize with what the client has struggled all his or her life, the attempts at mastering this struggle, and the unrelenting pain suffered nevertheless. The central issue is presented to the client using a "time-bound self-image" (Mann & Goldman, 1982) that includes three components: time, affect, and the image of the self. The central issue should communicate three important messages: (1) the therapist is aware of the client's very real efforts to master the present and chronically endured pain; (2) the therapist recognizes that despite the client's best efforts, he or she still experiences the pain; and (3) the work of therapy will be devoted to a mutual exploration of how the client has come to feel this way. In this way, the client feels that a painfully hidden part of himself or herself has been brought to light in an empathic and nonthreatening manner.

Sequence of Dynamic Events

The strict 12-session agreement arouses both a "sense of optimistic urgency and a sense of pessimism" (Mann, 1973, p. 31). Mann proposed that the single focus and explicit construction of time sets into motion a well-organized sequence of dynamic events that transpire across beginning, middle, and ending phases of treatment. The therapist's goal in phase 1 is to establish an explicit therapeutic contract through the central issue and to foster a strong working alliance by using empathy and support. The short duration of therapy requires the fast establishment of a strong working alliance. Accordingly, therapist style congruent with the ACT Style 3, low directive behavior/high supportive behavior, is implemented in this first phase of treatment. As client and therapist move into the second phase of treatment, the therapist actively continues to guide the treatment toward the central issue. Accordingly, the therapist's style, especially in the first and second phases of treatment, incorporates more consistent and active use of interpretation and support (ACT S 2/S 3 responses) than would be expected from a classical psychoanalytic model.

As the therapist continues to refocus the client directly on the central issue, therapist style more closely mirrors Style 2, high directive behavior/high supportive behavior. The therapist attempts to teach the client to view his or her situation in a certain way. Activity level is fairly high, as shown in the encouragement of the client to focus consistently on the central issue, the confrontation of resistance to this issue, and the continual use of interpretation regarding the central theme. While directiveness level is not high as compared, for example, with a behavioral model, the therapist is considerably more directive than a classical analyst. In the second phase, it is predicted that the client's initial enthusiasm will begin to wane and that a negative transference will emerge, as evidenced by discouragement, frustration, and disappointment. Working through these feelings and the impend-

86   *Steven B. Robbins and Karen P. Lese*

ing separation from the therapist marks the third stage of treatment. In this last stage, encouragement of affective expression occurs in the context of the client's difficulty letting go of, or separating from, significant early relationships. The therapist again uses Style 3, with extensive use of empathy. The client is therefore supported in working through his or her feelings about loss and separation.

Rationale for Client Selection

This approach is geared toward college age people who are experiencing "maturational crises" that are related to the separation-individuation process. As such, an explicit set of criteria exists to assess client readiness for the treatment. The set of client selection criteria includes the following:

1. Is not severe borderline or schizoid personality organization (i.e., can form and tolerate significant relationships).
2. Has had no recent suicide attempts.
3. Does not manifest certain psychosomatic conditions such as ulcerative colitis or rheumatoid arthritis.
4. Is not psychotic.
5. Is not severely depressed.
6. Has the capacity to tolerate loss (e.g., someone with extreme dependency needs who does not want to rid himself or herself of this would be inappropriate).
7. Has the capacity for rapid affective involvement.

The ACT model suggests the use of three criteria to guide client selection. These criteria are a useful adjunct to those proposed by Mann. The first of these is client *willingness.* Is the client willing to accept the dynamic formulation, the terms of therapy, and the responsibility for continuing to focus on the central issue? Without this willingness, therapeutic growth is unlikely. The second factor is the *ability* to engage in the emotional and cognitive requirements of the therapy. As has been noted, the client must be able to form and sustain intimate relationships, must manifest a certain degree of impulse control, and must have the ability to tolerate the impending loss of the therapist. Third, ACT suggests the client must have the necessary *confidence* that he or she will be able to do what is necessary to meet the therapeutic goals. Mann's approach emphasizes this factor to a lesser degree than the others; however, the approach in no way precludes its use. Assessment of these factors not only yields information about the appropriateness of the treatment for the client in question; it also gives the therapist an indication of how much support and direction the client needs.

COMMONALITIES BETWEEN MANN AND ACT

The overlap between the Mann approach and the approach suggested by ACT is apparent in the systematic variation by both of therapist support and directiveness, and in the explicit focus of each on selection issues. In terms of selection issues, ACT suggests an overall eclectic orientation, matching therapist approach to client needs. Mann's approach uses a reversal of this approach; it emphasizes the need to find the right client to fit the model. A client with little ability to tolerate loss, for example, might not attain the positive results experienced by the client described later in this chapter. Such a client might benefit more from other therapeutic styles. ACT would be useful in suggesting alternative approaches.

Therapist style in Mann's approach varies with the phase of treatment and with client needs. Similarly, ACT suggests that the therapist's style change with the task of therapy and with the client's readiness. A general overview of Mann's system suggests the use of therapist Styles 2 and 3. However, there are not proscriptions, as would be the case in a traditional analytic approach, on the degree of therapist direction, and/or support, and/or activity level. Certain behaviors by necessity fall within Style 1—Telling. The therapist determines such things as length and focus of treatment. Style 2—Teaching behaviors, such as interpretation and encouragement to explore the central issue, are widely used. Style 3—Supportive behaviors are used in initial stages to form the working alliance, and they also are used later in treatment to facilitate termination. Within the treatment process, supportive behaviors are used liberally as an encouragement for the client to explore the affective components of the central issue. Finally, Style 4—Delegating behaviors may be used intermittently to allow the client to freely explore thoughts and feelings associated with the central issue or the overall themes of loss and separation-individuation.

CURTIS: A CASE OF MEASURING UP

In this section, information about the client and the central issue that was formulated for this person will be presented. Following this section will be a description of the course of treatment.

Preliminary Information

The client, Curtis, is a 24-year-old single white male currently in the third year of training as a health professional. He is engaged to be married. Curtis

88   *Steven B. Robbins and Karen P. Lese*

sought treatment from a university counseling service after experiencing considerable distress in school and upon the referral of a psychiatrist.

Presenting Complaints

During the evaluation session with the therapist, Curtis indicated that he began to feel some anxiety and fear of failure several months prior to the intake interview and as he began a new school year where he would have to "apply" his knowledge for the first time. The event that precipitated seeking out counseling was the manifestation of a constellation of symptoms of extreme anxiety, an overwhelming fear of failure, and a sense of loss of control. These symptoms escalated into several full-blown panic attacks several days before the start of a new assignment. Other known disturbances in the client's life included a strained relationship with his parents and fiancee, and obsessional anxiety about work and achievement. Prior to evaluation with the therapist, Curtis had received anti-anxiety medication from a psychiatrist and had decided to take several weeks off from school.

Predisposing Influences and History

Curtis is the eldest of two sons in an intact family. His younger brother, age 18, recently has begun his education at a prestigious university. His parents live out of state, residing several hours away. The father, a medical professional, is described as hardworking, stoic, and emotionally neglectful and has always pushed his son toward academic achievement. The mother, a homemaker, is described as overly invested in her children's achievement both in the academic and social realms. Curtis always has been successful academically and continues to receive high grades in professional school. He reports that he always has tried to please his parents but always experienced a pervasive feeling that despite his efforts, it just wasn't "good enough."

Condition for Which Help Is Needed

The client's presenting problems, coupled with additional assessment information (clinically significant scores on depression, anxiety, phobic anxiety, interpersonal sensitivity, and obsessive-compulsiveness), suggest a person who is anxious, depressed, and prone to feelings of inadequacy and loss of control. Additionally, an obsessive-compulsive personality style is evident. Based on the aforementioned information, a diagnosis of panic disorder and adjustment dis-

Time-Limited Psychodynamic Counseling   **89**

order with mixed emotional features was given (DSM-III-R, American Psychiatric Association, 1987 [this same diagnosis meets DSM-IV classification, 1994]).

Central Issue Formulation

From a psychodynamic perspective, the anxiety attacks are the result of underlying emotional conflict. The basic conflict was formulated as a tendency to use performance to obtain love and by his concurrent fear about the withdrawal of love if he fails. There is a preoccupation with meeting the perceived demands of others and an inability to assert one's own opinion. At the conclusion of the evaluation session, the following central issue was formulated and presented to Curtis: "Although you have worked so hard and have been successful in your life, you have always felt inadequate and afraid to let yourself and others down."

A set of criteria also was specified to help operationalize maximum improvement in the central issue:

1. improvement in relationship with parents,
2. loss of obsessional anxiety about work and achievement,
3. disappearance of panic attacks,
4. evidence of a more positive self-image (i.e., increased self-esteem and decreased feelings of inadequacy),
5. increased expression about self and self-assertions, and
6. improvement in relationship with fiancee.

In this evaluation session, a central formulation of the hypothesis was set, as were goals for therapy. While the client had input into the formulation with the presentation of his story, the therapist defined the conflict and presented it to the client in a teaching (S 2) manner. This manner is consistent with Mann's approach, which defines specific boundaries for therapy. The client had more input into the definition of goals, which were defined using both the therapist's conceptualization and the client's stated goals for therapy.

Course of Treatment

Phase one. In this case, the client displayed a moderately high readiness. He presented as a self-motivated individual who, in general, was willing to do the tasks required by therapy. Furthermore, he had the abilities necessary to engage in a working alliance with the therapist and confront the conflict areas as defined by the dynamic formulation. However, he lacked confidence in his role in the thera-

90   *Steven B. Robbins and Karen P. Lese*

peutic process. This was evidenced in his shame regarding his participation in therapy and in his initial uncertainty in session. A supportive style, S 3, therefore was employed in the first phase of treatment.

Tasks of the first phase of treatment, as defined by Mann, are to clarify and elaborate the central issue. This is done with considerable use of support and a moderate use of interpretation. The first two therapy sessions were characterized by an optimistic tone and a reported decrease in symptoms. Curtis further elaborated on issues discussed in the evaluation session. We will highlight the presentation and elaboration of the central issue through two interactions.

Therapist: *What about this girl you dated who broke your heart?*

Client: *She was just prettier than anyone I'd ever been out with, nicer than anyone I'd ever been out with. And I think that I was just so infatuated with her. She was of a higher social class than anybody I'd ever been out with.*

T: *This was your freshman year.*

C: *We went to different schools. I probably saw her about eight straight weekends in my fall semester. . . . Then she started dating us both at the same time and that was really tearing me apart to do it, but I dated her with her dating another guy. After I tried so hard, I felt like, well, she knows—she's seen the best of me and she's seen what I've got to offer. If she's gonna run around like that, it wasn't worth—*

T: *Isn't this really becoming the main theme we're hearing, that you're a person who's worked very hard and successfully but have always felt inadequate and really afraid that you'd lose the support of others?*

In another example, the therapist reframes the client's concern within the context of the central issue.

C: *And another thing that's sort of bothering me, not as much, is just looking around me, seeing how much all these other people know. I mean, I did well on my national tests this summer and I did well in my first two years, but just seeing how much these people know and when they're treating patients and me not being able to put it together as well as they can, I feel like I'm going to be working my entire life to catch up with everybody else or something.*

Time-Limited Psychodynamic Counseling **91**

T: *I wonder if you feel like you've been working your entire life to get people to love and care for you, and that your work has been your way—your gift to your parents. And you'd wonder if it was enough.*

C: *I think you're right. I don't know what else—I just—I've always tried to work hard and I just—the last couple months I've felt so ignorant, I guess like everybody else in my class, but instead of rolling with the punches and laughing it off, I just put on my pressure to try to learn harder to catch up.*

T: *And the fact that you turned to your parents Monday but were unable to talk to them about how you're really doing—that it's only your successes that you can share with them.*

C: *Well, I'd like to share with them the downside, but for some reason, whenever I get ready to do it, I get all emotional. And if I could just tell them when things are going good but I feel like I've got a lot to learn and I feel lonely way out here in the middle of nowhere and things like that—if I could just do it and say it, it'd be all right. But I feel like—for some reason I can't really express my true negative emotions—I don't know. It's even telling them that I love them. I guess that is not negative. But expressing emotions that you don't normally; it just makes me feel like crying for some reason, so I just don't ever express them.*

T: *I wonder if your tears are tears of a lonely boy, a boy who never really felt he could get a hug when he wanted one. When he got a hug, it was because he brought an "A" home. And wouldn't that lonely boy be afraid that if he told his parents Monday night that there was more going on than whether he passed a class, he would have to find out whether his parents would still give him a hug?*

C: *I know my parents are always there for me and they're going to stand by me and logically I can think it through but I guess sort of subconsciously—I just—I don't—I've just always told them—I haven't covered up things. I don't lie to my parents. But whenever I talk to them, I always try to tell them the positive things that are going on. And unless it's really important, like me taking time off from school, I try to not talk as much about the negative. I had a really—I told you—I think my mother's always pressured me more into, I guess, being more sociable. I mean, I'm friendly and I like talking to people, but I guess I have trouble meeting people.*

92   *Steven B. Robbins and Karen P. Lese*

In the first four sessions, a major theme that emerged was the client's relationship with his father, which had always felt strained and discordant. The therapist described the father's insensitivity and inability to provide emotional support within the context of the central issue. The client's *resistance,* or difficulty with painful material, was confronted to help enable him to explore more fully his affective experience of highly critical and conditionally loving parents. An example of this is as follows:

C: *Seems like everything I do, I can't be sure if it's totally the right way.*

T: *You have got to be as sure in here you're working the "right way." You're describing a lot of uncertainty in your feelings.*

C: *I just wish I could snap my fingers and everything would be all right.*

T: *It'd be easier than having to talk about this stuff and work it through, wouldn't it?*

C: *I mean, I don't feel that uptight. I just—I sort of thought I might feel like this but I just—this week, I guess, I hadn't felt as much about talking about problems and talk—I feel like I don't want to open up this week for some reason. Sort of like it takes a lot of energy and relaxing and—to open up. And sort of wish I could make myself do it but I—*

T: *You'd wish a little bit that I would make you as well.*

C: *Sort of hoping things, I guess, would flow better but. . . . And I wonder even if we get to the point where I feel good about myself at work, sort of wonder, I guess, what type of person I am or if I am sort of weird or am sort of half crazy or something or if there's some big diagnosis I should have over my head.*

T: *So you have a lot of self doubts that are coming out, and rather than having the uncertainty of becoming more and more open about your self doubts and frustrations, you'd rather work nonstop, focus in on specific tasks in here or at work, and take your mind off your doubts and uncertainty.*

Phase two.   In the middle phase of treatment, the therapist carefully listens for the ambivalences that signify disappointment in the childlike hope that the therapist will "make everything better." Identification and clarification of this ambivalence toward treatment helps to promote the individuation-separation process. Curtis, at this point, was more accustomed to the therapeutic process. He had started accepting and articulating his ambivalence, and no longer needed as much support as he did on beginning therapy. The working alliance had strengthened to the point that Curtis could tolerate direct consideration of transference responses. Therefore, the therapist could adopt the delegating role, which is low in directive and supportive behaviors. Curtis was both willing and able at this point—with some assistance in the forms of clarification and interpretation—to direct the therapeutic process himself.

In this example, Curtis has just described an upsetting day at work:

T: *Wouldn't your fear be that if you called me last night that you wouldn't have kept up with my expectations? That you couldn't turn to me because you would have showed me a side that hadn't done well, that had failed?*

C: *I don't remember why—I just remember I thought about it because, well, I got home and my roommate was, had the radio playing a lot of rock music. I was sort of hoping it'd be quiet and hoping I could walk in and have things the way I wanted them. And I had a write-up to do and I had to start another one and I had to unpack clothes. . . . I tried to call my fiancee but she wasn't home. She was out shopping and I just felt like everything wasn't peaceful. My roommate's across the—one thing that bugs me is he's across the hall whistling and just him whistling, well, that's perfectly all right. I always feel like telling him to cut it out. He's been doing it for months and it just drives me up the wall to sit there and try to study while he whistles. Sort of like when I had those panic attacks. I don't know why I have them. It's just like all these little things build up. I feel like I'm no longer in control and things aren't going the way I want them to go. And I just—it's almost like it feels good to have somebody to cry to. It wasn't that I chickened out from calling you—*

T: *No, and I think the reality is that you handled the situation and you didn't need to call. But to get a sense of what's going on inside you, we would look at what your thoughts were about calling me.*

C: *Well, I feel like if I wouldn't be seeing you today, I might have called you but I felt like I was seeing you today and it was something I could depend on. . . . Sometimes I feel like if I didn't have this to come and talk to and didn't have my fiancee to talk to about all my problems, I don't think I could make it in school.*

T: *You are expressing some doubts about whether you're strong enough to manage without your fiancee or me.*

94   *Steven B. Robbins and Karen P. Lese*

C: *And I've been thinking, I wonder, what if I get—what's going to happen at the 12th session. Am I just gonna be dumped out on my own? I wonder if I'm gonna be one of those people who needs to talk to somebody once a month to get things in perspective.*

For this client, anger and disappointment at important others is extremely dangerous, as the withdrawal of love could result. These negative feelings about the therapist serve as a springboard to understanding the client's feelings about his father. An example from the 7th session can illustrate:

C: *I also—another thing that sort of frustrated me with this—I feel like most of the time I talk and you listen but I get frustrated when I feel like you're playing games with me. Like that one time when you started talking about something in the last session and didn't tell me what it was, sort of seeing if I would remember what we were talking about at the end. Or when you sat in the chair the last time waiting for me to get up. I mean, I'm sure gonna pop out of my chair this week but I don't—*

T: *What I said, was, are you waiting for my permission to leave.*

C: *I think there is a lot to what you've been—well, what we've been talking about, of not liking to live under other people's rules, especially when—like I accept the rules in here type thing or at school and at home, I think I do get frustrated a lot, trying to play by their rules and—*

T: *But you're trying to play by my rules too, aren't you?*

C: *Well, I'm trying to play by them but I don't think there are too many rules in here—I always enjoy the security of going home and being around people that I love and things, but I spend a lot of the weekend or whatever self-conscious, hoping that my fiancee and I say the right things. I sit there and start squeezing her hand when she starts to say things that are wrong; I sit there and start squeezing her hand because I feel like my parents are judging her, just like maybe—I don't know.*

T: (A few minutes later in the session.) *But you say people. You'd rather say people than focus on the specific people who are disapproving.*

C: *My grandmother is, in her own little way, under the covers—is giving me a hard time about her being Catholic. And what I'm gonna do about it and all that. But she's sort of a manipulator. My father doesn't get along with her that well. That's—I don't know. We were talking about my father*

Time-Limited Psychodynamic Counseling **95**

last week and I was really ragging on him pretty bad. That's sort of another area where I think he could enjoy life better is not—is not worrying about my mother's mother. He doesn't like going to visit them and he—every time we have to go, he sort of piddles around and we end up leaving 30 minutes late and he makes fun of her.

T: *Ragging on your father is—I think the theme today has to do with the part of you that, to use your words, would like to slap your father around.*

C: *I really would. In a way, I guess I sort of felt like maybe I shouldn't have said all those things about him, but it's completely true. It frustrates the hell out of me to go home and watch him do all these things where I think he could be so much happier if he would enjoy things and experience feelings instead of being sort of mean—I mean pinching people and sitting on their laps and squishing them while you pinch their thighs and giving them arm burns and tickling them and all that crap.*

T: *He's basically neglected you emotionally, hasn't he, all these years?*

C: *I want to get to the point that I don't quote need my parents anymore. I mean I—my da—my father's basically—he makes a good living and he's basically put money in the bank when I've needed it and paid for my school. But every—whenever my fiance wants to go out to eat, I always feel guilty that I'm wasting his money or anything. I'm just waiting for the day when I can give back to them and don't feel like I owe them something and that I'm under—I still feel like there's some—there's—I still feel like—I don't know how to—I still feel like their son who lives at home and has to answer to his parents for everything he does.*

Phase three. During the last phase of treatment, Curtis was able to acknowledge the father's limitations, deal with his feelings of grief, and see how he blamed himself for his father's limitations. Feelings of sadness and anger were explored within the context of parental and therapist relationships. With the client's continued self-directiveness, the therapist was able to continue utilizing the delegating style. However, as Curtis started addressing issues of loss and separation—typical issues to emerge as termination approaches—the therapist employed a more extensive use of support. This use of support facilitated the client's ability to do the work of termination, addressing fears of being alone and what loss meant to him. An example from session 10 follows:

C: *I don't want my brother to fall into the same trap that I have. I don't think that I've solved all my problems. I still get insecure about leaving home.*

96 *Steven B. Robbins and Karen P. Lese*

And when I left yesterday, I cried a little bit, which I don't understand but I guess I can live with it. I got tired hiding it and I went ahead and just cried in front of my mother and told her that the reason—that I wasn't upset or anything. It's just that I—I just said that I loved them a lot and it hurt to leave. And I get teary-eyed now talking about it and I'm not upset and I think it's sort of dumb but I guess it's part of me.

T: *And what's dumb? Go with your thought.*

C: *I think if you're real happy or you're real sad, then, there's I guess, quite a good reason to cry, then it's sort of acceptable. But I feel like I'm crying without a reason when I talk about how I feel about my parents or when I talk about how I know that they love me type things or get into really deep feelings; I end up crying and I really feel like I don't have a reason to. . . . There's a big difference between the slap-on-the-back I love you and the—which I can do when—and not worry about—and look them in the—I don't know. I don't know why I don't like crying. But the look-them-in-the-eye, hold-their-hand I love you that I want to hear so bad. I don't know why the slap-them-on-the-back at the end of a phone call type isn't good enough for me.*

T: *But the little boy who would want to be picked up and held and squeezed and said to, I really love you, son—that little boy's never gotten that.*

C: *Well, three-fourths of the world doesn't get it and I don't think they're gonna see a psychologist because of it.*

T: *What you said is a wonderful insight into why you feel so inadequate; you've made the assumption that because you desperately, as a boy, wanted to be picked up and squeezed and hugged that there must be something wrong with you.*

Later in the hour, the therapist begins to relate this topic of "saying goodbye" to completing therapy:

T: *I wonder if you're expressing some fear now of whether you're gonna be able to keep this balance, and we haven't really specifically raised the topic of our finishing up here. And this whole theme of saying goodbye, and are you gonna be able to do it, would fit your thought of having to be on your own in a very short period.*

C: *I still got that thing in the back of my head saying, what do I do? But I feel like eventually, it'd start coming natural. Like my father says, he's not willing to change, and I sort of feel like I am willing to change because I don't think the way that I've been going is the right way. I think I'm funner too—when I let that emotional side through. I'm funner to be with; I enjoy what I'm doing; I don't feel like I have to impress people as much. But it's still—you're taking chances when you show that side of you. And sometimes you go over the edge and show that side too much and get yourself in trouble and it's just sort of keeping the balance.*

T: *And you'd wonder if you can manage on your own without our work.*

C: *I think for the first time—I always get in this trap of trying to look at the big picture and getting overwhelmed. And I think I've had—my three months in my next assignment that starts in five weeks—it's sort of swinging like a pendulum up here ready to chop my head off. . . . I think that I can get things situated and I've gotten things in perspective through the 12 or 13 meetings, that I've sort of gotten prepared. But it's sort of like taking parachuting lessons, being thrown out of the airplane. There aren't gonna be check stations on the way down to the ground to make sure your parachute's come out. It's just gonna be a sink or swim type thing.*

T: *It's a pretty strong picture you're painting of being—of me shoving you out of an airplane and saying, I hope you—*

C: *That's just what came to mind.*

T: *But you laugh. You wanna take back that image and it's an important one. It is a sign of your ability to start expressing those images—it took a risk to let me in on that image.*

Termination and follow-up.   The last sessions were used to help Curtis express fears of being alone and to experience saying goodbye in a meaningful way. An example from the beginning of the last session highlights the client's effort at separating from the therapy process by beginning to reflect on the future.

C: *Well, I feel pretty good. I tried to—I didn't give it as much time as I wanted to but I tried to make a point of thinking about this being our last session and what I was gonna do after this and how I'd changed because I was busy and I never got around to it, but I really feel good about myself*

> now. And I try to put myself in the shoes of thinking that I do resent this being our last session. But I really can't identify with it. Maybe I'm avoiding it, but I don't feel like I am. I feel like I haven't had those insecure feelings in a couple months. And I feel like things are going well. I've tried to reset my priorities and look at things a little different and it's nice—I feel like—I like coming to these sessions because I feel like it sort of does a bookkeeping type job of putting things back in order and put this book in here and this one there and get it all nice and neat. But I feel like I sort of, during the last month or so, learned to start doing that myself, and I think I've become less dependent on these, less dependent on my fiance, don't run to my Tranzine every time I get nervous. I don't know—I've just tried to—something that's really helped me is, my goal is to do my best and sort of say to myself, well, if he doesn't like it, then screw him because I'm doing my best and what they think doesn't matter as long as I know that I'm doing what I should be doing and I'm not—something I think I did before and I still do a lot but not as much is sit around and think, what do I have to do to get honors, or what do I have to do to impress this person, or what do I have to do to make this person like me, as opposed to showing them the real me and not worrying about it.

A two month follow-up appointment was conducted, with Curtis reporting successful completion of a previous work assignment and entry into a new assignment. He reported that he continued to struggle with some obsessional anxiety about work and achievement but that the severity of the anxiety had lessened considerably, with no additional panic attacks. Despite several recent stressors, including contracting a mild case of Tuberculosis, Curtis reported significant progress in communication with his parents and fiancee. He stated that as a result of therapy, "I now realize that I'm a good person."

CONCLUSION

This chapter illustrates the way in which the ACT approach can be used to help structure and systematize James Mann's short-term model of psychodynamic therapy. Both approaches are useful. The psychodynamic approach, which is theoretically-driven, allows us to understand the clients' problems from a developmental perspective that proposes that symptom formation is the consequence of underlying conflict. ACT, in turn, provides a means for identifying important client and therapist factors that must be taken into account over the course of treatment.

Mann's approach broadens the level of therapist activity, making the contributions of ACT to the selection of therapist behavior especially valuable. Mann's model calls for a higher level of support and directiveness than is implemented in traditional analytic approaches. This strategy encourages a transference resolution that occurs through the identification, clarification, and interpretation of the shifts in transference from positive to negative and back to positive that correspond to the beginning, middle, and end of treatment. ACT allows the use of client and therapist behaviors to be systematically guided by the particular client's needs. In this example, the client entered therapy with a low level of confidence. Accordingly, a larger amount of support was used in the early stages of therapy. When the client displayed increased confidence, shown in his willingness to vocalize ambivalence about the process, the therapist could take a more delegating role, thereby encouraging the client's increasing autonomy. Within a more traditional psychoanalytic perspective, the therapist would not have become more delegating but would rather have encouraged the dependency of client on therapist through supportive behaviors.

Because establishing a time limit is central in evoking the "sequence of dynamic events," careful identification and elaboration of a central issue is vital. In this case the initial assessment appeared to be on target. If a reformulation was necessary, it should have occurred as part of the process of treatment, with modification of the central issue accomplished through trial clarifications and interpretations. The therapist must have confidence that the 12-session limit will be adequate to accomplish the goal of resolving the central issue while "working through" issues of separation with the client.

Client readiness, as can be seen, is critical to this approach. Resistance was not exceedingly high and resulted in an absence of S 1, or highly directive, therapist activity. In this example, the ACT model facilitated the adaption of a psychodynamic therapeutic style to a particular client's needs. This matching process is crucial if the client, as consumer, experiences treatment as an effective and gratifying experience. Both client and therapist must be aware that resolution of the central issue does not equate with the complete amelioration of all present or future client complaints and concerns. The client, rather, is prepared to face the inevitable life stresses with a full confidence and an access to his or her native talents and skills.

REFERENCES

American Psychiatric Association. (1987). *Diagnostic and statistical manual of mental disorders* (3rd ed., revised). Washington, DC: American Psychiatric Association.

American Psychiatric Association. (1994). *Diagnostic and statistical manual of mental disorders* (4th ed.). Washington, DC: American Psychiatric Association.

Davanloo, H. (1980). *Short-term dynamic psychotherapy.* New York: Aronson.

Howard, G., Nance, D., & Myers, P. (1986). Adaptive counseling and therapy: An integrative model. *The Counseling Psychologist, 14,* 363–442.

Mann, J. (1973). *Time-limited psychotherapy.* Cambridge, MA: Harvard University Press.

Mann, J., & Goldman, R. (1982). *A casebook in time-limited psychotherapy.* New York: McGraw-Hill.

Patton, M., & Meara, N. (1993). *A textbook of psychoanalytic counseling.* New York: John Wiley and Sons.

Robbins, S. (1989). Role of contemporary psychoanalysis in counseling psychology. *Journal of Counseling Psychology, 36,* 267–278.

Sifneos, P. (1979). *Short term dynamic psychotherapy: Evaluation and technique.* New York: Plenum.

COMMENTS

Psychodynamic Approach and ACT

Don W. Nance

A central theme of ACT is matching the form and style of treatment to the readiness of the client. Chapters 2 and 3 illustrated the match being achieved by therapist adapting the treatment to fit the client. This chapter illustrated **an alternate path to the necessary match.** For Dr. Robbins and Dr. Lese, the parameters of this treatment process are set. Thus, the therapist and the treatment process do not adapt to the client. Rather the client is selected for the treatment. The therapist is very clear about the criteria used for evaluating the appropriateness of a client for this brief psychodynamic treatment. Those criteria are used to select clients who are able to tolerate the intensity of the process, able to access feelings, and able to accept the limits of treatment. The client is willing to commit to the treatment process, willing to work actively on the central issue, and willing to tolerate interpretations. For Curtis, his anxiety and discomfort initially provided the major motivation for change. The client must have some confidence in the therapist, in the treatment, and in the importance of the central issue.

Intentional use of ACT adds to the effectiveness of the brief psychodynamic therapy process by assisting the therapist to systematically vary the amounts of direction and support provided at each stage in the process. The Style 3 behaviors in the early sessions match the purpose of developing the positive transference. The use of Style 1 and 2 interpretations matches the purpose of affectively exposing the central issue. The use of Style 4 to promote Curtis' doubts and fears is intentional and matches the phase or stage of treatment. The clarity of the therapeutic contract, the limits set, and the structured anticipated sequence of therapy are noteworthy. After the initial intake, assessment, and evaluation, the therapist behaves much like an oncologist describing a course of chemotherapy.

> After evaluating your condition, I feel that you are an appropriate candidate for a course of brief dynamic therapy. We will be treating (**the central issue**). The treatment will last 12 weeks. You are likely to experience both relief and pain in the course of treatment. If you agree sign here.

The treatment uses expert power and emphasizes the position power of the therapist role rather than the personal power of Dr. Steve Robbins, the therapist.

The brief psychodynamic model also exemplifies the differentiation between a conceptual framework and the methods associated with the theory. The brief model retains the psychodynamic conceptualization while importing a range of therapist behaviors extending out from Style 4 to all quadrants of the ACT model. The expanded range of therapist behaviors increases the fit between ACT and psychodynamic models. Traditional psychoanalytic methods, which rely on free association and interpretation, have an overreliance on Style 4 and a relative absence of active Support (S 3) or Teaching (S 2). The free association and interpretation process of classical analysis seems an S 4, S 1, S 4 sequence. That is, say little and observe (S 4); make an interpretation (S 1); and return to the previous style (S 4). The ACT model would predict inefficiency in this process and progress with only the most motivated of clients who have high ability at introspection.

The improved efficiency of the Mann model over more traditional psychodynamic treatment seems well demonstrated in the case presented in this chapter. Efficiency is achieved by limiting the content task to the central issue. That efficiency is implemented through the active intentionality of the therapist to behave in ways that move the dynamic process forward. ACT assists the therapist in orienting the systematic variations in direction and support.

QUESTIONS

1. How does the 12-session time limit impact the course of treatment? The ACT styles used?

2. How does it differ from the circumstantially imposed limit with Kevin (Chapter 3) or the lack of a set limit with Bill (Chapter 2)?

3. How does the way time limits are set impact the tasks, the pace, the progress of therapy?

4. What types of problems or clients would not benefit from the brief psychodynamic approach?

5. How adaptable is this approach to a more extensive or ongoing treatment process? What about Dr. Poland recommending Kevin seek out brief psychodynamic treatment for his next round of therapy (Chapter 3)?

6. What are the likely effects for the client of being selected for a specific treatment?
   On willingness?
   On commitment?
   On trust?
   On power?

7. When is it therapeutic to not decrease a client's emotional pain or turmoil?
   What role does your theoretical orientation play?
   What role does ACT play?

8. Would Bill or Kevin be an appropriate candidate for brief psychodynamic treatments? If so, would this approach be preferable?

9. How would the central issue be stated for both Bill and Kevin?

10. Would Dr. Robbins have selected Bill for the brief psychodynamic treatment? Would you? If so, how might Bill respond to the proposed central issue and contract?

Chapter 5

SYSTEMS THEORY AND ACT: A CASE OF PUBLIC COMMITMENT

Pennie Myers
Wichita State University

This chapter uses clinical casework to illustrate the value of integrating systems theory and Adaptive Counseling and Therapy (ACT) theory in clinical practice. Systems theory, the body of theoretical models for marital and family therapy, provides the conceptual orientation for understanding people psychologically and behaviorally. Systems theory helps therapists answer questions such as, How did the clients and the systems in which clients live develop? What needs to happen for the family, the marriage, to be more functional? What kinds of therapeutic goals do the clients need to accomplish?

ACT, on the other hand, provides a theoretical orientation for treatment selection. It helps therapists answer questions such as, What therapeutic interventions will have the highest likelihood of assisting clients to meet their identified goals efficiently and effectively? What therapist behaviors are most helpful for clients at various points in their therapy? Using the two theories in tandem offers practitioners a tool for both case conceptualization and treatment selection.

105

SYSTEMS THEORY AND ACT:
A SUCCESSFUL MARRIAGE

Systemic thinking and the ACT model (Howard, Nance, & Myers, 1986, 1987; Nance & Myers, 1991) blend well theoretically because both theories are rooted in an emphasis on the value of understanding the context within which behavior occurs. However, the two theories focus their attentions on different, but compatible, aspects of the therapeutic process. Systems theory relates to how systems function. ACT theory relates to how therapy functions. Systems theory is useful for assessing what tasks need to be accomplished. ACT is useful for designing appropriate task-specific interventions. Systems theory conceptualizes the client's relationship system and the functioning positions of the people who comprise the system (Friedman, 1991; Kerr, 1981). ACT conceptualizes the therapeutic system and suggests positions for therapists to take in order to best facilitate changing the client system. Systems theory helps therapists to understand. ACT theory helps therapists to behave.

Systems Theory

Systems theory (Bateson, 1972, 1979; Guttman, 1991) is an umbrella theory, sheltering diverse and numerous approaches to biological, sociological and psychological phenomena. Within the field of psychotherapy, specific systems theories form the basis of family therapy practice and can be divided into four primary schools of thought. These include strategic family therapy (Haley, 1976; Madanes, 1991; Palazzoli-Selvini, Boscolo, Cecchin, & Prata, 1978); structural family therapy (Colapinto, 1991; Minuchin, 1974); experiential family therapy (Roberto, 1991; Satir, 1972; Whitaker & Keith, 1981); and transgenerational family therapy (Bowen, 1978; Framo, 1965; Friedman, 1991; Kerr, 1981; Papero, 1990). All of these theories have a number of things in common. A systems perspective focuses on the relationships within the system. The contextual nature of behavior—the belief that behavior develops and occurs within some setting and within a complex relationship system rather than in isolation—is emphasized. A systemic orientation also involves the recognition that the problems and issues brought to therapy involve differing perspectives. The people who come for counseling are not right or wrong, good or bad, villains or heroines in any simplistic sense. They are earnest people working as hard as they know how to make relationships work. What is "real" is less important than the clients' perspectives about their lives; their views of their relationships; their behavior toward and feelings about each other; and their relationships with people outside their families, including their relationships with therapists. A systemic orientation implies that the therapist understand her or his own role in the client system (Tomm, 1984).

An Organizing Integrative Perspective

In family therapy, as in other areas of clinical practice, debates still occur as to which approach is the best way to do therapy. Many practitioners have ceased fighting over this issue and recognize the value of having more than one perspective through which to view any clinical problem. Inevitably, having multiple choices leads to problems in decision making. Confusion resulting from the range of available approaches to therapy has led to the search for viable integrated models (Norcross, 1986).

ACT is one such integrative model. Applied to systems theory, it can be helpful in two ways: (1) for organizing and categorizing the various sub-theories within general systems theory and (2) for selecting treatment interventions from the range of systems theories by matching them to the readiness levels of clients.

In systems work such as marital and family therapy, the problem of complexity is compounded by the fact that while the number of people in therapy may be only increasing arithmetically, the effect is far greater. Three people in the consultation room are more likely to be experienced as nine (three squared) than as three (one plus one plus one). Applying ACT to a system's approach is one way of taking the "mountain" of problematic systemic dynamics and breaking it down into a series of "molehills."

THE SCHOOLS OF FAMILY THERAPY

It is possible to assign particular schools of systems theory (family therapy theory) to particular styles of the ACT model (Myers, in progress). The psychoanalytic and transgenerational schools of family therapy are Style 4 approaches to family therapy. The goal of psychoanalytic family therapy (Fairbairn, 1954; Freud, 1961) is to enable the individual family members to be able to interact with one another without the intrusions of unconscious images of the past. In order to accomplish this goal, the focus is on changing the personality structure of family members. The goal of Bowen's (1978) transgenerational family therapy is increased differentiation of self. These are long-term goals involving structural personality change in family members. Both approaches require highly motivated

108 *Pennie Myers*

clients who are verbal and psychologically sophisticated. In fact, Bowen and other transgenerational family therapists often will work only with the family's most capable members. Bowenians believe that therapists work best when they have achieved a high level of personal differentiation so that they will not become triangulated into the family's emotional life. The therapist's maintenance of low emotional involvement translates into the ACT concept of low support. Many of the therapeutic techniques of transgenerational family therapy such as objectivity, transference analysis, family of origin work, and interpretation utilize less directive interventions than other schools of family therapy.

Proponents of experiential family therapy (Satir, 1967; Whitaker & Keith, 1981) provide the clearest examples of Style 3 systems therapists. The principle goal of therapy for the experientialists is that of growth for family members—greater life experience, more independence, a wider range of choices. Congruency and uniqueness of family members are valued. Experiential family therapy relies upon the therapist's ability to be forceful, accepting, and emotionally evocative (high support, low direction). Unlike Bowen, experiential therapists such as Satir and Whitaker do not work to stay uninvolved and cerebral but rather work to be completely involved with the family (high support). I observed Whitaker illustrating supportive emotional involvement at a program at which he did a live family demonstration. The family came on stage during a coffee break. The break had been inordinately long; the audience chatting and relaxing for far more than the 15 minutes allotted. Whitaker did nothing to reconvene the group. It would be difficult to imagine much less direction on his part to get the session under way. Finally, someone in the audience went to the microphone and angrily asked the audience to return to its seats so that the demonstration could get started. Once the session began, Whitaker, in his most remarkable way, immediately joined the family by denouncing the audience for its rudeness and lack of consideration. He completely empathized with the family's anxiety which, he suggested, had to have been exacerbated by the long wait (high support). Within moments, Whitaker had a most cooperative and relaxed family with which to work.

The structural school of family therapy (Aponte & Van Deusen, 1981; Colapinto, 1991; Minuchin, 1974) is founded on the belief that faulty structure is responsible for systemic problems. Therefore, the goals of therapy focus on altering the system's or the family's structure. Joining the family (high support) and then activating interventions aimed specifically at reorganizing family structure, such as assigning Dad rather than Mom to get the children ready for bed (high direction), earmark the process. Minuchin (1974) maintained a similar structural view of the larger community system within which families operate. High direction on the part of the therapist may be necessary for assisting the family in navigating the difficult currents present in the world of social services, medical services, and so forth.

Behavioral family therapy (Falloon, 1991; Holtzworth-Munroe & Jacobson, 1991) joins the structural school in the Style 2 quadrant of ACT. Problems are seen as serving a familial function and as being maintained by behavior (Levant, 1980). Behavioral family therapists focus more on dyadic interactions than do other systemic theorists who attend more to triadic relationships (Nichols, 1984). The goals of behavioral therapists are limited to working to alter the specific behavior patterns that produce the family's presenting symptoms. The vehicle for change is skill development. Therefore, teaching and training are significant parts of the process. Teaching is highly directive and requires significant reinforcement from the teacher (high support).

Behavioral family therapists include those who focus on communication (Rappaport, 1976; Stuart, 1980). For these therapists, behavior *is* communication, and the goal is to prohibit behaviors that are likely to stimulate or reinforce symptoms. The role of the therapist is to point out problematic sequences in the family's communication process and then to train the family to use different, more functional sequences. This is accomplished through modeling, instruction, practice, and feedback (high direction). Like other behavioral family therapists, those focusing on communication skill development provide reinforcement in the training process.

The strategic school of family therapy (Haley, 1963, 1976; Papp, 1980; Watzlawick, Weakland, & Fisch, 1974) is behaviorally oriented and totally absorbed with solving the family's presenting problem. The therapist has primary responsibility for developing a strategy to solve the presenting problem. Strategic therapy is often brief with little time being wasted on establishing significant relationships with family members (low support). The major technique is tactical maneuvering by the therapist (high direction). Strategic therapists can be more oblique and indirect in their directiveness. This is best illustrated by the use of paradoxical interventions (Palazzoli-Selvini et al., 1978) and the use of prescriptions from the therapist's team located behind the one-way mirror (Papp, 1980).

THE PROCESS OF FAMILY THERAPY

Family therapy, like individual therapy, is a process and, as such, has a developmental life of its own. Systems oriented therapists can utilize interventions

110   *Pennie Myers*

from the different schools of family therapy in different parts of the therapeutic process. Whitaker and Keith (1981) described the process of family therapy and, in so doing, unwittingly described therapy as the analog of ACT. In their view, family therapy is quite structured in the beginning phase as the therapist takes charge and works to get the family to take responsibility. In the middle phase of family therapy, according to Whitaker and Keith (1981), there is active involvement with the family. A part of this phase involves the teaching style, with the therapist providing a lot of support and some direction. Finally, in the end phase of family therapy, Whitaker and Keith suggested that the family is developing independence. At this point the therapist begins to disengage, and the family takes over more and more responsibility for itself as it moves to termination.

GREG AND SUZANNE: A CASE OF PUBLIC COMMITMENT

The case of Greg and Suzanne will serve to illustrate the use of ACT for a systems oriented therapist. This case involved an unmarried couple who had been involved in a significant relationship for about four years. Each had family of origin issues that were interfering with each one's ability to work out the relationship with one another. Therapy involved a variety of tasks for the couple and for each of the partners. Readiness levels varied by task for the couple and by task for each individual. This couple initially was seen conjointly. After several months, occasional separate sessions for each of them involved family of origin work. Several times their children also participated in the counseling process.

The Couple

At the time of their first appointment, the nature of the relationship between Greg and Suzanne was a secret shared only by one or two of their closest friends. Greg was legally separated from a wife of 19 years. The presenting problem was that Suzanne wanted a public commitment from Greg, who claimed that he too would like to be able to divorce his wife and make a more public commitment to Suzanne. However, he stated that a number of factors were keeping him from doing so. Greg wanted Suzanne to let him work things out on his own time schedule. Suzanne, who was seven years younger, felt that if she left Greg to his own time schedule, no changes would ever take place. Suzanne was dissatisfied with the status quo and was agitating for change. Greg was defensive, and while he claimed to be satisfied with keeping their relationship as it had been for a while longer, he too was not satisfied with the nature of their current relationship.

Greg and Suzanne presented themselves as eager to have the escalating conflict about this issue resolved. In ACT terms, they were willing to participate in couples' counseling. They also appeared to be capable of participating actively in their counseling, as both were verbal and articulate. Both were hopeful about the counseling. Therapy began with the therapist operating from a Style 3 position. After joining with the couple to establish a relationship with them, information about the history and current status of the relationship, as well as about each of them individually, was gently elicited.

The conjoint therapy highlighted some fundamental differences between Suzanne and Greg. These differences, which had initially attracted them to one another, had now begun to chafe. In the first few conjoint sessions, it also became clear that these chafing differences were deeply rooted in family of origin issues. Therefore, changes in the relationship were going to involve changes for each of them individually.

Forty-six-year-old Greg had, for the last eight years, resided in a city other than the one in which his wife and children lived. He and his wife, from whom he was separated, had been married for 19 years. He claimed that there was no open conflict in the marriage—just apathy and lack of involvement. Greg stated that he and his wife had been about to divorce at the time that she became pregnant with their first child. A second child was born three years later. Greg vowed that he would never abandon his own children no matter what the cost. Unresolved childhood feelings that his father had emotionally abandoned him immobilized Greg from moving ahead with divorce once he had children. Unwittingly, he was perpetuating his father's pattern of abandonment by staying away from home for the better part of eight years.

Suzanne had been divorced for several years. Her marriage had been a very brief, right out of high school, had-to-get-away-from-home kind of marriage. It lasted seven years, during which time she and her husband adopted two children. Suzanne had custody of the children. Their father did not provide for them in any way, although every now and then he would see them. At the time of her divorce, Suzanne had only a high school education. Her family of origin had been very poor and uneducated, as had her husband. Suzanne returned to school, eventually completing a master's degree. She proceeded to gain self-confidence and respect as a high functioning, independent professional woman, living on her own and raising her two children. She had several brief dating relationships, but until she

112   *Pennie Myers*

met Greg she was not particularly interested in getting involved in a long-term, serious relationship. The relationship with Greg evolved slowly over time.

Greg and Suzanne were in agreement that the purpose of counseling would be either to assist Greg in moving ahead with divorce so that he could make a public commitment to Suzanne or to assist Suzanne in ending the relationship. Within a few sessions, it became apparent that Greg and Suzanne were reenacting with one another a number of the unresolved issues from their families of origin and from their previous relationships.

Greg

Greg had never had any kind of therapy before he participated in the joint sessions with Suzanne. He volunteered that he came to counseling both because he didn't want to lose Suzanne and because at some level he recognized that he was stuck in a situation that was no longer working satisfactorily for him. Despite Greg's 46 years, he had been naive about himself, describing himself as emotionally constricted prior to meeting Suzanne. The relationship with Suzanne had begun a process of self-examination that continued with therapy—looking at such things as his emotions, his family, his relationships, his fears, and his motivations.

Greg surprised himself with the level of emotion he experienced during the sessions. Most of his life he had prided himself on being cool, detached, and unemotional. One strong affective trigger for Greg was his feeling about his relationship with his father. When he would talk about how unhappy he was in his marriage and begin to talk of legally divorcing, he would tear up almost immediately. His focus would shift to how cut off he was from his own father and how he didn't want his children to feel that way about their relationship with him. Not surprisingly, I learned that Greg's father was very unhappy in his own marriage but stayed for Greg's sake. Greg is an only child.

Greg had not wanted children. He constantly felt guilty, as if he had to make something up to his children (ages 11 and 14) because he had not wanted them. Guilt was the primary motivator for his behavior towards his children. Greg was very willing to change this pattern of interaction with his children because he didn't like the way he felt and because he wanted to be different from his parents whom he saw as also having been guilt-driven. However, Greg appeared to be unable to change his guilt orientation, which was rooted in the legacy inherited from his family of origin. Greg had never been able to think of guilt in any way except the one in which he had been programmed. Greg's readiness, willing but unable, suggested that Style 2 would be most helpful for the task of assisting Greg

Systems Theory and ACT **113**

to give up guilt as his primary parenting motivation. Such an educational approach to Greg also would be in keeping with Peggy Papp's (1983) suggestion that therapists intervene directly when clients are not resisting (i.e., when they are willing). The following conversation was from the session in which the guilt issue was introduced. Suzanne was present in the session.

Pennie: *Guilt has two different kinds of functions, you know, Greg. One of those is a future oriented perspective where we sometimes don't do something because we project ourselves into the future and say to ourselves, "If I do that, I'm very likely to feel tremendously guilty." But you know, guilt can also be a retrospective process where we look back at things that we've done and feel real guilty about them.*

Greg: *Boy, do I know that. I don't know how many times . . . and in fact even when it came to the conception of my son, I beat myself for having let lust get in the way . . . let my body get in the way, and I've been mad at myself about that ever since.*

P: *Well, that's exactly my point. I'm not sure that all of that guilt about what's already happened, about conceiving your children, is serving much of a purpose for you. Don't you think you've done enough penance by now?*

G: (Laughs.) *Well, I never thought of it that way.*

P: *You know, I remember when my kids were young, sometimes I'd get so caught up in being guilty about how I acted yesterday that I couldn't function very well today. And you know, that only had me be guilty again tomorrow about how I behaved today. And so the next day, I'd have to be guilty about yesterday. That can go on and on.*

G: (Laughs.) *Well, I can certainly identify with that! I'm still doing it.*

P: *I'm glad you can have a sense of humor about it and can recognize your own behavior, Greg, but, you know, I think what I would ask you to think about is, "What function is my guilt serving?" In a way, you're evaluating now some things about how you want to behave with your children so that from a futures perspective, you don't have to look back and feel guilty. It might feel real powerful to say, "I'm going to go home and see my kids this weekend and do some things with them because if I don't do that, I'm going to feel guilty." That's really looking ahead into the future and letting the possibility of guilt motivate positive behavior on your*

114 *Pennie Myers*

part. I really can't see where continuing to be guilty for a conception that took place 14 years ago is any longer serving much function. I'd like you to try at least throughout this week, when you're feeling guilty, to stop and ask yourself, "Is this guilt serving any purpose?"

G: *That feels like something I could do pretty easily. I think I do understand what you're saying.*

As the session continued, the focus shifted to a discussion about how we behave in particular ways and feel particular ways as a result of things back in our family that we've absorbed without even knowing it, and how part of therapy is understanding what those learnings are and making adult decisions about what we want to keep and what we want to discard. At that point, Greg took off by telling me a variety of stories that indicated to me that he didn't need much direction from me. In fact, the only support he required was an occasional head nod and my attention. He was not only motivated, he also was able to look back and begin to sort out some issues for himself. He was willing and able, and I could shift into a Style 4. While listening to Greg's stories and observing him, I would promote an affective focus when feelings bubbled near the surface.

G: *I remember that my Mom would dress me in the morning immaculately, and she would point her finger at me and kind of shake her finger in my face and say, "Now when you come home at the end of the day, young man, I expect you to look exactly like you look now. I want you to be just as clean when you come home as you are when you leave the house this morning." And so I remember, like at recess time, I wouldn't get down like the other kids and play marbles. Even a teacher remarked once that I was too neat and clean. And you know, a bunch of years ago I was with a friend. We'd gone to a football game and we were in the bleachers and he had his two- or three-year-old daughter with him—this was long before I had kids—and his daughter got down under the bleachers with these two little boys and they were playing, and they were just filthy! I mean, you know it was hot, and the sweat and the dirt were running down their faces kind of mixed together—I mean, they were just a mess. And after a while, the mother of those two little boys came over and grabbed those kids. . . .* (As Greg was saying this, he began to choke up and to tear, continuing to try to plow on with the story.)

P: *Stop a minute, Greg. I want you to stop and try to get in touch with what's going on with you.*

G: (After several minutes of silence, choking back, and crying.) *You know, this is really a strange thing. At that moment, I remember thinking that that mother was right to yell at those kids. And my friend got down from the bleachers and he was playing with his kid—he thought it was great fun. And I remember thinking that that other mother was really right and that what my friend needed to do was give that kid a good pop on the ass. (More silence and then . . .) And I feel so sad now, and I think there was a part of me that really wished I could be that little kid playing in the dirt and not have had to stay so clean. That's what my tears are about.*

Greg was able to take the learning about family legacy messages and begin to talk about how he thinks sometimes—about how he's done so many things just like his parents without ever thinking about them. Then he talked about his hope that he would now be able to be a little looser with his children—in this case about the cleanliness issue. I was now providing almost no direction, providing support only as necessary. It was Greg's ball, and he took it and ran with it. (If several sessions later, he would have said he was having trouble loosening up with his kids, I would have needed to revert back to Style 2 and provided more direction as to how he might attempt such changes.)

In a session several weeks later, Greg remembered and talked about another pertinent piece from his childhood. Since he was willing and able to engage in the task of working through family of origin issues, I provided little direction in this session, and what support I provided was mostly related to wanting to reinforce Greg's new learnings.

G: *I remember Santa Claus coming to my house. When I got older, I realized how hard my mother worked to make the Santa Claus suit. Then she'd get a neighbor to be Santa—it was so wonderful when Santa actually came and I could see him and all. I feel all warm inside just thinking about Santa Claus coming into the house. I wouldn't want to give up those feelings.*

P: *I'm glad you have such happy memories and feelings. And, I'm very impressed that you can see some things you want to hold onto as well as things you are ready to give up.*

In this session, ACT provided the basis of the in-session *behavior.* The *theoretical* basis for systemically conceptualizing Greg's problem was multi-generational—how feelings and behaviors are passed from one generation to another, and how to help the client differentiate himself from his family of origin

116 *Pennie Myers*

in order to be able to operate more independently of emotional responses now that he is an adult. Greg was giving himself a new story, a new way of looking at things—particularly in relationship to his parenting. The process began with the direction and support coming from me (S 2). Eventually all of the direction and most of the support came from Greg (S 4).

Greg moved so far as to put the legal wheels into motion for his divorce and began talking with his children about his relationship with Suzanne. In a session with Greg and his 14-year-old daughter, who had been staying with him for the summer, the following took place:

G: *I think Jennifer and I have done real well together these last few weeks. It's the first time we've ever really spent this much time together.*

J: *Yeah!*

G: *We talked last night about Suzanne—my relationship with her.*

P: *What was your reaction, Jennifer?*

J: *I wasn't surprised. I could tell they didn't only work together. The way they are together is real different than the way it is when my dad and my mom are together. With Mom and Dad there is so much tension—no fights, just tension. I hate it!*

G: (To therapist.) *You kept telling me that kids are smart and know a lot about what is really going on, but I was sure that my kids weren't aware of my relationship with Suzanne.*

J: *Geez, Dad! Why didn't you just ask? Think of all the money you would have saved if you'd of asked instead of seeing a shrink.*

Suzanne

Suzanne appeared to be slightly ahead of Greg in terms of her differentiation from her family of origin, in part because of previous individual therapy. The previous therapy had focused on helping her to work out issues with her mother who was psychologically unsophisticated, overinvolved, and critical. Suzanne still struggled when she asserted herself with her mother although her assertive behavior had definitely increased. One Thanksgiving during the period that I was seeing Suzanne and Greg together, Suzanne decided that she was no longer interested in attending Thanksgiving at her mother's home where everybody got angry and fought and where there was very little holiday pleasure. Despite agonizing beforehand about how to tell her mother she wouldn't be coming for Thanksgiving, Suzanne did call her mother and inform her that she would be having Thanksgiving at home with her own family. When her mother got upset and angry, Suzanne maintained her position and expressed good feelings about what she had done.

Within the context of the couple's counseling, Suzanne identified her lack of self-esteem as an area on which she wished to focus. Though she had experienced much improvement in this area over time, she was seeing unlimited possibilities for her future hampered only by limitations she placed upon herself. Since she had made significant changes in her educational and professional status, she did not believe her self-esteem issues were related to competency. Rather, she felt her workaholic behavior was compensatory for some basic belief she held that she was not a worthwhile individual. When I began to delve into the origins of Suzanne's feelings of insignificance, she began to pull back from the therapeutic process. Suddenly, she was not her usual highly motivated self. Although she had agreed to a contract to focus on issues related to improvement of self-esteem, we seemed to be dead-ended unless we could explore the origins of and reinforcers for her poor self-esteem. Both she and I believed that the roots of her poor self-image were buried in her family of origin and had continued to grow in her family with her children, her relationship with her first husband, and her relationship with Greg.

Suzanne's unwillingness to look at the past was the result of the pain she experienced whenever she allowed herself access to these painful areas at an emotional level. The following dialogue is from a session in which I had to get more directive to balance Suzanne's lower readiness level for this task.

P: *Suzanne, it seems like you really clam up when we get to talking about how you feel about yourself in relationships.*

Suzanne: (Nonverbally agrees with a head nod and lots of tears.)

P: *I think it's important we keep at this a little. Of course, I'll back off if you prefer.*

S: *No.* (Followed by a negative shake of the head.)

P: *I'd appreciate it if you'd hang in here with me. Try to talk about this. Try to answer some of my questions.*

118 *Pennie Myers*

S: *OK.*

P: *Where would you guess your bad feelings about yourself come from?*

S: *I don't know. I guess my family just wasn't very good at expressing their feelings.*

P: (At this point, I decided I was not being directive enough. Suzanne was struggling, and I needed to take better charge of the session.) *Suzanne, can you describe a scene to me from your family when you were a little girl, something that you remember feeling strongly about?*

S: (Took some time thinking.) *I'm not sure if this is what you mean, but when I was little, my mother was always telling me I was ugly. Oh, she never said it real directly, but the message was obvious. Like, she'd say, "You have a fat belly just like me." And we were so poor, so very poor. I was only a marginal student then because I hated to go to school. My clothes were shabby, and I knew from what my mother said that I was basically unattractive.*

Suzanne was beginning to open up. We both had struggled when my questions were too vague, not directive enough. Once I could see that asking more specific questions was helping Suzanne to talk about an area that, because of its painfulness, was difficult to share, the session progressed productively. At one point the individual issue for Suzanne merged with the relationship issue.

S: *How can I expect Greg to love me?* (Quiet tears fill her eyes and she begins to dab at them with a wad of kleenex.) *It seems nobody has ever really loved me.*

P: *Can you remember feeling that way when you were little too?*

S: *No. Mostly I don't remember feeling much of anything when I was little. Life was just so hard. We lived in such dreary poverty. My parents trudged through grimly. I just tried to have no feelings and get through life. Nobody cared about me. They were too caught up in their own problems.*

P: *And now?*

S: *I feel like no one loves me now either.*

P: *It's sad to feel so alone.* (Suzanne cries for a while, then stops and blows her nose. I decide that in addition to supporting her feelings, I also want to do something to begin to change her perception of herself as unlovable/unloved.) *Can you move away from the feelings for a moment and think about who loves you now?*

S: *My mom doesn't love me because she isn't capable of love. Brian and Kim* (her children) *love me. And I guess I know Greg loves me even if I don't always feel it. When I feel like he doesn't love me, I just want to hurry up and end things so it won't hurt so bad when he leaves me.*

Suzanne's first husband had been totally irresponsible. That was one of the reasons she had left him. I was able to congratulate Suzanne for having learned something from her first marriage. In choosing Greg, she had chosen a man who was clearly more responsible. Unlike her first husband, who left her with two young children and never provided for any of them again, Greg had been providing for his children for the last eight years even if he didn't live with them. I suggested that she was caught on the horns of a dilemma. The very quality that she found so infuriating in Greg was also a quality that she admired greatly. Suzanne said she had never thought of it that way before.

Greg and Suzanne

At the time that Greg and Suzanne came into couple's counseling, they claimed to love each other but felt as if their relationship was going nowhere. Greg was unable to legally divorce (in his family of origin, one behaved "responsibly" no matter what). Suzanne, feeling rejected by Greg's inability to divorce (just as she had felt rejected and unloved as a child), would tell herself that Greg really didn't love her. She would attempt to move away from Greg—threatening to start dating again and cutting off the sexual relationship. Then Greg would become further immobilized by guilt about Suzanne and about his children. This dance with Greg and Suzanne each taking the same steps had been repeating itself throughout their years together. Within the context of conjoint therapy, Greg and Suzanne both made significant progress in working out some deep-rooted emotional issues for themselves. The fact that each was sometimes privy to the other person's personal battle was helpful to their understanding of one another, their intimacy, and the relationship.

Relationship problems that stemmed directly from the interaction of some of their individual personality traits were also addressed in this couple's therapy.

120 *Pennie Myers*

Suzanne tended to believe that one should set goals, make a plan, and then take action. After all, that is exactly how she had gotten herself out of poverty and out of a problematic marriage. In contrast, the only action Greg ever took was in reaction to something else. Greg had learned not to be proactive as a child. Any action he did take was met with criticism by his parents.

Greg and Suzanne certainly needed the balance their different styles provided. Still, their differences in this area were a cause of dissension. Like most of us, they had the good sense to pick a partner who provided balance in an essential area. Also, like most of us, they then spent much of their time trying to make their partner into a person just like themselves. Exacerbating this style conflict was their negative self-talk. Suzanne, angry at Greg for his inability to set goals and to act, would turn around and negate her own goal oriented, proactive behavior by calling herself a "castrating bitch." Similarly Greg would refer to himself as a "wimp," at the same time devaluing Suzanne for her lack of sensitivity. Traditional gender stereotyping, rather than an appreciation of the adaptive and survivalist nature of some of their behaviors, fed into their feelings about themselves. Their relationship, which at one time had them admiring of one another's differences and feeling good about themselves and each other, had deteriorated. Greg and Suzanne were suffering.

The issue of their style differences was addressed partially through direct discussion about how each of their individual patterns of behavior had been useful and how these behavior patterns had been problematic—what parts of their styles did they really want to keep; what did they want to work on changing. A Style 2 educational approach on my part was well received by both of them. They were willing learners whose ability to change some parts of themselves while maintaining others was somewhat enhanced through discussion and understanding. This is an area that continues to require attention.

The issue of Greg's feelings of responsibility surfaced somewhat differently when he realized, with some surprise, what an enormous sense of responsibility he felt for Suzanne. Since he was still feeling overwhelmed by a sense of responsibility for his wife and children, he recognized long-standing feelings that he might be jumping out of the frying pan and into the fire—replacing one set of burdens for another. These feelings were old and familiar. He had not been a carefree child. Internal and external responsibilities burdened him throughout his childhood and throughout his adult life. Multigenerational messages had been passed from parents to children for at least the last four generations in Greg's family. He could hear his parents and grandparents saying, "work, don't play" and "always do your duty." (Ironically, Greg eventually reacted to his over-parented sense of responsibility by behaving less responsibly, by moving away from his wife and children,

Systems Theory and ACT **121**

by being unable to make a commitment to Suzanne.) Whenever Greg attempted to lower his expectations of himself in terms of responsibility, the trade-off became the burden of guilt. He felt caught between a rock and a hard place and responded by being totally immobilized. He was willing, but did not know how, to change. He needed direction.

In keeping with his need for increased direction, I suggested he talk to himself in such a way as to reduce his reactivity to Suzanne's problems—even going so far as to give him lines to say to himself. "It is not my responsibility to remind Suzanne to get her car serviced. If her car develops problems, it is not my responsibility to take it in to be fixed." Over time, the new self-talk did impact his feelings of responsibility towards Suzanne. He began to change his behavior with her. As Greg's feelings of responsibility lessened, I moved to Style 3—giving Greg occasional direction but primarily a lot of support to help him maintain new and unfamiliar feelings and behaviors. On one occasion, I suggested that Greg had been so responsible as a child, he had even been responsible for keeping his unhappy father stuck in his marriage. After all, his father had said he only stayed married for Greg. In dismay, Greg responded that he sure didn't want his own children to feel responsible for their father's unhappiness. This was a new way for Greg to start to think about what it means to "stay married for the children."

As of this writing, there is still work to be done within the context of couple therapy to make the connection between Suzanne's experience with men as irresponsible and Greg's experience with men as overresponsible fall into place. Predictably, Suzanne became unnerved by the changes in Greg's behavior, deciding, despite what he told her, that they meant he was wanting to end the relationship. She had to fight her natural tendency to retreat in preparation for the eventual demise of the relationship. Some of the ammunition for this fight against her natural tendency came from her being able to hear about Greg's internal struggle.

Suzanne continues to fight against trying to get things happening as quickly as possible and against the kind of discouragement that has her leave relationships when she fears she might get left. Not acting on these habitual reactions is a real battle for her. It helps when she is able to remind herself that part of the problem resides with Greg and his family legacy rather than with her perceived unlovableness.

Greg and Suzanne continue to be motivated to work on themselves and their relationship. Their overall readiness for therapy was (and remains) high. They voluntarily came into therapy and asked for help. They understood the therapeutic process and the value of therapy. They were bright and verbal. They liked therapy. They were unable to figure out how to change their relationship in the desired direction. Their failed attempts to move their relationship resulted in a lack of

122 *Pennie Myers*

confidence in their own ability to salvage things. Suzanne and Greg were willing to change the nature of their relationship—they just could not do so. A task-by-task assessment of their willingness, their ability, and their confidence level assisted me in my decisions about how to approach various treatment goals.

COMMITMENT TO AN INTEGRATIVE SYSTEMIC APPROACH

In a discussion of the play, "Six Characters in Search of an Author," Johnson (1990) said that the essential constructivist dilemma is that each of our languages describes only our own internal world and that the listener interprets them based on his or her own internal world. "Thus, given that, how can we ever live harmoniously with others, as families, as couples, as neighbors, friends?" One aspect of the importance of systemic therapy is that it allows members of the system increased access to the internal world of their significant others. Systemic therapy increases our chances of living together more harmoniously. Greg and Suzanne learned about each others' internal worlds. These two parents and their children are learning more about their cross-generational internal worlds. And if I'm doing my job, all of them are also learning how to continue to dialogue about their internal worlds long after therapy terminates.

No one exists in isolation. Therapy must recognize the interactive effect of individuals in their current time and space and across the generations in order to address the reality of people's lives. Greg and Suzanne each say they want to be together. Wishing for it is not enough. The two of them and their children will have to learn to live together if Greg and Suzanne's relationship is to survive. Parents, grandparents, aunts, uncles, cousins, ex-spouses, friends, etc. also need to be considered for their interactive effect. We would be remiss as therapists if we forgot this. It does not always matter who is present in therapy. It does matter that the impact of others in the system be part of the therapeutic consideration.

ACT can be a helpful tool for systems oriented therapy. We can use this integrative model to determine the task readiness of couples and families for whom we provide therapy. We can make treatment selections using ACT—selecting from the large array of systemic intervention, from the various schools of family therapy, those approaches that best meet our clients' needs in terms of directiveness and support. We can calibrate our style as therapists so that our style has the highest likelihood for assisting appropriate change . . . a little more or less direction here, a little more or less support there.

REFERENCES

Aponte, H., & Van Deusen, J. (1981). In A.S. Gurman & D.P. Kniskern (Eds.), *Handbook of family therapy.* New York: Brunner/Mazel.

Bateson, G. (1972). *Steps to an ecology of the mind.* New York: Ballantine Books.

Bateson, G. (1979). *Mind and nature: A necessary unit.* New York: Bantam Books.

Bowen, M. (1978). *Family therapy in clinical practice.* New York: Aronson.

Colapinto, J. (1991). Structural family therapy. In A.S. Gurman & D.P. Kniskern (Eds.), *Handbook of family therapy* (Vol II). New York: Brunner/Mazel.

Fairbairn, W. (1954). *An object-relations theory of the personality.* New York: Basic Books.

Falloon, I.R.H. (1991). Behavioral family therapy. In A.S. Gurman & D.P. Kniskern (Eds.), *Handbook of family therapy* (Vol II). New York: Brunner/Mazel.

Framo, J.L. (1965). Rationale and techniques of intensive family therapy. In I. Boszormenyi-Nagy & J.L. Framo (Eds.), *Intensive family therapy: Theoretical and practical aspects.* Hagerstown, MD: Harper & Row.

Freud, S. (1961). The ego and the id. In J. Strachey (Ed.), *The standard edition of the complete psychological works of Sigmund Freud* (Vol. 19, pp. 3–66). London: Hogarth Press.

Friedman, E.H. (1991). Bowen theory and therapy. In A.S. Gurman & D.P.Kniskern (Eds.). *Handbook of family therapy* (Vol. II, pp. 134–170). New York: Brunner/Mazel.

Guttman, H.A. (1991). Systems theory, cybernetics and epistemology. In A.S. Gurman & D.P. Kniskern (Eds.), *Handbook of family therapy* (Vol. II, pp. 41–62). New York: Brunner/Mazel.

Haley, J. (1963). *Strategies of psychotherapy.* New York: Grune & Stratton.

Haley, J. (1976). *Problem-solving therapy: New strategies for effective family therapy.* San Francisco: Jossey-Bass.

124 *Pennie Myers*

Holtzworth-Munroe, A., & Jacobson, N.S. (1991). Behavioral marital therapy. In A.S. Gurman & D.P. Kniskern (Eds.), *Handbook of family therapy* (Vol II). New York: Brunner/Mazel.

Howard, G.S., Nance, D.W., & Myers, P. (1986). Adaptive counseling and therapy: An integrative, metatheoretical approach. *The Counseling Psychologist, 14,* 363–442.

Howard, G.S., Nance, D.W., & Myers, P. (1987). *Adaptive counseling and therapy.* San Francisco: Jossey-Bass.

Johnson, S. (1990). Six characters in search of an author: A constructivist view. *Family Process, 29,* 297–308.

Kerr, M.E. (1981). Family systems theory and therapy. In A.S. Gurman & D.P. Kniskern (Eds.), *Handbook of family therapy.* New York: Brunner/Mazel.

Levant, R.E. (1980). A classification of the field of family therapy: A review of prior attempts and a new paradigmatic model. *American Journal of Family Therapy, 8,* 3–16.

Madanes, C. (1991). Strategic family therapy. In A.S. Gurman & D.P. Kniskern (Eds.), *Handbook of family therapy* (Vol. II). New York: Brunner/Mazel.

Minuchin, S. (1974). *Families and family therapy.* Cambridge, MA: Harvard University Press.

Myers, P. (In progress). *Adaptive counseling and therapy: An integrative model for marital and family therapy.*

Nance, D.W., & Myers, P. (1991). Continuing the eclectic journey. *Journal of Mental Health Counseling, 13,* 119–130.

Nichols, M.P. (1984). *Family therapy: Concepts and methods.* New York: Gardner Press.

Norcross, J.C. (1986). Eclectic psychotherapy. In J.C. Norcross (Ed.), *Handbook of eclectic psychotherapy.* New York: Brunner/Mazel.

Palazzoli-Selvini, M., Boscolo, L., Cecchin, G., & Prata, G. (1978). *Paradox and counterparadox.* New York: Aronson.

Papero, D.V. (1990). *Bowen family systems theory.* Boston: Allyn and Bacon.

Papp, P. (1980). The Greek chorus and other techniques of paradoxical therapy. *Family Process, 19,* 45–57.

Papp, P. (1983). *The process of change.* New York: The Guilford Press.

Rappaport, A.F. (1976). Conjugal relationship enhancement program. In D.H.L. Olson (Ed.), *Treating relationships* (pp. 41–66). Lake Mills, IA: Graphic Publishing Company.

Roberto, L.G. (1991). Symbolic-experiential family therapy. In A.S. Gurman & D.P. Kniskern (Eds.), *Handbook of family therapy* (Vol. II, pp. 444–476). New York: Brunner/Mazel.

Satir, V. (1967). *Conjoint family therapy.* Palo Alto, CA: Science and Behavior Books.

Satir, V. (1972). *Peoplemaking.* Palo Alto, CA: Science and Behavior Books.

Stuart, R.B. (1980). *Helping couples change: A social learning approach for marital therapy.* New York: Guilford Press.

Tomm, K.M. (1984). One perspective on the Milan systemic approach: Part I—Overview of development, theory, and practice. *Journal of Marital and Family Therapy, 10,* 113–125.

Watzlawick, P., Weakland, J., & Fisch, R. (1974). *Change.* New York: Norton.

Whitaker, C.A., & Keith, D.V. (1981). Symbolic-experiential family therapy. In A.S. Gurman & D.P. Kniskern (Eds.), *Handbook of family therapy* (pp. 187–225). New York: Brunner/Mazel.

COMMENTS

Systems and ACT

Don W. Nance

This chapter involves much more than an explanation and illustration of how ACT can be useful with a systemic orientation. Dr. Myers utilizes ACT concepts to categorize the major schools of family therapy. The categories correspond well to those previously identified for other major theoretical approaches (Howard et al., 1987). While almost all family therapy schools share one parent, the systemic perspective or orientation, the other parent comes from different theoretical roots. This family of theoretical origin work, categorized by Dr. Myers, is likely to increase our understanding of how ACT, schools of family therapy, and other theoretical orientations are related. Certainly, I gained additional clarity from reading her chapter.

The concepts of *flexibility* and ***range,*** central in the ACT model, are extended in Dr. Myers' description of her work with Suzanne and Greg. Therapist flexibility was extended to include adapting the configuration of participants to the tasks emerging in the course of treatment. The initial client was the couple, their relationship. The initial task was to change the current status of that relationship. The change could be more public commitment, i.e., marriage, or bringing the relationship to a close. After working with the couple for a while, it became apparent to the therapist that this "stuckness" in the relationship was held in place by issues brought to the relationship by each individual from his or her respective family of origin. If Greg weren't so guilty and responsible he could get divorced and express his love for Suzanne more publicly. Suzanne's struggles would be lessened significantly if the security she felt in her professional life extended to her personal relationships.

The therapist altered the format. In conjoint sessions, she focused on the relationship. The impact of individual issues on the relationship was explored. In individual sessions, she focused on individual issues in order to give more flexibility in how each person approached the relationship. Initially these changes in configuration were accomplished with S 2 direction and support. Over the course of therapy, the decision about who would be at an appointment was decided by the couple—R 4. The format and configuration of therapy was adapted to fit tasks—ACT at its best.

The systems approach can be used to understand and intervene from the individual level to the global level. The therapist showed flexibility in conceptualizing the couple, the individuals, and how each of their backgrounds impacted on the current relationship. As therapist, she broke the rules of some schools of family therapy. She saw the couple together and individually plus at least one child.

The combination of family of origin work, behavioral prescriptions, modeling, clarification of individual needs, and couples communication was intriguing. The negotiation, clarification, renegotiation of the therapeutic contract, content, format, boundaries, and confidentiality with the clients was parallel to the processes going on internally with the therapist. The process was a systematic one of conceptualization, intervention, gaining new information, leading to reconceptualization, new intervention, etc. This circular process keeps the therapist and the clients engaged in an active exploration of the issues.

The systems chapter also marks a transition to more eclectic approaches as conceptualizations and interventions are utilized from a variety of schools and approaches. The role of the therapist is less clearly defined; the nature of the problem seems to emerge and change rather than being clear from initial points in the therapy process. While the role of ACT may also be less clear at times, its organizing and integrating properties may be more important under these conditions than in the clearly identified process of Mann's brief psychodynamic model or when the cognitive behavioral tasks are clear. ACT helps the therapist focus, refocus, intervene, and reassess.

QUESTIONS

1. Who is the client when working with a couple or a family?
   How are individual needs/issues taken into account?

2. If a family has a family physician, a family clergy person, a family attorney, then what are the pluses and minuses of having a family therapist?
   How is therapy different?
   How did Dr. Myers manage the potential problems?
   How did seeing several family members assist the therapy process?

3. Under what circumstances might a therapist engage in
   a. Family focused therapy in an individual context?
   b. Couples counseling while seeing only one partner?
   c. Couples counseling in a family therapy context?
   d. Individual therapy within a couples context?
   e. Individual therapy within a family context?
   Which of the above were employed by Dr. Myers?

4. What rules do you have about who must be present for couples or family treatment?

5. What are the potential impacts on a system, couple, or family of one person changing due to therapy?

6. What are the family systems elements of each of the clients from previous chapters?
   Bill (Chapter 2)—Single parent needing to fill system roles formerly occupied by wife/mother?
   Kevin (Chapter 3)—He and Cathy exchanged roles in the relationship when she did what he had been doing? What role did family pressures to join family business play on Kevin's difficulties with commitment?
   Curtis (Chapter 4)—Found the role of family hero more and more difficult to maintain? Curtis changed his needs for love and acceptance in family of origin? How would a more systemic view impact the course of treatment in each of these previous cases?

7. How can a therapist employ ACT styles in order to produce equilibrium, disequilibrium, and change?

8. How does a therapist adjust ACT styles based on the differential readiness of individual family members?

9. In what ways is the ACT focus on power applicable to a systems approach?

10. What concepts from cognitive behavioral therapy, psychodynamic, and humanistic approaches did you notice operating in process of Dr. Myers working from a Systems/ACT perspective?

Chapter 6

AN ECLECTIC APPROACH TO COUNSELING WOMEN: A CASE OF MOVEMENT OUT FROM A CLOISTERED LIFE AND A CASE OF MOVEMENT OUT OF THE PAST

Eileen T. Nickerson
Boston University

In this chapter my theoretical orientation will be delineated briefly and used in conjunction with the Adaptive Counseling and Therapy (ACT) model as a framework for conceptualizing and understanding my work with two middle-aged women of ethnically-oriented and working-class backgrounds. The ways in which the ACT model informed and expanded upon the therapist's formulations will be examined as a way of illustrating the usefulness of ACT for those working with women.

THEORETICAL PERSPECTIVES

My therapeutic theoretical orientation is eclectic and multifaceted. It is influenced heavily by developmental, feminist, psychodynamic, multicultural, and systems-oriented considerations. By virtue of my initial training as a counseling psychologist, I am developmentally oriented. I view education, counseling, therapy, and helping interventions as psycho-educational stratagems for optimizing human development across the life span. I believe that the potential for human growth is never ending and that our therapeutic skills should be utilized in assisting people to fuller self-purpose, no mater what their age, gender, ethnicity, or station in life. Employing a developmental framework, a therapist is allied with a client as a facilitator of his or her optimal development (Blocher, 1986). A client is not seen merely in terms of dysfunction or pathology. The strengths, assets and skills that a client brings to therapy are given equal attention and validation. A developmental framework also provides a sense of developmental periods, developmental tasks, and the intertwining of personally derived and societally derived expectations and directives.

I am persuaded by a number of psychodynamic formulations, which seem to be compatible with the notion of development or becoming. The idea of prior experiences shaping present attitudes, behavior, and functioning is one example. Client and therapist need to unite in their efforts to uncover and comprehend the nature of influential prior experiences. The behaviors modeled and the messages and scripts that permeate one's family of origin are particularly relevant. And when employing a multicultural or a multi-pluralistic perspective, one acknowledges that the "family of origin" concept needs to be broadened to include all relevant familial and community members. Human development takes place in interaction with others, and the perceptions and values of those "others" color our sense of ourselves (self-concept) and how we value ourselves (self-esteem).

Feminist theorists and therapists have raised our collective therapeutic consciousness (Ballou & Gabalac, 1985; Jaggar & Rothenberg, 1984; Rawlings & Carter, 1977; Rosewater & Walker, 1985). Our awareness has increased about the ways in which psychological theories, research, and psychotherapeutic practices have tended to compound women's difficulties in achieving a sense of first-class citizenship. I view most women as having been externally socialized into gender roles that imply a second-class or inferior status. Helping women differentiate between the external and internal sources of some of their dilemmas is crucial. Women need to be helped to understand that some of their struggles are related to societal rather than self pathology.

Of particular concern for feminist-oriented helping professionals has been the evidence that traditional helping practices, such as counseling and psychotherapy, often have operated to keep the status quo and to inhibit change in the social and vocational roles of women (Broverman, Broverman, Clarkson, Rosenkrantz, & Vogel, 1970; Chesler, 1973; Nickerson, 1988). Feminist therapists, by training and understanding, assist their clients to feel differently and better about themselves.

Self-valuing of oneself and one's gender, just as valuing of one's color, seems to be essential for healthy self-definition and self-acceptance. ACT, as I will discuss near the conclusion of the chapter, assists in organizing my behavior with clients and helps maintain a therapeutic focus.

SELECTION OF CLIENTS

I have chosen to write about my work with two women—Marie and Lily. The study of Marie's and Lily's lives affords an opportunity to apply the ACT model and an eclectic orientation to working with women often neglected in more traditionally-oriented clinical deliberation—that is, middle-aged women of working-class and ethnic-minority backgrounds. Contemporary developmental psychologists point to the middle years of adulthood as years of continuing change and transition (Goldhaber, 1986; Norman & Scaramella, 1980). For many women, their middle years present the first real opportunity to move out into the world in meaningful ways (Baruch, Barnett, & Rivers, 1983; Giele, 1982).

Although Marie and Lily are from similar working-class, highly ethnically identified (French Canadian, French speaking) backgrounds, they differed in some significant respects. Lily, for example, married when 20 (before finishing college) and proceeded to give birth to five children—the rearing of which took considerable time and energy. Marie, in contrast, entered a religious order upon completion of high school, when she was 18 years old. Like Lily, Marie lived a life of service to others, though not for her own children. Marie did not leave the order until she was 42 years old, although she first experienced doubts regarding the nature of her vocation some nine years prior to her actual departure. Lily experienced doubts about her life situation earlier and for more years. She managed to complete a college education and to move out gradually into the world of work. Despite multiple and seemingly never ending responsibilities to others, they somehow reached a point in their lives where they realized that after all of their caretaking of others, they now needed to care for themselves. Seeking out therapy was one of the ways in which Marie and Lily—at 45 and 49 respectively—sought to more fully care for themselves.

MARIE: MOVEMENT OUT FROM A CLOISTERED LIFE

Marie was the oldest of two female siblings. Her younger sister was a premature infant and was reputedly "sickly," requiring much of her mother's

132 *Eileen T. Nickerson*

attention. Her mother also was portrayed as "sickly," and Marie claimed that she was essentially raised by an aunt, her mother's sister, in a protective, close-knit family setting.

Her grandparents had migrated from the French speaking province of Canada to a small city in the Northeastern part of the United States "in search of a better life." Both of Marie's parents, who had eighth-grade educations, grew up, married and worked in the same close-knit, French speaking, working-class neighborhood in which Marie was raised. Family, work and church constituted their world. Her father was employed as a plumber and her mother stayed at home. The home environment was seemingly stable, self-contained, and unremarkable, except for the poor health of her mother and her sister.

Marie attended parochial schools where the instruction was conducted in French and English. Marie portrayed herself as a fairly quiet, serious, compliant and deeply religious child, who did well in school and was desirous of pleasing her parents and teachers. About this period, she notes, "My parents made it clear that I was to associate with French Catholic girls only. I had friends . . . but no interest in dating."

Marie entered a religious order directly after graduating from a parochial high school. She never really entertained any other options at that time except a religious life of devotion and service. After 15 years in the convent, Marie began to experience doubts about her choice. Over the next few years, she became progressively more depressed, with crying spells, insomnia, weight gain, occasional ideas of suicide, and poor job performance. For the last three of these years, she was in weekly therapy and her depression gradually lifted. During this later time period, she founded a day-care center under the auspices of her religious order. By the time she was 41, she had resolved to leave the religious order. She moved into a boarding house in the same city, continuing her work at the day-care center. At this time, she met Warren, a divorced, free-lance engineer, with whom she eventually developed her first adult heterosexual relationship.

A year later, 24 years after she entered the religious community, she formally left the order and moved to a large urban center in a nearby state. She returned to school, earning a master's degree in education. After her master's degree program, she found employment at a nursery school. She continued her relationship with Warren, though it was unsatisfactory in a number of ways. After a year she entered a doctoral program, and shortly thereafter, she came to see me.

Marie's View of Her Problems

By the time Marie had sought counseling with me, she had become acutely aware that she wanted to make some changes in her life. She wanted marriage, a home of her own, and more financial independence. She felt that she had to make some kind of job move that would allow her to afford a place of her own. She wanted to develop adult relationships that were more egalitarian in nature and in which she functioned more as an adult, rather than as a needy child. She also wanted to either change the nature of her relationship with a man in her life, Warren, or to move onto a relationship that held the promise of commitment, marriage, and a traditional home life.

In a requested "Family of Origin" review, Marie described her "short-term goals" as follows:

> I need to continue to practice stress-management techniques and relaxation to help reduce anxiety. I have recently joined a weight reduction program and am learning when I eat to reduce and meet emotional needs. Food is often love, comfort or security. It is also a way to deal with anger, frustration. As I continue to deal with these emotions in more constructive ways, they ought to become less important in this respect. I need to better pace myself to reach my goals. In speaking with family members, I need to be aware of my interaction patterns. I further need to anticipate problems or reactions so that I will be better prepared to deal with them. I need to continue to develop assertion techniques at home and at school. I need to discipline myself in making a budget to feel more in control of my finances.

As to longer range goals she wrote the following:

> Value clarification in order to continue to grow in self-awareness and self-understanding in developing a greater sense of personal identity. I want to continue to develop more adult relationships in my family of origin, my transition family and my work situation. My career goals include completing my degree work in order to feel more competent and to open up and expand my options. I hope to eventually enter a marital relationship with the possibility of children depending on the nature of the relationship.

For Marie's stated goals, ACT Styles 2 and 3 were indicated. Consistent with my conceptual goal of balancing autonomous and intimacy striving, a large part of the initial treatment plan was to assist Marie in implementing a more satisfying

134   *Eileen T. Nickerson*

and viable living, relational and work situation. Marie's approach to therapy was willing and able to present and explore issues. Marie needed little teaching (S 2) and was able to make progress with more of a supportive (S 3) and even delegating (S 4) stance with respect to forming a therapeutic relationship. Marie essentially had learned from her three prior years of intensive therapy to use therapy in a concerted manner.

Marie's career direction and employment situation were crucially intertwined with her ability to afford to live independently. These areas were a major focus in the first three months of therapy. On these issues Marie reported confusion and difficulty focusing. Her report served to indicate that I should use more structured Style 2—Teaching and Style 1—Telling interventions. A career assessment was conducted. Several sessions were devoted to an interpretation of test results and other available autobiographical and informational data (e.g., scholastic records and test data). Essentially the career assessment validated Marie's previously selected career pathway. Detailed considerations of additional educational and training needs to obtain her employment goals were discussed, as well as appropriate employment transitions. Marie has proceeded along with her career planning and job improvement endeavors, periodically refocusing on these topics as needed. My therapeutic style at these later times was primarily supportive (S 3).

Marie next tackled the business of finding an affordable apartment and moving out of her single parent friend's household. This task was complicated by external realities—Marie's limited finances and the scarcity of reasonably priced housing. Eventually Marie came into a session and announced the following:

Marie: *I did it! I answered this ad. . . . It's the upstairs of this elderly couple's home with a separate entrance. It's been newly decorated. It costs more than I had hoped, but . . . it's close to my job . . . to the university. . . . I'm really excited, but . . . I have to get out of this lease with . . .* (roommate) *though . . . and. . . .*

Therapist: *How is that working out between you two?*

M: *Well . . . she's not happy. . . . There is a lot of tension between us . . . but I'm trying to be fair. I've waited until after the holidays and . . . it feels like I'm deserting her, but . . . we've outgrown our need to live together . . . . We both have. I know I have to work out something regarding the lease, the financial arrangements around the lease. . . .*

T: *Sounds like your long apartment search has paid off and you've found a reasonable apartment; but now you need to negotiate the transition with your roommate.*

M: *Yes, and.* . . . (She goes on to detail what she feels is a reasonable way out of the lease for both her and her roommate, who has herself indicated some thoughts of a housing change.)

By the end of the first year of weekly therapy, Marie had made some significant strides in her life. She had (1) moved into her own apartment, her "first home"; (2) come to terms with Warren's disinclination towards a committed relationship; (3) made a concerted attempt to meet new men and to date more; (4) developed a regime of exercising, attending Weight Watchers, and paying more attention to her appearance; and (5) made progress toward completing her doctoral degree work.

Marie and Her Relationship with Her Mother

In the next phase of therapy the major issues were

1. her need to individuate more, while making peace with her family, particularly her mother;
2. her neediness and dependence on others and her desire to live her life on her own terms and to be in more egalitarian relationships; and
3. her need to balance more her work and relational requirements, as well as what she referred to as the "feminine and masculine parts" of her personality.

The mother-daughter relationship is often posited to be a crucial developmental link for women (Nickerson, 1988). Marie's previous three years of therapy, while in her thirties, seem to have been very helpful in understanding this pivotal relationship.

M: *With the support and insight of that time in therapy, I realized that subconsciously I was living out my mother's unfulfilled desire to be a nun . . . . This was . . . truly . . . the beginning of my differentiation from my mother. . . . I had been frightened of her anger. Her tactic was withdrawal of love. . . .*

T: *M-m-m.*

136   *Eileen T. Nickerson*

M: *In retrospect, I can increasingly see . . . see how enmeshed I was in my family . . . my family life. I had never lived my life apart from my family you know . . . and at mid-life, I started . . . slowly, slowly . . . to take charge. The first year away from the community was hard. . . . There was lots of stress and I coped poorly. And at that time I lived about a hour away from my family. Visits there were always stressful. They did afford me though . . . some emotional support which I needed and financial benefits. This was my mother's . . . my mother's way . . . way of giving me love.*

Financial considerations continued to figure in her deliberations about her mother. Marie wanted to support herself and her graduate education. She often resisted accepting financial aid, even though she was in great monetary need. As Marie became better able to support herself, money became less of an issue in her relationship with her mother. In fact, it became easier for Marie to accept, in an uncomplicated fashion, financial aid from her mother at several crucial points.

Then during this therapeutic period, Marie's mother became ill. She was diagnosed as having cancer of the large intestine. She was operated on, and the prognosis was between three and five years. Marie summarized the experience as, "I was jolted into the realization of how emotionally over-attached and dependent I still am. . . . The thought . . . the thought of my mother not being there for me is devastation." Marie worked hard all during this phase of therapy to come to terms with her relationship with her mother and her sister, who was now living with her mother. A gradual acceptance and fuller understanding of her mother and her mother's limitations has taken place. Marie now seems more at peace with a mother who in turn now shows her more respect and appreciation. Marie at one point said this about her relationship with her mother:

> Though she exemplifies many stereotypic female behaviors, I think she is gradually learning to respect my nontraditional ways of being in the world. In fact, I think she admires my courage and my determination in trying to meet my own life goals.

In some sense, as often happens when mothers and their adult daughters age, Marie has come to the awareness that she is now a kind of "mother" to her own mother. She said it simply and clearly at one point: "she is more like the child now." Generally supportive (S 3) and delegating (S 4) types of interventions also have been interspersed in these therapeutic interactions with some more structured activities, including familial role and dream analysis (S 2). Were Marie's mother's health better, I would have even suggested the notion of some joint sessions with Marie and her mother.

Marie, Money, and Interrelated Employment Considerations

Just as the issue of money regularly arose in the context of examinations of her relationship with her mother, it regularly arose in conjunction with Marie's attempts to become more autonomous and individuated. One of the complications for many women's struggles for independence is their financial as well as their emotional dependence on important others in their life. Marie, at the age of 42, found herself with only one thousand dollars for some 24 years of labor. She wanted to get a place of her own, to complete further education—reasonable goals, but seemingly impossible with such minimal resources.

Though Marie was not married, her plight was not dissimilar from the divorced woman who arrives at middle age to find that she must make her way with minimal income and income-earning skills. Frequently such a woman feels forced to turn, as did Marie, to family of origin members, who often have misgivings about their adult child's new status and ability to cope. Permeating this phase of therapy were portrayals of her struggle to juggle job(s), studies, and social life. Marie was constantly "on the look-out" for a better paying job—preferably one with more career potential. As a feminist therapist, attuned to the reality of many women's lives, I regularly would take therapy time to look at this "meaningful work" dimension of Marie's life—with my interventions ranging from Style 1—Telling through the full range of stylistic interventions to Style 4—Delegation. We examined the pro(s) and con(s) of each job move she contemplated, the timing of her graduate comprehensive and dissertation projects, the resources she might tap to fund her course of study, etc. A feminist developmental perspective informed my work with Marie. To ignore the external realities of a woman who arrives at mid-life needing to learn to take care of herself in many survival-related ways would further compound the obstacles to her autonomous strivings. The ACT model, in turn, helped me decide the level and nature of the interventions that would best assist Marie in advancing in her therapeutic goal attainments within this overall theoretical perspective.

Marie and the Men in Her Life: The Search for Intimate Connectedness

Our sessions have focused frequently on the topic of the men in her life and her search for a committed love relationship. Despite her reputedly "closer" relationship with her father, Marie went on to note, "Though he was a warm and caring person, he was not very much involved in my parenting." Much of Marie's formative years was spent in the company of females. . . . She was raised with a sister. In her close-knit family, aunts were around, and her father was the only

138 *Eileen T. Nickerson*

male in the household. She attended parochial schools, was encouraged to associate only with her own kind (i.e., French Canadian girls), and entered a religious order at 18, never having dated.

Not until Marie left the religious order did relationships with men become an important issue. It is not surprising then, that Marie experienced discomfort in the presence of men. A specific example involved a male academic advisor. She reported an incident in which she had not heard or understood something he said to her in an advising session.

M: *I was too afraid or too uneasy to ask. I said nothing. I nodded my head and hurried away.*

T: *You didn't understand, yet you didn't ask for clarification?*

M: *Yes . . . I was afraid to, afraid of what he might think. I'm really uncomfortable when I am with him. It's this old thing about men in authority. I even keep putting off setting up a meeting with him, but I know I need to. . . .*

What may be more surprising is the willingness and perseverance Marie has shown in connection with improving her relationships with men and in seeking a committed heterosexual relationship. She describes the process of change that started in her mid-thirties.

M: *I was beginning to get a sense of myself as a person. I changed from religious garb into regular clothing. I became conscious of my womanhood in a totally new way. During these years, I started thinking about marriage, about childbirth and about them as choices. . . . That's something I had never thought about before.*

Recently Warren, her first romantic partner, has reentered her life. Marie announced

M: *Warren is back in my life.*

T: *Warren is back?*

M: *Yes . . . he contacted me recently.* (Marie goes on at some length to describe how Warren contacted her, how they got together, what Warren is doing now, etc. And she added) *I do think he has changed in some ways, and I can see that I can become more of a person in the relationship now.*

An Eclectic Approach to Counseling Women **139**

This "third beginning" in their relationship, as she referred to it, has also been the stimulus for her to do a good deal of further exploration of her relationships with men in general. She says, for example

M: *I've also been more conscious of my relationships with men. I've tended to cater to them, to rely on them for everything. I still find it difficult with men. I more easily give up my power.*

More recently Marie has been vacillating about her relationship with Warren and whether she should stay in the relationship and see what its potential is. We end a session, after lengthy exploration, concurring that they are both in process, both are gradually changing.

T: *And now you both seem to be examining what the possibilities of the relationship might be. You both sound like you are giving each other some space and yet support in which to do that.*

At this point, therapy has not been concluded with Marie. She continues to come monthly, to review with me recent developments, and to explore her sense of how things are for her and how she is doing. The phasing out of therapy often involves this type of spaced appointments, resulting in eventual total client delegation and termination. She mostly talks, directs the nature and narrative of the session, and periodically asks me for my impression. My predominant style is delegating (S 4). Sometimes after 20 to 25 minutes of a recital of some aspect of her situation, she turns to me and says, "Well, that's what I've been thinking—that's how I see it. . . . That's what I think I need to do now. How does it seem to you? How does that sound to you?"

In one area, her dissertation, she seeks specific Style 1 and Style 2 guidance. Marie has asked to see me monthly until the dissertation process is complete. In this respect, we have moved from a therapist-client relationship into one more akin to a consultant-consultee. In this role, I have functioned more as a paid consultant—a position some professional helpers might question, though I obviously feel it is appropriate and relevant. I argue that it is a deviation from orthodoxy, required by some mature adult women who can benefit from a kind of therapeutic mentoring since professional women tend to have fewer role models and mentors available to them than do their male counterparts.

Marie is no longer doubtful about her ability to complete her doctoral program, to provide reasonably for herself, and to be in a meaningful relationship. She feels that she has made peace with her mother and sister; thus, she has met her second goal of therapy. As she puts it,

140   *Eileen T. Nickerson*

> I no longer see my mother solely out of a sense of duty. Rather, I
> feel that my mother is entitled to a reasonable amount of my time
> now. And her demands are much more reasonable now. As a result,
> I don't feel used or choked. I am more able to acknowledge her own
> and my self-worth. I find myself doing this with my sister and my
> aunts and uncles as well.

Marie feels increasingly comfortable and confident in her relationship with men. She has contracted for a new dissertation advisor, and her relationship with him is a respectful, supportive and empowering one. She is also reasonably hopeful that she will be able to accomplish all of her original short- and longer-term goals, including marriage and a home. Some of the continuing issues and struggles for Marie center around her sense of urgency—the need to catch up on adult developmental tasks and learnings, learnings that she felt most adults her age had already accomplished.

I have developed considerable respect and compassion for this woman who, at the age of 42, left a religious order and courageously moved herself out into a more autonomous existence in a world for which her prior experiences had not adequately prepared her. Marie's life, in a sense, is a testament to the female condition, spirit and willingness to grow.

LILY: MOVEMENT OUT OF THE PAST

Lily was a 49-year-old married female with five grown children when she originally came to see me. Her husband was an educator. Lily also had been an educator but had moved into a corporate managerial position 12 years earlier. She had a number of job promotions since joining the firm, each leaving her feeling more tenuous in her ability to cope. Her promotions also resulted in a higher income than that of her husband and necessitated some out-of-town trips.

In her family of origin Lily was the seventh of nine children. The family's financial circumstances were marginal although both her French-Canadian, Catholic parents worked. Lily indicated that her parents were "always working." Household management was often left to her, including her two younger and her two next older brothers. The first four children were somewhat older and seemed to have formed their own sibling subsystem, moving quickly out and away from the family home. In therapy, she repeatedly decried her early years of deprivation and neglect.

Lily particularly portrayed her father in unflattering terms—"a broken man who had lots of bad luck." She described him as a "weak man who made crude

An Eclectic Approach to Counseling Women **141**

sexual jokes at the expense of my mother." She painted her mother in shadowy, martyrish terms such as, "My mother was a hard working, sacrificing woman." She had no recollection of parental encouragement, nor sibling or other types of familial support—only yelling, scolding and, occasionally, beatings if things went wrong.

Despite the travails of growing up in this large, hectic, and seemingly chaotic and nonsupportive household with "overwhelming" home responsibilities, she did well in school, becoming the only one to get a college education. She also reported that all but one of her eight siblings has had a "nervous breakdown or problems with alcohol."

Lily met her husband while attending the state college. She became pregnant before she married him in her junior year of college. They had four more children in the next four years, until she "went on the pill." Each pregnancy she described as "difficult." Lily portrayed herself initially as a "good wife who tried to do and be everything." She recalled "feeling overwhelmed, depressed and gradually rebelling," with the aid of periodic visits with a psychiatric nurse, followed by two years of sporadic visits with a therapist. During this time period, she made the decision to return to teaching full time, as finances were tight and the children were of school age.

Financial concerns, as well as meeting family obligations, have figured significantly in Lily's home life, just as they did for her parents. Her husband is also from a large extended immigrant family. Trying to get ahead and to survive economically seems to have consumed much of his energy. He has usually been involved in at least two jobs. Meeting the perceived needs of both of these extended clans, as well as those of her own five children, has been a repeated theme in therapy. The sense of overwhelming familial responsibility also has been played out against the backdrop of resentment about never ending familial expectations.

Lily's View of Her Problems

Lily came to therapy with me when a number of changes had coincided in her life to produce a crisis. These changes included

1. a recent job promotion, which left her feeling "overwhelmed";
2. a recent move to the suburban "home of my dreams" after some "20 years in a shabby house. . . . I always felt embarrassed to be living in it";
3. the movement of all but her youngest child out of the family home;

142 *Eileen T. Nickerson*

4. a number of achievement/autonomy-related fears and concerns, including fears of failing, doing poorly, and being assertive;
5. a number of interrelated affiliated intimacy issues, which were described as fears of antagonizing and offending others, of standing out and expressing her opinions, and of abandonment and/or retaliation by others;
6. concerns regarding relationships with the important men in her life (e.g., her husband, her father, her father-in-law, her male superiors) and authority figures in general; and
7. unfocused, recurring feelings of guilt, shame, and embarrassment.

In addition to being ready to seek therapeutic help because of prior experiences with helping professionals, Lily was also ready because she was experiencing "inner turmoil." She did not feel at peace with herself.

Lily's Readiness for Therapy

When Lily initially came to see me, she expressed readiness for seriously engaging herself in a program of self-change. She also reported feeling "stuck" and unable to make progress with her concerns on her own. Initially I saw Lily and Marie as equally ready for therapy. I even tentatively thought of Lily as "readier" than Marie for therapeutic change. Lily was articulate, intelligent, and able to verbalize her goals for therapy. She spoke of feeling like "I'm in pain all the time" and of feeling that "I am the savior of my family" (referring both to her own family and her family of origin). She focused on needing to become more self-confident and self-assertive, though simultaneously expressing fears of people's anger. Lily and I initially contracted to work on an every other week basis on her concerns. My initial therapist style, as with Marie, was a combination of Styles 2 and 3.

It soon became apparent that Lily had contracted for appointments once every two weeks partly in an attempt to contain or control the pace of therapy for her own sense of security. Though Lily was consciously desirous of making changes, there were deep-seated resistances to revealing and unveiling some aspects of her life, particularly those of her earlier years. Thus, it became apparent that Lily was less ready than Marie to probe into some of her less accessible psychic realms. She was less willing and less able for the type of uncovering necessary in this therapeutic endeavor. It became apparent that Lily would require a more directive (S 2 and S 1) therapeutic style, with more emphasis on structured interventions than I had originally surmised. Lily needed therapeutically designed opportunities to revisit and reexperience much of her earlier years. She had repressed and sup-

An Eclectic Approach to Counseling Women **143**

pressed many painful memories in order to survive. And in a sense, since she had never really been properly parented in her childhood, she needed to be "parented" or "reparented" (Minuchin,1974). This was a draining process—indeed Lily would sob uncontrollably at times as pieces from the past were exhumed. The ACT model and my intuitive sense propelled us to deviate from the original combination of primarily S 2—Teaching and S 3—Supporting to include more of a Style 1—Telling approach. Hence, a more structured treatment plan and set of therapeutic interventions were instituted as Lily slowly rebuilt the pieces of her life into a healthier, better integrated whole.

After approximately six months of every other week sessions, Lily became more ready, more willing, to engage more intensively in the uncovering aspects of our work, opting to meet weekly. This was not always easy. Her position required periodic out-of-town travel, all day and evening conference meetings, etc. We both juggled our schedules to make weekly sessions possible, which bonded us in a therapeutically effective way and which left her feeling supported, respected, and cared for.

Lily's Shame, Recall, and Recovery

During this next year and a half of weekly meetings, my style became more varied, ranging from the initial S 3 through S 2 to S 1 as needed. I remained structured in my overall approach, employing, at times, highly directive interventions while trying to supply a steady supportive base for our work. I used a combination of techniques in an effort to assist her to gradually identify and explore a series of "shame-filled" events in her life. Many of her earlier memories seem to have been virtually nonexistent or shrouded in a vague, fugue-like sense of unreality. In an effort to recall and reexperience some of her earlier life, we moved in the direction of a graduated series of explorations into the nature of a number of pain-filled incidents. In this connection, the interventions reflected the full range of ACT styles from free association (S 4) and dream/memory recall (S 4 and S 3), through guided Gestalt age regression (S 2), to diary keeping and other homework assignments (S 1).

I tended to bring Lily, in a very structured Style 1 manner, into recalling and reexperiencing earlier events, particularly those from her childhood. We employed the Gestalt "Empty Chair" technique (S 2), in which she would address either her mother or her father about her fears, her sense of abandonment, and her being overwhelmed by the duties assigned to her. At other times, I would take her on a Guided Fantasy (S 2) to some neighborhood scene in which she was a witness to and immobilized by some abusive and degrading action—such as the forcible

144   *Eileen T. Nickerson*

removal of the blue jeans of a neighbor girl by a neighborhood group of boys including some of her brothers.

I encouraged Lily at these times to reexperience these terror-filled incidents and her understandable impotence in the light of her now more empowered adult status. I assisted her in a very directive (yet supportive) manner to reenact, reexperience, and rework a series of dehumanizing childhood experiences. In this sense, I employed essentially a "telling" style (S 1) with elements of "teaching" (S 2) and "supporting" (S 3). One of the complications of employing the ACT model is that eclectic therapists, such as myself, are constantly shifting in a kaleidoscopic fashion between styles and techniques—even within one 50-minute period.

Through these structured interventions, various bits and pieces of Lily's shadowy childhood slowly and painfully have emerged to be exposed to the light of her present adult capacity to recall, reexperience, and reintegrate into an emerging and more resourceful adult self. We are still not clear on all the details of the combination of neglect and physical and sexual abuse that were a part of her growing up.

What does seem abundantly clear is that a central core of Lily's difficulties in her adult existence stems from the lack of reasonable safety that she experienced as a child. It has been hard for Lily to talk in certain ways about her childhood and her parents. While Lily has become quite aware of and able to express her anger at their neglect, the expression has been compounded by a sense of loyalty and a real recognition that her parents in turn, especially her father, "had a rotten childhood." At one point, she poignantly declared: "They were victims too!"

While not being able to give specific captions for all the "nameless terrors" Lily has recalled, what has become clearer are

1. Incidents of silent acquiescence in abusive activities in which she identified with the victim (including herself) and didn't intervene or voice objections for fear of retaliation, rejection and accompanying feelings of powerlessness, shame and being "overwhelmed" (one of her most common expressions).
2. The recognition that her father was alternatively physically abusive; sexually abusive by joke, word, and some actions (e.g., pinching her mother's breasts); and neglectful. Her father coupled these behaviors with unreasonable expectations for responsible behavior on her part and that of her siblings.

An Eclectic Approach to Counseling Women **145**

3. The recognition of her own victimization in a myriad number of ways, including the still fuzzy recollection of a "cellar rape" by possibly a neighbor boy, when about three or four. In recalling this event, she has been racked by sobbing and choking, and frequently refers to the symbolism of a "black hole," even more recently saying, "I still think I was in that dark hole," and relating it to fantasies of being raped or incest when first married.

It is apparent then that a large part of Lily's dilemma in growing up was the lack of reasonable parental supervision and guidance. This parental and home neglect led her to an almost incessant feeling of being overwhelmed, of having her space violated, and of being unable to cope with (control) persons in her environs (brothers, parents, neighborhood kids), which is related to her present adult fears and issues. These early circumstances of Lily's history may explain the differential levels of readiness exhibited by Lily and Marie.

In general, the treatment plan for Lily required an intensive reparenting process of rebuilding the personality structure (Cohen, 1984; Howard, Nance, & Myers, 1987; Minuchin, 1974) in which the major tasks of therapy included

> building trust in the therapeutic relationship as a foundation of the developmental process; retrieval of childhood memory; expression of affect (particularly anger and grief); integration of the splitting process, and; helping the client develop a differentiated identity. (Howard et al., 1987, p. 114)

We have continued our work together in weekly sessions, to which we have added periodic additional intensive therapeutic sessions as we continue the uncovering and rebuilding process. This combination has allowed us to continue a "looking backward" process as needed, with an exploration of more "here and now" concerns and issues. Such an evolution of therapeutic emphasis has been made more possible by the earlier rebuilding phases. Such a phase also allows more Style 3 and even Style 4 interventions to be mixed with the previously predominant Style 2 and Style 1 interventions.

We have focused on her "cognitive tapes and scripts," including her pronounced tendency towards "negative self-talk." In an effort to change these negating self-aspirations, a series of in-therapy and homework exercises have been prescribed. We have also focused on converting her "should(s)" to "could(s)" and her "ought(s)" to "might be(s)," etc. This new and demanding therapeutic task, for which Lily has been "less ready" than for some others, has required a shift to Style 1 behaviors in which I have provided Lily with instructions and homework prescriptions.

146 *Eileen T. Nickerson*

Lily and I have taken up in some detail her job and family interactions and concerns, a kind of dualistic intimacy and autonomy orientation (Nickerson, 1984). The goal has been to aid Lily in simultaneously balancing autonomous and intimacy needs. I have allowed Lily to be needy of relationships, including our therapeutic interactions, even if imperfect. The therapeutic process also involves improving her ability to be in a relationship. The goal is to be intimately connected, yet autonomous and independent. Providing support and validation for being an "OK" parent has been important. I have affirmed that she has reasonably and responsibly parented her children. Along with the frustrations and the pain of therapy, there have been pleasure-filled moments and satisfactions. Building on these for herself has been an important part of our work.

MARIE AND LILY: SOME COMPARISONS

Marie and Lily were similar in that they were both middle-aged women who came from working-class, extended ethnic clans that emphasized the virtues of family and church loyalty, hard work, and traditional gender role prescriptions. Their parents struggled in varying ways to meet their families' needs. In both households, the fathers seem to have been preoccupied with earning a living. Marie's father appears to have been both more successful in doing so and less burdened with family responsibilities, partly as a consequence of having two compared to nine children. For whatever set of reasons, Marie's father also seems to have been somewhat more available to her in some ways that left her with more of a sense of caring. Lily's father seems to have modeled more inept, neglectful, physically and sexually abusive behavior—the physical abuse being meted out more towards the boys and the psychological and sexual abuse towards the females in the family in the form of crude jokes, put-downs, etc.

While Marie periodically complained of her parents "overprotection," Lily bitterly resented the "under-protection." Lily's adult issues around vulnerability, safety, and abandonment seem to have their root causes in these early parental failures to protect, nurture, and meet her understandable needs for guidance and support. Both Marie and Lily saw their mothers as self-sacrificing but ineffectual. Both mothers seemingly modeled deference and resignation to their husbands and their lot in life. Neither was proactive in providing her daughter with other than a kind of downtrodden, suffering stance. Neither daughter grew up wanting to emulate her mother, her father, or any immediate family member.

Interestingly, despite a lack of positive modeling of traditional female behavior, both Lily and Marie pursued traditionally prescribed female avenues. Marie

An Eclectic Approach to Counseling Women   **147**

retreated to the safety and security of religious order and Lily to the imagined comfort and security of family life, though Lily had not seen family life as a haven in her own childhood. Both then reached their middle adults years, having not yet found "the promised land." Both were dissatisfied with their present lives centered around more traditional serving of others. Both wanted to reap more meaning and pleasure out of their lives. Both expressed a need to escape from the tyranny of their own fears and passivity, and both chose to enter therapy as a means to that end.

Clients' Reactions

As a part of this process, I have shared with Marie and Lily my review of my work with them. Their responses to the foregoing assessments have been instructive. In general, Marie has validated my sense of my work with her and my assessment of her readiness level. She has indicated that I have given a "meaningful account of our time together." "It really is interesting and encouraging to read of my development from your perspective." She felt that "the enormous role and impact the Catholic church had on my life" merited more emphasis.

> You can't have any ideas/think for yourself. There was no way I was going to test that. It still gets in the way . . . stops me a lot. . . . The idea of doing critical . . . doing critical thinking on papers terrified me. I was very idealistic. . . . It's a strength of mine, in a way, but I needed to ground it in reality.

Lily's initial reactions were different from those of Marie. She indicated that she "hated it with the first reading. I felt like I have been unfair to my parents." Lily remains impaled between her inability to forgive her parents and her recognition of their own victimization and fragility. Seeing this dilemma so starkly etched in print brought it painfully home to her. Her reaction typifies much of her present approach to life—she accents the negative, the deficiencies, and finds it difficult to appreciate her growth. We concur that these features in her psychic functioning need to be altered.

REFLECTIONS ON ACT

The opportunity to apply ACT in my work with Marie and Lily and report the work here was well worth the effort. Reviewing my own work with these clients was revealing to me in a number of ways. The way in which ACT was most illuminating to me lies in my heightened consciousness as to the central impor-

148 *Eileen T. Nickerson*

tance of the concept of client readiness, particularly as it impacts Therapist Style, Treatment Planning, and accompanying interventions. I was reminded repeatedly of the need to respect where a client is developmentally and to view this readiness as an essential key to where we could be psychotherapeutically. Therapy goals need to be regularly reexamined and consensually revised in the context of the client's goals and task readiness.

One of the major benefits of the application of ACT, for beginning and experienced therapists alike, is the assistance it provides in formulating a treatment plan. ACT provides a conceptual framework for deciding how to proceed and how to continue proceeding with a client. This is no small matter given the proliferation of theories and techniques presently advocated. Making sense out of all the myriad inputs that go into a therapist's training and understanding, in a way that is most beneficial to a variety of clients, is a considerable undertaking. The ACT model is a crucial organizing and integrative tool for the therapist involved in the sensitive and demanding human undertaking of therapy—that is, assisting in another person's developmental, growth-enhancing endeavors.

In reviewing my work with Marie and Lily, the employment of the ACT model was helpful in a number of ways. The ACT model was useful, for example, in dealing with my own "counter-transference" issues. There were points at which I became impatient with the progress we were making or the resistance I felt I was encountering. There were times when I wanted Lily and Marie to almost magically be leading the lives they claimed they wanted. Reviewing their readiness for certain changes and the nature of my intervention efforts reinforced my developmental conception of these clients, thereby lessening my impatience.

In several instances, I misread Lily's readiness to explore some aspects of her life. At one particularly sticky point, toward the end of the session and after our mutual recognition of the need to delve more deeply into her sexual history, I asked her to spend the next week jotting down her remembrances of her sexual development and to bring it into the next therapy session. A review of this enabled me to see that she was neither willing nor able to complete this task.

Lily: *I just don't think I can do that yet. I know we need to talk about this, but I know I won't be able to do that just yet. And you know how I feel about "home assignments"!* (Laughs.)

Therapist: *Yes . . . I should know!* (Laughs also.) *We agree that we need to talk about your sexual development more, but you're not ready yet to be sent out on your own to do this.*

An Eclectic Approach to Counseling Women   **149**

L: *Yes . . . I know we need to go into this area more . . . I know . . . but . . .* (eyes tearing).

T: *It's OK . . . we'll come back to this* together *. . . when we get together next week. . . . I know that much of this is hard . . . hard for you to talk and even think about.*

Reflecting on my work with Lily and my studied attempt to apply the ACT model reminds me of the ease of minimizing a client's neediness and exaggerating motivational confidence and readiness for a therapeutic venture. I have had to regularly reasses and reconceptualize my efforts with her. I have needed at points to try to match more nearly where Lily was rather than where we both would have liked her to be.

One of the significant benefits of using the ACT model within one's theoretical perspective is that it can help a therapist deal with technique and style of intervention. A conceptual perspective helps us understand how people grow and change. It does not necessarily teach us to intervene in such a way as to maximize a match with the client's ability, confidence, and motivational readiness to move and grow in certain directions.

While the ACT model was extremely helpful from a number of perspectives, it can only go so far in informing therapist judgment. ACT's usefulness seemed most apparent at the beginning and ending phases of the therapeutic process. In the middle phases of my work with Marie and Lily, it appeared most helpful in the understanding and negotiating of the impasses or "stuck periods" we would encounter. On the whole though, the conceptualization of client readiness matched with therapist style became murkier during these middle stages. It may well be too much to expect of any integrative therapeutic model that equally valuable assistance be available to the therapist for each and every decision that constitutes the real work of therapy.

In a sense, one of the major virtues of ACT also may be a key to some of its limitations. That is, while it is important to develop integrative therapeutic models that encompass all psychotherapeutic theories, it is simultaneously stretching a model's creditability to expect it to cover all aspects of the ebb and flow of therapeutic transactions. There are times when the therapeutic decision making process is so complex, no one theory can attend to all relevant variables. The endless cultural, ethnic, and linguistic nuances, in and of themselves, almost defy cataloging, let alone integrating.

In closing, the opportunity to analyze my work with these two clients continued to sensitize me to the struggles and impasses that female clients wage, periodically retreating from and surging forward while trying to grow personally in their relational and work lives. Given both the internal and external "baggage" often foisted on women, it is a testimony to the human spirit and personal strength of these women that they strove to prevail. One becomes truly respectful and in awe of the courage and character of one's clientele. I found myself at times spontaneously and enthusiastically validating and supporting their efforts, their insights, and their perseverance. I often was moved in my work with Marie and Lily by their formulations of themselves, their dilemmas, and their willingness to push aside the barriers of injustice and unfairness in their quest for saneness and wholeness. I learn from my clients, and I grow humble in the face of their spirit. I have become, I hope, a better person and therapist as a result of this opportunity to explore my work with Marie and Lily.

BIBLIOGRAPHY

Ballou, M., & Gabalac, N.W. (1985). *A feminist position on mental health.* Springfield, IL: Chas. C. Thomas.

Baruch, G.K., Barnett, R.C., & Rivers, C. (1983). *Lifeprints: New patterns of love and work in today's woman.* NY: McGraw Hill.

Blocher, D.H. (1966). *Developmental counseling.* NY: Ronald Press.

Broverman, I.K., Broverman, D.M., Clarkson, F.E., Rosenkrantz, P., & Vogel, S.R. (1970). Sex-role stereotypes and clinical judgments of mental health. *Journal of Consulting Psychology, 34,* 1–7.

Chesler, P. (1973). *Women and madness.* Garden City, NY: Doubleday.

Chodorow, N. (1978). *The reproduction of mothering: Psychoanalysis and the sociology of gender.* Berkeley, CA: University of California Press.

Cohen, P.M. (1984). Violence in the family: An act of loyalty. *Psychotherapy, 21,* 249–253.

Enns, C.Z., & Hackett, G. (1990). Comparison of feminist and nonfeminist women's reactions to variants of non-sexist and feminist counseling. *Journal of Counseling Psychology, 37,* 33–40.

Giele, J.Z. (1982). *Women in the middle years.* NY: Wiley.

Gilligan, C. (1982). *In a different voice.* Cambridge, MA: Harvard University.

Goldhaber, D. (1986). *Life-span human development.* NY: Harcourt, Brace.

Howard, G.S., Nance, D.W., & Myers, P. (1987). *Adaptive counseling and therapy.* San Francisco: Jossey-Bass.

Jaggar, A.M., & Rothenberg, P.S. (1984). *Feminist frameworks* (2nd ed.). NY: McGraw Hill.

Miller, J.B. (1986). *Toward a new psychology of women.* Boston: Beacon Press.

152   *Eileen T. Nickerson*

Minuchin, S. (1974). *Families and family therapy.* Cambridge, MA: Harvard University Press.

Nickerson, E.T. (1984). *Intimacy and autonomy: A dualistic perspective.* Presidential Address, New England Psychological Association.

Nickerson, E.T. (1988). *Mothers and daughters, daughters and mothers: The unbroken cycle in female development.* Paper presented at the International Council for Psychologists, Singapore, July; and the International Congress of Psychology, Sydney, Australia.

Norman, W.H., & Scaramella, T.J. (Eds.). (1980). *Mid-life: Developmental and clinical issues.* NY: Brunner/Mazel.

Rawlings, E., & Carter, D. (1977). *Psychotherapy for women: Treatment toward equality.* Springfield, IL: Chas. C. Thomas.

Rosewater, L.B., & Walker, L.E. (Eds.). (1985). *Handbook of feminist therapy.* NY: Springer.

COMMENTS

Eclectic Approach to Counseling Women

Don W. Nance

The work of Dr. Nickerson presents further extensions of several of the themes found among the previous chapters as well as some new issues. Dr. Nickerson is keenly attuned to the ways in which societal, ethnic and religious influences impact the expectations, experiences, feelings, skills, and problems that women bring to therapy. The use of a feminist developmental perspective helps the therapist view these challenges as appropriate and necessary developmental tasks. In Marie's life, the task of independent living was delayed for about 20 years given the nature of her religious community. For Lily, the task of understanding and integrating issues from her childhood can be viewed as delayed by the struggles of parenthood and economic striving. Thus, client readiness to address a particular task is, in part, a function of how developmentally necessary the task is and how much psychic, emotional, mental, and physical energy the client has available to devote to the task.

The work with Lily and Marie demonstrates how the nature of the problems, and therefore the nature of the tasks, evolve in the course of treatment. The therapist initially takes a developmental approach with both clients. There are new challenges, stresses, and issues associated with Marie's movement out of religious life and Lily's climb up the corporate ladder. The therapist's role is to support, teach, and occasionally tell the client as she or he masters the cognitive, behavioral, and emotional elements of those developmental tasks. The course of treatment with Marie, while replete with many struggles and twists, essentially remained on a developmental track. The therapy with Lily, however, was significantly modified by two factors. The first factor was therapy not having the effect sought by either therapist or client. She was not feeling better about herself or her life. The second factor was the emergence of information, new to the client and the therapist, about events and feelings from Lily's childhood. These emerging problems stood in the way of her accomplishing the more developmental tasks. In this instance, the client and therapist agreed that a new, more intensive approach was needed. The style of treatment changed as did the therapist behaviors. The client was reluctantly willing to engage in therapeutic processes and experience images and feelings that were new and often painful. The therapist made the decision to expand the therapy rather than bracket or limit the scope of treatment. She also agreed to direct (S 1/S 2) and support (S 3) the client through what was a difficult, emotional process.

154 *Eileen T. Nickerson*

Dr. Nickerson's care, concern, and appreciation of the clients was an underlying tone in her writing. She is willing to become an advisor on urban living, an information and referral source, a dissertation coach, a transferential mother figure, an organizational consultant, a career counselor, and a mentor. She is willing and able (therapist readiness) to operate from a wide range of roles and to bring much of her varied knowledge into the therapy process. She becomes a significant person in the client's life for years.

The range of therapist behaviors and roles described by Dr. Nickerson is extensive, overlapping, and evolving. Dr. Nickerson is keenly aware of the ***multiple roles*** she serves with clients. This range of roles contrasts to the roles played by the therapist in the cognitive behavioral and brief psychodynamic approaches. In those approaches, Dr. Deffenbacher (Chapter 2) and Dr. Robbins (Chapter 4) are in roles that are clear, are limited, and remain fairly constant. Dr. Poland (Chapter 3) demonstrates how an overlap in roles can block progress. The resolution was accomplished by addressing the issue directly in therapy. Dr. Poland also argues that the therapist's personhood is an important and integral part of the humanistic therapeutic process. In the systems chapter (Chapter 5), Dr. Myers does not form a confidential, exclusive relationship with one client. Her role is therapist to the couple and to each individual. Are there potential role conflicts? Certainly. Can conflicts be managed therapeutically? Usually. Can the benefits be worth the potential role conflicts? Absolutely.

An Eclectic Approach to Counseling Women   **155**

QUESTIONS

1. What are your reactions regarding the range of roles and the range of topics/issues represented in this approach to therapy?

2. How does this open-ended approach compare to time-limited approaches?

3. As a therapist, how would you know when your assessment of client readiness needs to be revised? Because the client is less ready? More ready? How would you adjust your behavior?

4. If you are seeing a client for an extended period, what would be the likely effects of teaching the client the ACT model?

5. What role do your own religious beliefs and background play in your work with clients?

6. What are the effects of religious teachings about the roles of women on women clients? On women therapists? On the therapy process?

7. What are the relative merits of focusing on strengths vs. weaknesses? Developmental vs. remedial? Normality vs. pathology? How are those dimensions reflected with Marie and Lily?

8. How is dependency on a therapist different from dependency on family? Friends? Church? School? Alcohol and drugs?

9. How would you work with a woman client who has interests and skills in a field that pays poorly? Would your approach be different if the client were a man?

10. How do the financial aspects of treatment enter into
    the therapeutic contract?
    the pace of therapy?
    client readiness?
    the ACT styles used?

11. How does the therapy change if insurance is involved?

Chapter 7

DEVELOPMENTAL ECLECTIC COUNSELING WITH MEN: A CASE OF HIGH EXPECTATIONS

Gordon M. Hart

Temple University

I became interested in the issues facing men about ten years ago when several events happened to me. For one thing, my best friend died suddenly, at the age of 38. Not only did I experience a feeling of tremendous loss, but also I became aware that I had few people whom I could consider "real friends." Maybe men don't make so many friends, I wondered. Secondly, I realized that I enjoyed the companionship and intimacy with a group of male psychologists whom I saw only once a year at a conference that we all attended. I began to see how important men's relationships with men could be. Thirdly, my oldest son, Keith, entered high school, and I began to see that eventually he (and later my other son and my daughter) would be leaving home. If I was experiencing these interpersonal upheavals, then what about the men I was seeing professionally?

The developmental approach in my work, which is primarily with couples and families and with individual men, is based on my belief that behavior, either satisfying or dissatisfying, develops over time and is the result of an accumulation

158   *Gordon M. Hart*

of events. Behavior is not, in my opinion, a result of a single incident, nor is it shaped primarily in a particular time period (such as childhood). Behavior is cumulative. Furthermore, behavior is shaped and defined in a social context that adds meaning to all interactions (Guttman, 1991).

Howard, Nance, and Myers (1986, 1987) and Nance and Myers (1991) provide a solid rationale for working with the feelings, thoughts, and behavior of clients using a range of theoretical concepts. Many counselors work with various aspects of clients' lives with a variety of approaches and have adopted an eclectic label. For eclectic counselors and therapists it is important to match the approach to the problem and the client. Adaptive Counseling and Therapy (ACT) assists counselors in selecting a particular technique or strategy based on a careful analysis of the client's readiness.

My dominant style, in ACT terminology, is Supportive (S 3) with a strong reliance on Teaching (S 2). Most clients with whom I work have the ability to achieve some greater level of emotional awareness, understanding, and appropriate expression by means of a supportive exploration. I believe that it is most helpful to anchor this awareness in some beliefs or self-statements that guide them in daily actions. Of course, some clients need more support than teaching and others need more teaching than support. Furthermore, what a client needs at the beginning of treatment is not necessarily what he or she needs later in the process.

As I move among the domains of thoughts, feelings, and actions, I use the ACT concept of match and move. ACT suggests that it is helpful to start with the amount of structure and support that is needed and to move toward less structure and less support. Another way of viewing this progression would be to say that clients in ACT ideally would move from dependence (on either structure or support or both) to greater independence (from structure and support). This movement is the overall process goal with the clients with whom I work.

Most of the men with whom I have worked have been overly reliant on their external environment and have neglected information from their internal senses (Pasick, Gordon, & Meth, 1990; Silverberg, 1986). Thus, they are more able to provide information about events and actions than express their feelings. Consequently, I often begin with a relatively high amount of direction and data analysis about their life situation and later move into helping them identify and express feelings they experience. With a few clients, I offer a higher amount of support and offer it earlier in the counseling process because these clients are ready for this style. They are in touch with their feelings, and their feelings strongly and directly influence their behavior. Later, I would help them use their cognitions for problem-solving and rational behavior. Regardless of the stated reason for seeking help

Developmental Eclectic Counseling with Men **159**

and of the particular style of relating to the world, men face a variety of issues that pervade their lives and the treatment process. These issues must be conscious in the mind of the therapist, as well as directly discussed in counseling, if success at any specific treatment goal is to be long-lasting.

The field of psychology has been somewhat slow in entering the issues that affect adult men. The popular literature initially outpaced the professional literature and remains a valuable resource for clients. For general reading about men and how they live their lives, I suggest the works of Bly (1990), Emerson (1985), Farrell (1986), Garfinkel (1985), Keen (1991), Klein and Erickson (1987), and Rose (1980). For a more specific look at men's conflicts and particularly their conflicts with women, I recommend Goldberg (1976, 1980, 1983). In the area of father-son relationships, I refer clients to Cosby (1986) and Sifford (1982). More clinical and academic works of importance include those written by Fine (1988), Kiley (1983), Kimmel and Messner (1989), Meth and Pasick (1990), Scher, Stevens, Good, and Eichenfield (1987), Silverberg (1986), and Solomon and Levy (1982). Books written primarily on father-son issues include Osherson (1986), Voght and Stirridge (1991), and Yablonsky (1990). The issues that have been identified anecdotally have yet to be researched fully. Issues such as power, intimacy, career struggle, marriage and family establishment, and retirement are all worthy of more extensive research and clinical review.

DEVELOPMENTAL ISSUES FOR MEN

The issues facing adult men are viewed in this chapter as developmental; that is, they are seen as part of an ongoing process of learning about oneself and about the world. Men approach each new life event as the sum of their successes and failures in previous situations. Accumulated experiences form the context by which subsequent incidents are defined and understood (Vaillant, 1977). Although developmental theory has been described by authors with various points of view, the work of Erickson (1963), Kohlberg (1981), Loevinger, Wessler, and Redmore (1970), and Piaget (1955) are major influences of the developmental approach. More contemporary modifications have been offered by Gilligan (1982) and Kegan (1982). Applications to psychotherapy have been made by Ivey (1986) and Kelly (1955).

In general, adult men face the following issues:

1. **The search for power.** Power is the ability to achieve one's wishes and desires. It is measured either by the influence a man has over other

160 *Gordon M. Hart*

people or by the wealth he has accumulated, although definitions vary (Bateson, 1972). In present-day America, men are expected to gain power through competition in which one person (or company, department, team, etc.) wins and one loses (Silverberg, 1986). This competition is based on the assumption that there are not enough resources (prizes, promotions, raises, attractive women, etc.) for everyone. Men have been taught that power (measured by goods or status) can be achieved most effectively by acting confidently, assertively or aggressively, and energetically. They should never show feelings such as sympathy, sadness, worry, or doubt, which might be perceived as signs of weakness. Nontraditional definitions of power and how to achieve it (Rogers, 1977) have existed for some time but go against the mainstream of contemporary culture.

2. **The search for intimacy.** Intimacy is the degree of closeness people feel toward each other and is attained through openness, honesty, and tentativeness especially in the expression of feelings toward each other such as warmth, vulnerability, and closeness. Intimacy is not achieved through competition but instead through cooperation in which each person gets some of what he or she needs (McGill, 1985).

3. **Establishment of an effective protector/provider role.** Early societal messages have told men that they must take on the role of protecting women and children from physical and economic harm (Goldberg, 1980). This means that they must be alert, wary, and good at solving problems effectively. As providers, men must be aggressive, competitive, and ready to take any economic gain that comes along.

4. **Creating a life outside one's career and family.** The high stress reported among adult men in the work force accompanied by low job satisfaction has led to burnout, inappropriate job changes, and substance abuse. One way of coping with existing job stress and dissatisfaction or preventing stress and dissatisfaction is to establish resources that can sustain a person in the face of career problems.

   Family stress and problems also can seem to be overwhelming. If adequate activities and relationships are available outside the home, relief from family pressures can be achieved, at least temporarily. Creating a life outside one's career and family consists of maintaining (or establishing) friendships and leisure activities that provide diversion, alternative satisfaction, and a sense of well-being that cannot be attained solely by means of one's career and family, no matter how great a career or family one has (Gordon & Pasick, 1990).

5. **Developing a workable style (from thinking and acting to feeling and experiencing).** A man with the best of goals may fail if he uses the

wrong approach to accomplish those goals. Many men attempt to use a rational, logical approach to interpersonal situations. They conceptualize interactions as being a problem needing fixing; if no problem exists, then people around them are ignored. If a problem is acknowledged, then an approach to solving it usually includes analysis, generation of alternatives, and a plan of action. Sadly, this approach both to conceptualizing interpersonal interactions and solving a perceived problem often ignores the feelings of the people involved and their need to be heard and acknowledged (Balswick, 1982). Some men learn to approach interpersonal situations not as problems to be solved or otherwise ignored but as situations to be experienced. Their feelings, not their thoughts, are the means of analyzing the situation. For example, if they feel uncomfortable in some situation, then they may wish to change this state but do not sense an obligation to fix anything. Instead, they may wish to talk about how they feel or ask others how they feel.

The five issues described interact in a complex matrix. Men face a struggle between meeting their needs for power and intimacy (Fine, 1988). Often they face this struggle with few resources and a style that is ineffective. For years men have learned that only power is important. The nature of the man as strong and silent is taught from one generation to the next (Garfinkel, 1985) and is glorified in the spirit of the Old West as portrayed in films and books. Men who want both power and intimacy face a daily conflict resulting in a variety of intrapsychic and interpersonal conflicts (Goldberg, 1983). By understanding men as people who want to meet their needs and perform their social roles as best they can, counselors are able to respond to these men and help them attain a more effective way of living their lives (Scher et al., 1987).

The ACT approach allows for attention to both concrete goal attainment desired by a client, such as a better relationship with a spouse, as well as more abstract goal attainment, such as feeling better about oneself. Effective clinical outcomes that really last must include attention to immediate and often person-specific concerns as well as to more ongoing and often pervasive issues. The individual and the system in which the individual functions both deserve attention. Specifically, men who enter treatment must be assisted to reduce the symptoms and problems that caused them to seek help. In addition, these men are likely to need help in developing understanding, emotional awareness, and new behavior with regard to the roles and relationship style they have developed that quite likely contribute to their current symptoms or problems (Allen & Gordon, 1990).

162   *Gordon M. Hart*

DAVID: A CASE OF HIGH EXPECTATIONS

David is 34 years old, Jewish but not very religious. He is in a first marriage (and for his wife Sarah also) for 10 years, has an infant son, and is employed as an attorney in a large and very prestigious (and highly competitive) Philadelphia law firm. Physically, David is about five feet ten inches tall, brown hair, good-looking and with an easy smile. He's a fashionable dresser, wearing the appropriate tie, shirt, and expensive suit. Sarah, whom I met some weeks later, is the same age as David. She is from an upper-class Jewish home and works as an account executive in advertising with an MBA (obtained three years ago). She recently entered the work force in a small but respected firm in center city Philadelphia. She came from a family where she was the younger of two children, her older sibling being a brother three years her senior. She is a well-dressed, tall (five feet seven inches), slim, and very attractive woman.

David grew up in a suburban middle-class home outside of Philadelphia, where his father was a salesman and his mother was a housewife. His father is now retired. David has an older brother and a younger sister. He describes his childhood and adolescence as uneventful, with family members spending time with each other but not relating very closely with each other. Although David thought about careers other than law, such as teaching or business, none of these seemed likely to bring in the amount of money that he desired. David seemed to sense while growing up that he had the intelligence and work habits to attain success in a variety of careers but didn't think much about what would be emotionally satisfying to him. He also knew that he had the support from his family to attain higher education and a career with prestige. It was a traditional family in which "getting ahead" was important, especially for the boys.

David works hard but does not express concern about it other than saying that he has too little time for his family and friends. He said that he likes people and enjoys parties, going out to dinner with friends, and having people visit him at his home or theirs. He does not enjoy athletic activities as recreation (nor does he exercise at all). Instead, David enjoys reading current nonfiction best-sellers and biographies or sitting on the beach at the seashore on weekends during the summer. He seems to be a serious, intellectual, and cautious person who enjoys his career or, rather, what it has brought him. But now he wonders if he wants to practice law for the rest of his life. However, he has no idea about what other career might be more satisfying to him. His career doubts are a minor part of why he sought my help. His "real problem" is his relationship with his wife.

Developmental Eclectic Counseling with Men **163**

David came to see me because he was "very unhappy with" his wife and was now "attracted to another woman." He wasn't sure if he wanted to leave his wife or not but certainly would not for the other woman because she is already married. Coming to see me was designed "to help decide whether to leave Sarah or not."

After hearing this brief overview, I requested that he "fill me in" on his relationship with Sarah. He described his relationship with Sarah as being confining, filled with "taking care of her emotionally," and not enjoyable. He had fun with the other woman, although he felt guilty about doing so. He said that he was having very little fun in life, except that he enjoyed his infant son a great deal. David told me that he felt tired of dealing with Sarah's requests for emotional reassurance. Whenever she felt slighted by her friends, coworkers, family, or by David, she asked David to make her feel better. David saw this as excessive and increasingly tiresome for him. As David said, "I'm tired of taking care of her." He went on to suggest that, "Sarah just is too sensitive and wants everybody to like her—and like her all the time! It's like I have two children to take care of."

Furthermore, David believed that Sarah was disinterested in his friends and even competed with them for his attention. He described a recent incident in which Sarah angrily accused him of wanting to be with other people more than with her. Formerly, David would have spent days trying to reassure her, but now he dismissed her claim as being, "ridiculous" and not "worthy of discussing." Currently, David reports that Sarah either requests sweetly or demands angrily that David reassure her that he likes her better than his friends and apologize for being so insensitive for not offering this reassurance when she first requested it.

For the first five years of their marriage, David depicted a traditional relationship in which he took on the role of the breadwinner and decision-maker while Sarah became the homemaker (until she went back to school for her master's degree and then to work). David made the decisions, kept the checkbook, paid the bills, bought insurance and other major purchases, and so forth. Sarah cared for the house, played the hostess to David's clients and colleagues, and supported David's early struggles in his career. David continues these household responsibilities, but Sarah's entry into the work force has meant that they obtain a housekeeper/babysitter.

Therapist Impressions and Conceptualization

Although David told me that he felt very "confused," "upset," and "in turmoil," the way he portrayed his situation in terms of content and affective expres-

164 *Gordon M. Hart*

sion suggested some of the early therapeutic issues that needed to be faced. First, he was "unhappy with" his wife—not his relationship with her, but "her." It was as if he were somehow unconnected to her or that he was not involved very much in the cause of his own distress. This description suggested a very linear or simple cause-and-effect way of thinking. It's a view that suggests that if David could just get Sarah to act differently (and he would remain the same, of course), then everything might work out for their marriage. In a systems view, David not only reacts to Sarah's behavior, but he provokes it as well and so is partially responsible for his unhappy marriage. I would need to work with David on his view of himself in his relationship if it turned out that this linear view was indicative of his thinking. Understanding and accepting the complexity of interpersonal behavior and then adopting new ways of behaving suggested by this more systemic view is needed in order for men to make lasting changes.

Secondly, David came to see me to "make a decision"—not to sort things out, not to improve the relationship if possible, but to decide by himself in a unilateral manner, apparently without input from his wife, about the future of their marriage. Men who handle interpersonal problems in this manner try to make the therapy process more rational and cognitive, and less painful, than I believe that it ever really is or can be. I would need to confront this belief if it were truly representative of David's mode of behavior. Making an independent decision and announcing it to Sarah would breed resentment and increase overt or covert conflict in their relationship.

David's style of expression showed several key points. First, he reported factual information and his feelings about the facts in the same manner. He was serious, thoughtful, concerned, and sincere but stayed controlled, calm, analytic, and introspective. Although not flat in affect, he was certainly under control. He talked about his feelings with little display of any depth of the emotions. It would need to be determined if David has an awareness of his feelings and finds it difficult to express them or has no awareness of feelings in the first place. Emotional awareness and expression are necessary for the successful attainment of any counseling goal that clients choose to work on.

Further evidence of his resistance to discussing or displaying feelings came when I offered a suggestion that something must have been painful, upsetting, or distressful. One of David's responses was to ignore or minimize my comment. As David said several times in the first few sessions, "Yes, but I try not to dwell on how I feel" or "Yes, but I don't feel that way too often." The clue I gained from this interaction is that I would not be able to focus on David's understanding and expression of his feelings for too long a time or at any great depth for several

Developmental Eclectic Counseling with Men   **165**

sessions. Providing emotional support for his feeling state would have to be done minimally and carefully.

Another of David's responses to my acknowledging his past and current feelings was to shift the focus to what could be done to make things better. David said, "So maybe I do feel bad. What do I do about it?" or "It's great that I've got so much insight into Sarah. Now how do I feel better?" It's the question asked by a man who doesn't want to feel badly anymore, which is fine, but also it may be a question asked by a man who wants a quick and easy solution to his immediate problem.

At the end of the first session, I knew that I wanted to meet Sarah to see for myself what she was like and also to gain her impressions of David and of their relationship. In addition, I wanted to assess her motivation for couples counseling at some point in the future. Seeing both of them together is the way, I believe, that couples can best solve the problems of their relationship, but I certainly recognized the developmental problems David was facing that could best be handled in individual meetings. I told David my reasons for meeting with Sarah alone before I met with him again, and he agreed to this plan but refused to commit to any joint sessions.

In my meeting with Sarah, I found a very tense, tearful, highly anxious person who expressed her deep need for David's support and approval. She told how she carefully monitors David's moods and wishes. Sensing his unhappiness, she urged him to seek marriage counseling with her. After he refused, she redoubled her efforts to be the person that she perceived he wanted. She went back to school for a graduate degree and then got a job in order to impress him as to her intellectual interests and abilities. If David would accept and reassure her then maybe life would work out, she believed. She went on to tell how David always resisted her depending on him and how he wanted her to be more independent. Her recent efforts to cater to his every whim met with failure. I believe this failure occurred for two reasons. David felt pressured to reassure her, and Sarah felt as though the fate of the marriage was at stake making her very nervous, awkward, and reactive.

After meeting with Sarah, I scheduled another meeting with David. My general plan was to meet with him individually on a regular basis and bring in Sarah later for joint sessions at a point in time we both agreed upon. My initial task in terms of the counseling process was to deal with David's expectations about the therapy process itself, because his beliefs and mine were quite different. When this task was achieved, he could move on to content goals that emerge directly from the problems he identified in the first session. These content and process goals are both examined in the next section.

166   *Gordon M. Hart*

Readiness

David was quite competent interpersonally in that he related to most people around him in an effective manner. He was usually polite, cooperative, and cheerful. His confidence level was high in most career and interpersonal situations with colleagues, friends, family, and acquaintances. His initial motivation to find a solution to his current dilemma also was good. Readiness, according to ACT, refers to a client's initial motivation to begin treatment and to his or her ability to engage in a type of therapeutic strategy that the counselor deems to be most appropriate at a particular point in the process.

Unfortunately, David's status in these three factors of readiness for therapy was of little value in determining the likelihood of his achieving any success in therapy or even of his staying in therapy more than a few sessions. Regardless of social skills or psychological sophistication, most men don't want to change or know how to do so. Consequently, David was ready to begin something to make himself feel better, but he had little awareness about what lay ahead in therapy. Perhaps ACT's general predictive ability with clients at the start of therapy is low; however, ACT's value in guiding the choice of therapeutic strategy during therapy is excellent.

In terms of initial readiness, David was ready to deal with the problem only as he had defined it and in a way in which he was comfortable. His definition of the problem was different from mine, and his way of solving problems was different from mine as well. David wanted to use the same old definitions and methods that hadn't worked before in his relationship with Sarah. David wanted to work harder at the same old ways; I wanted him to work differently. In order to work on process goals, I knew that I would have to teach, at least initially. If I were successful at attaining the process goals, then David's readiness to achieve the content goals would be significantly increased.

Process Goals

The process goals that I saw necessary to achieve were (1) to gain credibility as a therapist, (2) to change David's definition of the problem, (3) to help him lower his defenses and gain some awareness of the feelings he was experiencing, (4) to help him express these feelings, and (5) to help him understand therapy as an ongoing process of discovery and change.

Gaining credibility.   Gaining credibility as a therapist means that I must convince the client that it is worth his or her time, energy, and money to talk to me.

Developmental Eclectic Counseling with Men   **167**

With many clients, the use of empathic understanding of their feelings is a primary tool to accomplish this process goal. With many men, the tools are different. To be sure, empathic understanding is essential with men but more so of their thoughts than of their feelings. Too much emphasis on feelings will not only scare male clients but also portray the therapist as non-masculine and possibly one who might side with the client's wife if marital conflict is the presenting problem.

I tried very hard to understand what David thought was happening more than how he felt about what was happening. I communicated that understanding by means of simple paraphrasing—Style 3. In this way, David experienced that I understood what happened to him in his interactions with Sarah.

> As David said to me, "I told Sarah that I was going to stay late at work one night last week and then have dinner with my friend John who works with me. She blew up at me for not telling her farther ahead of time so she could have made plans to have dinner or something with one of her friends. She just resents my spending time with one of my friends rather than with her."
>
> I responded by saying, "So you think that Sarah was really out of line to blast you for something so simple?"
>
> "Damn right!" said David.
>
> "And you also think that she's being dependent on you for all of her social life but isn't really telling you that part?" I suggested.
>
> "Yeah, that's the communication part that's missing. Sarah's not being honest about what she wants from me. Or how much," David sadly commented.

In addition, I also tried to show that I saw parts of the puzzle that David hadn't seen. A brief example involved offering an explanation for a behavior of Sarah's that David didn't understand.

> David stated, "You know, I just don't understand why Sarah acts so needy all the time. She's smart and attractive, and does everything well."
>
> "Maybe she doesn't feel as smart or attractive as the other women she knows," I offered.
>
> "That's silly for her to feel that way, but maybe you're right. She does always look at other women—what they're wearing, wondering what they mean by what they say," David mused.

By demonstrating that I really understood him (S 3) and that I had some clues about Sarah's motivation or about their interaction (S 2), I was able to join with David at his current level of functioning. I only rarely and cautiously challenged

168   *Gordon M. Hart*

his externalized focus; that is, his blaming Sarah for their marital conflicts. Consequently, I gained some initial amount of credibility as a therapist.

Redefining the problem.   Here's where the situation heated up between therapist and client. I began to challenge not only David's definition of the problem but also his idea of what it would take to solve the problem. First, I challenged (S 1) his definition.

> David asserted, "I think that Sarah acts out all of her feelings on to me without ever thinking about how I will feel about it. Last week she pouted when I got home late from work, and then she didn't want to go out to dinner as we had planned. It was OK with me because I was tired and wanted to stay home."
>
> I suggested, "So do you think that she had any justification for feeling badly or feeling disappointed that you and she would not be alone together that evening?"
>
> "Well, sure," David mused, then quickly added, "but she didn't have to punish me for the rest of the evening because of it."
>
> "Sure," I agreed, "that wasn't very nice. But I wonder what she wanted you to do during that time?"
>
> "What do you mean?" David asked.
>
> "Well, I think that she may have been trying to send you a message that you didn't pick up on. Or maybe you didn't want to pick up on it," I offered.

By suggesting that Sarah had some intent in mind other than or in addition to punishing David, he began to move away from his view that he was the victim and she was the persecutor. My comment also indirectly challenged his view that he was the rational person and she was the irrational person in the relationship. Moving away from dichotomous or "black or white thinking" is an important step toward the achievement of both process and content goals.

The next part of redefining the problem was to challenge his notion of how to solve interpersonal problems. David's style was to confront problems head-on, decide on which person was guilty, have that person apologize, and have him or her promise to do things differently the next time. Showing him that this process wasn't working very well and that a different procedure might be viable was the task, and using an S 2 approach seemed appropriate.

> David reported, "When Sarah makes me feel guilty, I also resent her for doing that. I usually apologize, or at least I used to, for making her upset or disappointing her. But I also want her to see that she shouldn't try to make me feel guilty before I have a chance to talk to her."

Developmental Eclectic Counseling with Men   **169**

> "Maybe apologizing isn't the way to go," I suggested.
>
> "What so you mean?" David asked.
>
> "Well, maybe you and she should discuss what caused you to disappoint her or upset her in the first place," I offered.
>
> "I know what I did to upset her. She tells me very clearly," David replied.
>
> "I understand that, David. What I meant was that you and she might try to find out what caused you to say or do whatever Sarah disliked or disapproved of," I clarified. "And maybe wanting Sarah to apologize and promise to change her ways doesn't seem to work either," I added.

Seeking out an alternative cause for behavior can lead to acting very differently with each other by subtly challenging the way that a person tries to solve the presenting problem.

Attaining emotional awareness. Helping David to become more aware of his feelings in the sessions with me would help him to have more information about himself and so more information about his relationship with Sarah. In order to do this, I probed beneath David's smooth facade, a practice which I believe is directive and so is an S 1 style. The process would be frightening to him. Thus, this task was not addressed actively until progress had been made on the prior process tasks.

> "You know, I've been an excellent provider and supporter of Sarah and for a long time. She hasn't wanted for very much and has had life pretty easy," David contended.
>
> "It sounds like you're angry at her about that," I observed, focusing on the feeling.
>
> "Maybe I am. I guess so," David agreed cautiously. I took this response as a sign of some willingness to acknowledge his feelings.
>
> "I wonder if you're hurt that she hasn't thanked you for doing such a good job," I continued, increasing the heat by focusing on a feeling David was less ready to own than anger.
>
> "It's hard for me to admit that someone else has hurt me," David painfully and quietly confided.
>
> "I understand," I said.

This interchange was a powerful one in which David started to be in touch with a strong emotion that he felt uncomfortable in feeling and in admitting to me. It was the start of David's becoming more honest about himself and about his relationship with Sarah.

Expressing feelings. The goal in this area was not that David have a cathartic experience or tell Sarah his innermost feelings. The initial goal was for David's

170 *Gordon M. Hart*

verbal and nonverbal behavior to match during the session and hopefully outside of the session. Often when expressing a feeling, David would either smile or shrug his shoulders as if to minimize how intensely he actually felt. I tried to help him gain some congruence in this next example.

> "Well," David drawled, "I guess that I do feel kind of nervous about whether I'll have to take care of Sarah emotionally for the rest of her life."
>
> "When you say that, David—you know, you don't sound nervous or worried," I challenged in a puzzled way.
>
> "I guess it's hard for me to show people how I feel. Especially when I've just begun to figure out how I really feel," David admitted insightfully.

Without telling David directly that his words and actions didn't match, I tried to communicate that it was safe with me to show how he felt as well as talk about how he felt. No explanation of authenticity was necessary. He also told me, by his responses, that he was better able to know how he was feeling. I could support (S 3) that newly emerging ability.

Understanding therapy. David is like most men who are competent, confident, and motivated in the situations that are most familiar and most comfortable for them. They have adapted themselves to the demands of the world around them except for those situations that require more intimacy and emotional awareness than they have ever encountered before. I tried to teach (S 2) several concepts to David that were new to him or in contrast to what he believed about human behavior. The concepts highlighted here are (1) the multiple incident theory of causation, (2) the symbolism of events, (3) the idea of perception being more important than absolute reality, and (4) the belief that relationships evolve and are never static.

Many men believe that if they can isolate the one incident or recurring behavior that causes their distress that they will quickly be able to remedy the problem. I try to teach them that they should look for clusters of several incidents or patterns of behavior that cause conflict. The next section illustrates this lesson.

> David said, "If only I could find out what makes Sarah so needy of my reassurance."
>
> "Sometimes it's how a person was raised. Sometimes it's how a relationship is carried out. Sometimes it's a combination of a lot of things—an accumulation. Perhaps you'll never find one specific cause. Maybe all you'll ever know is that what Sarah wants you to do is very important to her," I offered.

Developmental Eclectic Counseling with Men   **171**

Men who are very concrete or literal in their thinking fail to understand that acts take on meanings that are not clearly observable to them but are nevertheless very important. I tried to help David look for additional meanings or symbols.

> "The other day when I suggested to Sarah that we rent a movie on Saturday night instead of going to that party my firm was throwing, she acted like it was a big deal. She was really grateful," David reported.
>
> "Maybe she thought that she had finally gotten through to you about how important it is to her to have you initiate some interaction with her. Especially if it's her over the firm," I suggested.

The idea of one's perception being more important than an absolute reality is difficult for some men to grasp. I find that I often make statements such as, "It doesn't matter what you said. It's what your wife heard or felt that is important." I tried to help David listen carefully to what Sarah was telling him.

> David angrily asserted, "But I didn't mean what Sarah perceived me to say. She inferred something that isn't true. I don't resent her for not working when we were first married."
>
> I responded, "I know, David. (S 3) Right now, Sarah is pretty worried about how you feel and what you'll do. And so she may make an inference that isn't true. And if that's how Sarah feels, then that's what you have to deal with. (S 2) Of course, in the absence of any reassurance from you, she may find it tough to know what to believe. I think that you have some responsibility to clarify how you really do feel about her not working. (S 1) What do you think?" (S 2)

A final part of understanding therapy is realizing that a satisfying relationship is not a plateau that once reached remains level forever. Relationships are fluid and so never remain the same. Events of a man's life, both dramatic and mundane, serve to change the context in which he relates to his spouse. Also, the natural and inevitable challenges of one's career and family demand responses that meet these challenges effectively. I attempted to teach David to anticipate that achieving an effective relationship with Sarah would not mean that he could stop working and return to old habits.

> "I don't know if Sarah and I can agree on how I can make her happy. She wants me to be somebody I'm not," complained David.
>
> "I guess you'll have to decide if you like the person you are now so much that you're willing to divorce Sarah to keep from changing," I commented. "I wonder if you'll be the same person ten years from now anyway," I wondered.

172   *Gordon M. Hart*

> "You know, people sometimes tell me that I'm not the same person they knew in high school or in college or when I first started to work here," David reflected. "I guess I change some things about myself without even knowing that I do," he considered.
>
> "So maybe you might want to be aware of and in control of the direction of these changes," I suggested.
>
> "I guess that I can never expect that Sarah and I will be locked in some freeze-dried state of eternal bliss," David said with mild sarcasm.
>
> "As much as this may disappoint you to hear it—no, I don't think so," I said in a warm and hopefully reassuring way.

All in all, process goals are very important to helping clients make the most of therapy and achieve long-lasting effects from their content goals. David was ready for the content goals of therapy, having achieved some measure of success at process goals. We returned to these process goals at various points in therapy in order to refresh his memory and to solidify the gains that had been made at the beginning of treatment.

Some of the issues described earlier facing most adult men, particularly power, intimacy, protector/provider role, and style of expression, are addressed during these interactions, sometimes very directly and at other times more indirectly. They will be addressed again during the work on the content goal. ACT provides a clear choice of options within which any counselor may fit his or her particular therapeutic interventions and which accommodate all theoretical orientations. ACT offers a conceptual outline that simplifies a counselor's choice of direction at any one point in time with a particular client.

Content Goals

The only content goal that David and I agreed upon initially was to improve his relationship with Sarah. If improvement in their relationship was impossible, then divorce was an option. In order to accomplish this overall goal, I suggested two sub-goals or tasks that he needed to achieve in order to accomplish the general goal. These tasks were (1) to understand his interaction with Sarah in terms of what she wanted and what he wanted, and (2) to express his feelings to Sarah more openly and directly. At this point I assessed his readiness to begin working on the primary goal and thought about which ACT style would be effective. With David, I believed that I would have to begin by using Style 3 with some minimal amount of direction. David's cognitive and intellectual problem-solving style would not tolerate an S 4 (Delegating—existential or psychoanalytic style). Using an S 1

Developmental Eclectic Counseling with Men   **173**

style at any point would be unlikely and unnecessary because David was a well-motivated and sophisticated client. Accomplishing the first task of helping David understand his relationship with Sarah and how he might act differently with her would require a major reliance on S 3 with some S 2 as needed.

David was more in touch with his need for power, information, and rationality than with intimacy, symbolism and feelings. I believed that David would not respect a therapist who offered no opinions or new points of view. "Expert" power was particularly useful. David wanted me to be an expert, just as he was an expert in the law. I would need to offer some suggestions, interpretations, confrontations, and definitions. This cognitive or didactic style (S 2) would make him feel less threatened and more in control of the sessions. This style also appealed to his practical nature as the following exchange illustrates.

> David asserted, "Gordon, I'm a 'bottom-line' kind of guy. Lay it out for me and I'll handle it."
>
> "I understand what you're saying. I'll be as clear and direct as I can be. But, you know, some things about relationships are complicated—especially when we talk about feelings," I warned.

I knew that I would have to offer support (S 3) as I probed for feelings under his facade of "I've got it together, except for this one problem with my wife." David told me that he was drinking too much, sleeping poorly, neglecting his work and generally feeling badly. With these admissions in hand, I was able to use them as a lever to get him to explore the feelings that were outside of his awareness.

In assessing David's readiness, I found that David was motivated to work on his relationship with Sarah for several reasons. First, he was tired of feeling upset; that is, angry and frustrated, lonely and sad, plus isolated. Secondly, David wanted to stay with Sarah, if at all possible, to honor the commitment he'd made to her when they married. Also, he wanted his child to be raised in a two-parent family. He didn't want to sacrifice his child's well-being for his own happiness. David's overall confidence appeared high because he had good relationships with other men and women in his life. I found him to be too smooth and actually overconfident; that is, more confident than he deserved to be. I believed that his air of confidence was insincere and might be covering up some insecurity about his ability to relate intimately to others.

On the third factor of readiness, competence, David was good interpersonally with acquaintances and poor with Sarah. David related well to others in social and business situations. He was articulate, insightful, forthright, and a good listener. Unfortunately, maintaining other than a superficial relationship was very difficult for him to do. Sarah wanted an intimate relationship, and David was not competent at the present time to conduct one with her or probably with anyone else.

Therefore, David's assessed readiness was similar for both tasks related to improving his marital relationship. He was willing to work but was currently unable to understand needs or communicate feelings directly. His confidence or self-assessment of his ability was higher than his current ability. The initial strategy was both to match David's more confident assessment of himself and to gather additional information on his readiness. I anticipated using Style 2—Teaching when he needed me to be an expert and as he struggled in building a more intimate, honest marital relationship.

Developmental Considerations

The content goal of improving his relationship with Sarah could be achieved by attending to the developmental issues that were identified earlier in this chapter. He was in good shape with respect to some of the issues, such as attaining and achieving a satisfactory protector/provider role, but needed work in gaining intimacy, creating a life outside of his career and family, and developing a more workable relationship style. To a great extent, David had satisfied his need for power in both his work life and personal life. To this point in his life, success in courtroom trials or in situations with his wife had demanded emotional distance, relational thinking, evaluation of facts, etc., which had resulted in a sense of fatigue, loneliness, and frustration.

David had married a woman he could protect and provide for financially. He felt secure in his ability to continue to provide for and protect her. David's need for intimacy went unmet. He could rarely let down his "pillar of strength" facade with Sarah or with anyone else. He was strong at the office and strong at home, and it was killing him. Similarly, David had little life outside of his home and could profit from the emotional resources from friendships and activities in the world around him.

The means by which David could alter his relationships in order to meet his need for intimacy would be to use the thinking and acting style less often and to use the feeling and experiencing style more often. By gaining awareness of his feelings and learning how to express them appropriately, he would be most likely to gain the intimacy that had eluded him.

Developmental Eclectic Counseling with Men   **175**

Improving the Marriage

As we began to focus on improving David's relationship with Sarah, first by understanding their interactions and then by expressing his feelings to her, a number of interactions between them needed attention if they were to establish more intimacy between themselves.

In David's words, "I don't talk to Sarah very often. Either I yell at her for something small, or else I withdraw from her completely." As David described his early marriage years, he began to understand that he spent much of the first half of his ten-year marriage trying to please Sarah by not telling her when he was upset with her or with anyone else. Unlike now, he usually was able to grin and bear it. In recent times he showed his anger through blowups but did not tell her what it was all about. Actually, he had little idea what his anger was about.

Initially, David made quick progress on the goal of understanding his relationship with Sara and his part in making it unpleasant. I used a very direct S 1 style to address various therapeutic issues such as David's belief that Sarah was fragile and needed his protection. He knew that he was angry with her for playing a weak and needy role but slowly realized that he was fearful of hurting her. I had ample evidence that he pulled no punches with men in his life but acted differently with women and particularly with Sarah. I planned to use this information to get him to understand his motivation for treating Sarah with kid gloves. I hoped that he would be forced to decide if Sarah was an emotional cripple or a competent adult. I wanted him to see that he was overdoing his protector role.

> I said to him at one point, "Do you really believe that Sarah would fall apart, have to be committed to a mental hospital, quit her job, move in with her parents?"
>
> David responded, "Well, no. It wouldn't be that extreme, but she would really be a mess for a while."
>
> I suggested, "Maybe you need to believe that she's fragile so you won't have to confront her with how you really feel."
>
> After a pause, he said somewhat defensively, "I guess you're telling me that I cause my own problems with Sarah."
>
> "To some extent, yes," I suggested.
>
> "Maybe I do," he weakly responded.
>
> "How about in the present situation you just told me about?" I pursued.

David said that he wanted to hear my honest opinion about his role in the problems with Sarah, and so I felt good about my use of the confrontive Style 1. I

176   *Gordon M. Hart*

continued by using the teaching style (S 2) now that he was willing to examine his own behavior. The focus of the teaching was to explain his actions in the developmental context and communicate that the issue was experienced by many men with whom I had worked.

A therapeutic issue that quickly followed David's fear of hurting Sarah by expressing his real feelings was the guilt that he experienced when Sarah got upset with what he had said to her. This issue cut quite deeply into David as it does into many other men. It's the notion that men shouldn't hurt women—at any cost. If they do, then they feel guilty or even ashamed. They must protect women not hurt them. As it worked with David, I tried to help him get past these feelings that cut off honest and direct emotional expression with Sarah.

> As David described, "Every time I've told her that I don't like her making these emotional demands on me, she cries and says that I don't love her and that I'm going to leave her. I'm not a cruel and unfaithful person. But I know what I feel."
>
> "David," I asked, "how do you feel after you've told Sarah how you felt—without blaming her for making you feel that way and without blasting her—and she's started to cry or look and sound sad?"
>
> "If I'm not mad at her for defending herself and putting it back on me, which is most of the time, I feel bad. You know, guilty," David admitted readily.
>
> "Many men avoid telling their wives how they feel because if the wife gets hurt then they feel really guilty or ashamed," I explained (S 2).

Hopefully, David would become increasingly able to take the risk to be more open and honest with Sarah. He seemed to be reassured to know that other men have such problems and that a solution, however difficult it may be, is available.

Another therapeutic issue was that David had become frustrated with giving assurance to Sarah, who never seemed to be satisfied for very long with the words that he gave her. The power that he previously had felt with her had diminished greatly. The strength that Sarah had gotten from his protector role probably had declined as she began to protect herself through her own actions and not by means of her husband's statements. After all, he's committed to protecting her no matter what his real opinion might be.

I chose to be supportive (S 3) rather than instructive (S 2) in the following example. I perceived sufficient pain in David's voice and facial expression that

Developmental Eclectic Counseling with Men **177**

moved me to focus on a painful loss for David that was right beneath his feeling of frustration.

> "I get really tired of propping Sarah up every few days," David complained with mild irritation.
>
> "It's really frustrating, as we identified a few minutes ago. I wonder if you're feeling anything else right now as you think about how you can no longer make Sarah feel good, at least for such brief periods of time?" I asked softly.
>
> "Hmmm," he sighed and then slouched back into the chair, "It just seems very empty, blank to me."
>
> "Sounds pretty painful, maybe sad." I offered.
>
> "I tried hard," David deflected but still showing the pain non-verbally. " Feel kind of useless and worthless, I suppose," he explored.
>
> "Yes," I acknowledged.

Eventually, David began to use more sensitivity when telling Sarah how he felt about something she had done or not done. As his understanding grew about his part in his interactions with Sarah, his anger and frustration diminished and gave way to sadness. The destructive spiral of anger and frustration had been broken. I then started to meet with both David and Sarah jointly every other week and continued to see David weekly. My focus with David shifted to the second task needed to improve their relationship.

The second task of helping David rebuild a relationship with Sarah was to help him express his feelings to Sarah, not only about her but also his feelings about his career and relationships with others. A related task was to help him hear Sarah's feelings. In this way, the chance for intimacy would be increased. Therapeutic issues emerged, such as David's fear of not keeping up with his partners at work. Again, I offered a balance of S 2 and S 3 styles.

> David reflected, "I feel very competitive with the other lawyers except for one man who's my best friend."
>
> "And how does that feel to you, going in there every day and knowing that your status and your bonus is on the line each day?" I dramatized a bit to increase the impact.
>
> "Well, sometimes I don't think about it, and other times I feel nervous and apprehensive about how much I should share with them. It makes me less cooperative than I ordinarily would be," he reasoned.
>
> I asked him, "Do you ever approach Sarah with the intent of sharing with her some emotional experience you'd had that day?"

178   *Gordon M. Hart*

> David said, "Not really, I guess. Sarah seems like the kind of person who is good at asking for things for herself, but I don't know if she would like to listen to me."

Sarah felt threatened because she wanted a responsible adult to protect and reassure her. For Sarah, David had to be the strong, silent type for whom nothing was a problem. He couldn't show fear or worry, nor could he act silly or irresponsible. Gradually, he had become closed to gaining nurturance from Sarah.

David had to take the risk to reveal his feelings to Sarah and find out if she really would reject him for doing so. If she refused to accept his being vulnerable and saw him as weak and immature, then the chances of his gaining a more intimate relationship with her were in doubt.

> "Honestly, Gordon, I would like sometimes to come home and complain about how everyone mistreated me or how I screwed up stuff and have Sarah take my side and sort of patch me up, I guess," David poured out. "But I'm not sure she wants to or is able to take care of me like that, even though I do a lot of that for her," he confided with a worried expression.
>
> In a Teacher style (S 2), close to S 1, I asked David, "What could you do each day that wouldn't take much effort on your part but would help you and Sarah?"
>
> After some thought, David suggested, "I could tell Sarah that I care for her and what she thinks and feels. But I'd have to also let her know somehow that times may be rough, and I'll be unhappy, and she'll be unhappy, and maybe we won't be married forever."
>
> "In other words, I love you now but don't take this as some lifelong guarantee of happiness," I suggested.
>
> "Exactly," said David.
>
> "OK, that's fine," I responded. "Now what if you told her what you wanted to about how you were feeling, about something that had happened that day, or something that had been on your mind for a while?" I suggested concretely.

Earlier in their relationship, David had offered general reassurance in a rather paternal way to Sarah. This nonspecific "pat on the head" response was no longer effective and needed to be changed. I chose to use the instructive S 2 style to help David understand the responses that might help him move closer to Sarah.

> "You know, when you take more time to understand exactly how Sarah feels, you may be more than halfway toward helping her feel better," I began.

Developmental Eclectic Counseling with Men **179**

> "I agree with that and I'll work on it," David accepted. "What else is there?" he questioned.
>
> "I think that you may move too quickly to solving the problem for her instead of letting her do that for herself," I suggested.
>
> "What do you mean, exactly?" he puzzled.
>
> "I've got an article here that you might find helpful, and there are several books that describe the patterns that you and Sarah apparently act out," I offered. "In general, men move too quickly to resolve the problem or fix whatever's wrong. Women want to be listened to and have their feelings acknowledged not whisked away," I simplified.

As openness increased; so did intimacy and confidence in David and Sarah's ability to nurture each other. In my individual sessions with David, we reached a point where David brought up a new issue—his unhappiness with his life outside of his marriage. As is so often the case, success at one goal allows other concerns to emerge.

Thus, a second content goal was established. The goal was to help David feel better about himself other than by gaining more money or status. I decided to work toward this goal by alternating problem-solving (direct suggestion, brainstorming, discussion of alternatives, and establishing goals [S 1 and S 2]) with support (S 3) for taking risks to act differently.

I suggested to David that this goal be achieved through professional and leisure time activities in which David would gain a sense of personal satisfaction. We discussed teaching a class, offering free legal service, tutoring kids in reading, writing a book, establishing or working with political action groups on a variety of causes, supporting political candidates in local elections, writing to friends, developing a new physical skill through exercise, and many more.

The thrust of these activities was to expand David's base of satisfaction from his career to include other activities. Instead of doing the same old activities more often, David got involved in new activities that could use his current talents and interests in noncompetitive ways.

Later, I tried the S 4 style in order to help him integrate his current understanding of himself in his marriage with his understanding of himself as a man in society at large. David was uncomfortable with this latter exploration either because of his concrete nature or of his resistance to feeling vulnerable in the session. I chose not to continue the S 4 style and switched to the S 2 style with a bit of S 1 to accomplish the goal we had established, which was to help him feel better about himself in his activities outside of his marriage.

180 *Gordon M. Hart*

Working on this goal led him into more administrative activities at his law firm for which he was not compensated monetarily, but felt as if he were really adding to the stability and integrity of the firm. Perhaps his increased understanding of his relationship with Sarah and his increased emotional expression with her supported him in behaving differently with others.

CONCLUSIONS AND REFLECTIONS

ACT is based on developmental principles that suggest that counseling is a process where clients are helped to move to a different point from the one where they found themselves at the beginning of the counseling process. ACT is a system of viewing this therapeutic movement or process. The ACT model reminds counselors that the client's readiness for change and his or her need for a particular ration of support and direction should guide the counselor's actions, not the counselor's adherence to a particular theoretical orientation to therapy, such as psychodynamic, humanistic, cognitive, or behavioral.

The ACT guidelines can be conceptualized as an overlay upon a counselor's dominant theoretical orientation. Where counseling theories provide general principles regarding the acquisition of client problems and how to eliminate them, they offer little help in deciding when a client might profit from specific techniques. ACT suggests that a counselor may use any technique in a systematic or carefully chosen eclectic way so long as the client is "ready" or likely to hear or use the information offered, thus continuing or advancing the therapeutic process. In essence, ACT helps counselors know when a client might be ready for a style of intervention. The range of styles extends from telling a client what to do, think, or feel to encouraging a client to verbalize whatever thoughts or feelings the client is experiencing at the moment with little comment by the counselor.

The simple ACT classification of counseling technique as ranging from support to direction makes ACT very useful for novice or expert counselors, for a variety of client problems, and for any point in the counseling process. However, I think that the use of readiness is clearest when clients begin treatment and are at major junctions in the treatment process. In contrast, the moment-by-moment choices of the most helpful degree of support or direction in a particular counseling session are very difficult to make. Perhaps reviewing audio tapes or videotapes of sessions will increase a counselor's sensitivity to the array of verbal and nonverbal cues that guide those artistic-like decisions. Making the process more conscious is certainly aided by using the ACT framework.

Developmental Eclectic Counseling with Men **181**

ACT was a dimension operating concurrently with my developmental orientation and concern for men's issues. This added dimension guided me to either support David's feelings, thoughts, or actions or confront these aspects of him. I knew what David was going through because he was like many other men whom I had worked with and read about. I had to find a way to get him to feel, think, and act differently without making him so defensive that he would terminate treatment. ACT helped me offer David a proportion of support and direction at the beginning of treatment when David was more defensive and anxious. This differed from the proportion I used later in the treatment process. ACT assisted me in blending support and direction throughout therapy while I also made choices about the specific content David brought up and about techniques such as the use of humor, self-disclosure, and so forth.

ACT also helped me feel confident that my movement from one style to another was legitimate, assuming that I had judged David's readiness appropriately. I think that David was able to profit from my direction and support because I assessed his cognitive nature accurately at the beginning of treatment and did not press him to be more disclosing of affect than he was willing to be throughout the counseling process. Perhaps the Socratic and nonthreatening nature of my teaching style was supportive in and of itself. I suspect that the manner in which a counselor applies any of the ACT styles is important and should be examined as another dimension. As one of my colleagues stated, "Some counselors have a heavy touch and some have a light touch," which I find to be a useful start at defining one's manner of applying any counseling technique.

ACT offered guidance and direction in moving through the counseling process, which is often confusing and defies precise definition and clear interpretation. I believe that ACT helped me expand my use of styles where I otherwise might have stayed within a more narrow band. Specifically, I used the S 4 and S 1 styles more often than I might have done not knowing about ACT. ACT did not just remind me of these styles but sanctioned their use when I judged that either of them might have been effective. I believe that ACT has become part of my ongoing counseling behavior, and I am grateful to the developers for their valuable addition to the field.

182 *Gordon M. Hart*

REFERENCES

Allen, J., & Gordon, S. (1990). Creating a framework for change. In R. Meth & R. Pasick (Eds.), *Men in therapy* (pp. 131–151). New York: Guilford.

Balswick, J. (1982). Male inexpressiveness. In K. Solomon & N. Levy (Eds.), *Men in transition* (pp. 131–150). New York: Plenum.

Bateson, G. (1972). *Steps to an ecology of mind.* New York: Ballantine.

Bly, R. (1990). *Iron John.* Reading, MA: Addison-Wesley.

Cosby, B. (1986). *Fatherhood.* New York: Doubleday.

Erickson, E. (1963). *Childhood and society.* New York: Norton.

Emerson, G. (1985). *Some American men.* New York: Simon and Schuster.

Farrell, W. (1986). *Why men are the way they are.* New York: McGraw-Hill.

Fine, R. (1988). *Troubled men.* San Francisco: Jossey-Bass.

Garfinkel, P. (1985). *In a man's world.* New York: New American Library.

Gilligan, C. (1982). *In a different voice.* Cambridge, MA: Harvard University Press.

Goldberg, H. (1976). *The hazards of being male.* New York: New American Library.

Goldberg, H. (1980). *The new male.* New York: William Morrow.

Goldberg, H. (1983). *The new male female relationship.* New York: William Morrow.

Gordon, B., & Pasick, R. (1990). Changing the nature of friendships between men. In R. Meth & R. Pasick (Eds.), *Men in therapy* (pp. 261–278). New York: Guilford.

Guttman, H. (1991). Systems theory, cybernetics, and epistemology. In A. Gurman & D. Kniskern (Eds.), *Handbook of family therapy* (pp. 41–62). New York: Brunner/Mazel.

Howard, G., Nance, D., & Myers, P. (1986). Adaptive counseling and therapy: An integrative, metatheoretical approach. *The Counseling Psychologist, 14,* 363–442.

Howard, G., Nance, D., & Myers, P. (1987). *Adaptive counseling and therapy.* San Francisco: Jossey-Bass.

Ivey, A. (1986). *Developmental therapy.* San Francisco: Jossey-Bass.

Kegan, R. (1982). *The evolving self.* Cambridge, MA: Harvard University Press.

Keen, S. (1991). *Fire in the belly.* New York: Bantam Books.

Kelly, G. (1955). *The psychology of personal constructs, Vols. 1 & 2.* New York: Norton.

Kiley, D. (1983). *The Peter Pan syndrome.* New York: Dodd, Mead.

Kimmel, M., & Messner, M. (Eds.). (1989). *Men's lives.* New York: Macmillan.

Klein, E., & Erickson, D. (Eds.). (1987). *About men.* New York: Poseidon.

Kohlberg, L. (1981). *The philosophy of moral development.* San Francisco: Harper & Row.

Loevinger, J., Wessler, R., & Redmore, C. (1970). *Measuring ego development, Vols. 1 & 2.* San Francisco: Jossey-Bass.

McGill, M. (1985). *The McGill report on male intimacy.* New York: Holt.

Meth, R., & Pasick, R. (Eds.). (1990). *Men in therapy.* New York: Guilford.

Nance, D., & Myers, P. (1991). Continuing the eclectic journey. *Journal of Mental Health Counseling, 13(1),* 119–130.

Osherson, S. (1986). *Finding our fathers.* New York: Free Press.

Pasick, R., Gordon, B., & Meth, R. (1990). Helping men understand themselves. In R. Meth & R. Pasick (Eds.), *Men in therapy* (pp. 152–180). New York: Guilford.

Piaget, J. (1955). *The language and thought of the child.* New York: New American Library.

184 *Gordon M. Hart*

Rogers, C. (1977). *Carl Rogers on personal power.* New York: New American Library.

Rose, F. (1980). *Real men.* New York: Doubleday.

Scher, M., Stevens, M., Good, G., & Eichenfield, G. (Eds.). (1987). *Handbook of counseling and psychotherapy with men.* Newbury Park, CA: Sage.

Sifford, D. (1982). *Father and son.* Philadelphia: Bridgebooks.

Silverberg, R. (1986). *Psychotherapy for men.* Springfield, IL: Charles C. Thomas.

Solomon, K., & Levy, N. (Eds.). (1982). *Men in transition.* New York: Plenum.

Vaillant, G. (1977). *Adaptation to life.* Boston: Little, Brown.

Voght, G., & Stirridge, S. (1991). *Like son, like father.* New York: Plenum.

Yablonsky, L. (1990). *Fathers and sons.* New York: Gardner.

Developmental Eclectic Counseling with Men   **185**

COMMENTS

Eclectic Approach to Counseling Men

Don W. Nance

Dr. Hart's understanding of developmental issues for men allows him to help David assess and address the power-intimacy issues in his life. In the process, Dr. Hart provides multiple examples of the ACT concept of ***match and move.*** He matches David's initial definition of the problem as a rational decision about his marriage and then moves him to explore his own role in the marriage, his feelings of responsibility, and his sense of emotional isolation. Dr. Hart matches David's expectations of the therapist as expert and moves that expertise from content— what to do with his marriage?—to process—here is how you need to proceed in examining this problem. The client was addressed at the cognitive level, his more comfortable mode, before moving increasingly into the affective domain.

The matching and moving is also evident at the interactional level, within the way Dr. Hart responds. One example from the transcript is

> David angrily asserted, "But I didn't mean what Sarah perceived me to say. She inferred something that isn't true. I don't resent her for not working when we were first married."
>   I responded, "I know, David. (S 3) Right now, Sarah is pretty worried about how you feel and what you'll do. And so she may make an inference that isn't true. And if that's how Sarah feels, then that's what you have to deal with. (S 2) Of course, in the absence of any reassurance from you, she may find it tough to know what to believe. I think that you have some responsibility to clarify how you really do feel about her not working. (S 1) What do you think?" (S 2)

The sex role socialization expectations for women identified by Dr. Nickerson (Chapter 6) find their mirror image and systemic counterpart in the expectations suggested by Dr. Hart. The primary training toward power for men and intimacy or relationships for women is evident in these two chapters. Those systemic reflections are clear also in the circular marital dynamics of David and Sarah. Sarah feels needy and asks for reassurance. David feels responsible, smothered. David responds with anger. Sarah is not reassured and feels needy. In the whole process, David is not directly aware of his own needs for reassurance and intimacy and Sarah is not aware of her own power. The systemic influences in the work of Dr. Hart are evident in the pattern described above. With David and Sarah,

186   *Gordon M. Hart*

an approach was taken that parallels the flexible, adaptive approach taken by Dr. Myers (Chapter 5) regarding the configurations in which clients are seen. In the case of Suzanne and Greg, the initial contact was with a couple, with subsequent work with each individually. With David, he was the initial client. Dr. Hart also saw Sarah individually and with David. The configuration matched the focus and the tasks.

Another issue illustrated in this chapter centers on the ***initial assessment of readiness.*** It would be easy to initially appraise David and his situation with a tone of envy. "Boy, has he got it made. Great career, big bucks, bright, attractive wife, good kids, right neighborhood. I should have such problems. He's one of the worried well." Your initial appraisal of David might not have this envious tone. Yet, he is the type of client, as is Lily (Chapter 6), who would be likely to present as more ready than proves to be the case. David is intellectually bright with a well developed set of logical thought processes. It might be tempting to approach the situation with a logical pro/con weighted checklist. If that were a successful path, why is he seeking therapy? Dr. Hart saw that David's experience and skill at accessing his feelings and needs was limited, as was his willingness. Thus, teaching (S 2) took place throughout therapy to build David's readiness in the affective domain. In the case of Lily, the early parts of therapy built a sufficient relationship (S 3) so that the client became more able to disclose to the therapist (and to herself) that the problem had more and deeper dimensions. *The general rule suggested by the ACT model is to prefer erring on the side of a more positive assessment of the client.* If the readiness is lower, the lack of progress will call for moving into a more directive style. On the other hand, the client may grow to fit the more positive set of expectations. Such a pattern also has the therapist on the side of the curve nearer the goal of willing, able, and confident (R 4).

Developmental Eclectic Counseling with Men **187**

QUESTIONS

1. How are the issues of power-intimacy experienced
      in your own life experience?
      for the clients in this book?

2. How are those issues impacted by the changing roles of men and women?

3. Identify developmental tasks or learnings that you were early, on schedule (with peers), and delayed in addressing? What were the effects of each pattern?

4. How were the circular systemic patterns of communication changed in the marriage? Who changed? How was the change balanced?

5. What are your predictions about how well David's therapy would have proceeded if he had been seen by Dr. Nickerson (Chapter 6)? Dr. Myers (Chapter 5)? Dr. Robbins (Chapter 4)? Dr. Poland (Chapter 3)? Dr. Deffenbacher (Chapter 2)?
      How would you rank order the matches?
      How would the focus, the readiness, the style, and the treatment have
        been similar and/or different?

6. What would be your prediction about David's happiness if he had left the marriage to pursue his attraction to another woman? With therapy? Without therapy?

7. What was the treatment contract regarding David, Sarah, and their marriage? How clear? What about a contract to "save the marriage"?

8. What would be the signs that the readiness assessment and style of therapist behavior were not off the mark? Too high? Too low?

9. What are the next developmental challenges for David, for Sarah, and for the marriage?

10. Whose therapist was Dr. Hart? David's therapist? Sarah's therapist? The couple's therapist? How is that different or similar to Dr. Myers with Greg and Suzanne (Chapter 5)?

Chapter 8

UPDATING ACT

Don W. Nance
Wichita State University

A model or theory evolves over time. Original concepts are revised or refined; new concepts are added. The evolving nature of many of the major approaches utilized in this book is easy to identify when viewed historically. Carl Rogers retained the core of his approach while changing the label from nondirective through client-centered to person-centered. Certainly the psychodynamic approach presented here represents significant movement, in technique and duration, from the methods of earlier psychoanalysts. The evolutionary roots of the various family therapy approaches were described in the systems chapter (Chapter 5). The perspectives employed by each of us as therapists and practicing professionals evolve, develop, and change. And so it is with the ACT model. The first evolution was from a business/organizational leadership model into one with clinical application for the mental health fields. The work and perspectives of the chapter contributors call for an updating of the model. The comments and criticisms of other professional colleagues also shape aspects of the additions, deletions, and refinements of this evolving perspective. In this final chapter, ten refinements, clarifications, additions, deletions, and cautions are identified and discussed briefly.

1. Organizing vs. Integrating

In the initial writings about ACT, the terms "integrative" and "metatheoretical" were used frequently as descriptors of the model. The wisdom brought from these intervening years and the additional experience in using ACT suggest the term "organizing" may be more appropriate than "integrative" in describing ACT.

189

190   *Don W. Nance*

The model does not integrate the conceptual, theoretical frameworks into one coherent, or even incoherent, whole.

The proponents of psychodynamic, humanistic, and cognitive behavioral perspectives have not put aside their differences and all joined together under the banner of ACT. Nor has the ACT model been used to develop the correct combination of approaches for being eclectic. To the extent that the term integrative carries such implications, a correction and clarification is needed. The ACT model does help the therapist organize his or her thinking about how to proceed in therapy. The ACT model is a tool for conceptualizing how to **act** or behave therapeutically. The ACT model is an organizing template for deciding or selecting from among varying degrees of direction and support.

2. ACT—A Compatible Additive

As demonstrated throughout the book, ACT functions compatibly with most theoretical approaches. The theory is used for conceptualizing the issues/problems and the necessary tasks of treatment. The ACT model helps organize and focus the approach used. An appropriate image for the ACT model is one of linked compatibility. In combination, a theoretical conceptualization and the ACT model are more powerful than either in isolation. In fact, ACT cannot function without some initial source of problem conceptualization. The ACT model can be viewed as an additive that potentiates and enhances the effectiveness of the conceptualization and treatment processes. Like another three-letter additive, STP, which purports to make engines run smoother, faster, and longer, ACT helps therapists be more focused, more flexible, and more effective in the course of treatment.

To some it may seem like a comedown to go from an integrative, meta-theoretical model to the relative of an engine additive. To me, it more accurately describes the important contribution of ACT and emphasizes ACT's compatibility with theoretical approaches. With the role and function of ACT more clearly established, let's turn to some insights about how the model functions in outpatient psychotherapy by focusing on ACT therapist styles.

3. Style 1—In the Structure vs. the Interaction

In Chapter 1, I indicated that Style 1 would be relatively absent from the cases because the clients presented were voluntary, self-referred, and functional for outpatient treatment. To an extent, that proved to be true on the verbal, interactive level as reflected in the verbatims. It became clear, at least to me, in reviewing the process of treatment, that Style 1 is alive and well in these cases. In the form of clinical work presented, Style 1 operates more in how the parameters, limits, and structure of therapy are set than in the verbal interactions between therapist and client. The nonnegotiable limits of the treatment process are very clear in the brief psychodynamic approach—12 sessions to address the central issue.

In other instances, the therapist experienced a need to change how therapy was being conducted. Most frequently, the therapist analyzed the situation, decided on the change, and told the client. For example, Eileen Nickerson may have said, "Lily, this isn't working. We need to meet more frequently, more intensively to focus on these childhood images and feelings." Pennie Myers communicated, "Suzanne and Greg, it's clear to me (and possibly to you) that some of the problems in this relationship have little to do with the relationship. Let's add individual sessions and do both individual and couples counseling." Will Poland shifted the focus of the therapy session by saying, "Kevin, focus on your need to appear together and your reluctance to really open up." In each instance, the fundamental communication was very structured and directive. The therapist was willing to discuss the client's reaction, resistance, or ambivalence, but little attempt was made to sell (S 2) the client on the change or the limit.

4. Style 2—Teach Them to Fish

The effectiveness of Style 2 therapist behavior is demonstrated throughout the therapy presented. The therapist has knowledge, information, and expertise about the process and/or the content of treatment. The therapist seeks to transfer that knowledge, information and perspective to the client. Once the client has learned what is being taught, the client can apply those perspectives and skills with little direction from the therapist. The teaching can take place very actively and directly about the content of the problem as in the cognitive behavioral approach. At other times, the teaching is less focused on content as in the Gestalt methods used to enhance and expand awareness. The client is taught a process that can be applied to a range of content issues. The one pattern that is likely to be ineffective exists when the content and the process are at odds.

T: *As we enter this phase of therapy, the goal is to reduce your dependency on me, become more independent* (content). *Therefore, we need to decrease the frequency of our therapy sessions* (process).

In the cases presented, clients learned new information (David, Marie), new skills (Bill, Marie), a new way of behaving and/or a different way to view issues (Greg, Susan). The client may confront and examine an internal conflict (Kevin)

192   *Don W. Nance*

or a central affective theme (Curtis). The teaching and therefore the learning may focus on the cognitive, affective, behavioral, or interpersonal domains.

5. Style 3—Home Base for the Outpatient Therapist

The high support and low direction of Style 3 can be considered a home base in most approaches used in an outpatient context. The active listening and attending behaviors provide an effective means of building a therapeutic relationship while gaining information about the client. Since these are frequently the initial tasks in therapy, the style matches well. Not coincidentally, Style 3 matches the preponderance of initial training in counseling methods. Thus, therapists are likely to be very ready to engage in this style.

Behaving in a highly supportive manner with low amounts of directive behavior is consistent with the first rule of medicine and health care—Do no harm. It seems a safe, low risk stance to take. With active listening as a major component of this style, it is also the place to return to if the therapist needs to clarify information, goals, or readiness. A frequent sequence for a therapy session involves asking (Style 3) the client about progress on issues and reinforcing that progress. A focus for the new work of the session is identified, and the therapist is likely to engage in more Style 2 behaviors in this phase of the session. If confrontation is involved, so may be Style 1. Most therapists are taught, "Don't confront at the end of the session. Give yourself and the client time to deal with the confrontation." Once the new work of the session is completed, the therapist supports the new insights, the plans made, etc. (Style 2 to Style 3). The session ends, and the client has the responsibility for utilizing the results of the therapy during the week (Style 4). This sequence matches well with the ACT principle of moving from style to style one step at a time.

6. Style 4—What Doesn't Need Attention

Style 4 is noticeable when a task of therapy, either content or process, receives less and less therapeutic attention. For example, when the client's questions and issues about trust are neither the content of therapy nor reflected in a reluctance to disclose, the task of establishing trust in the relationship is accomplished. So, in a sense, the presence of Style 4 in the therapy relationship is signaled by the absence of activity on the issue because the client is able, willing, and confident.

Style 4 behaviors are also appropriate when the issue is not resolved but the client is very able to do what is needed. When a client is actively grieving a loss, if the tears are flowing and the sobbing intense, the best stance is Style 4. The therapist says little or nothing to the client who is needing to grieve, is able to experience the loss, and is willing to express the feelings. The support is non-verbal, as is the unspoken permission to let the feelings flow.

Readiness.   The concept of readiness, its dimensions and methods of assessment, continues to evolve in several ways. One major addition from the original Situational Leadership model was made in the first presentation of ACT with the addition of confidence as a component of readiness. Confidence, which can be viewed as the client's assessment of ability and risk, may be more important in therapy and mental health considerations than in business and organizational contexts. The support of the therapeutic relationship allows the client to utilize and extend affective, behavioral, and interpersonal skills in ways too risky to consider without the support. New additions and corrections related to readiness have emerged from the ideas presented in this book.

7. Assessing Client Readiness—Just Ask

In the initial presentations of ACT, a somewhat elaborate system was proposed for assessing readiness. Potential sources of direction and support were identified and assessed. That process, akin to a full psychological assessment battery, may still be useful in some instances. Much of the time the process can be reduced to a very simple procedure—**ask the client.** Once the goals are identified and the path or tasks determined, the questions(from therapist to client) are: "How ready are you to do the task(s)? What needs to happen to increase your readiness?" The client and therapist then work together to remove obstacles to the client becoming willing, able, and confident.

8. Redefining the Tasks, Reassessing Readiness

In a couple of cases presented, Bill and Curtis, the initial conceptualization of the problem remained the same throughout treatment. The process also was carried out as originally planned. In the brief psychodynamic model, considerable attention is given to selecting the right clients and defining the right central issue. Once the process starts it is likely to remain on track. Attempts to prolong the process or shift the task are interpreted and confronted. While not demonstrated in the case presented, it is assumed that if it became clear that the treatment was not a fit and was not working, e.g., client was becoming delusional, an alternative plan would be implemented.

In several other instances, the tasks, the client's readiness, and the treatment plan were modified in the course of treatment. In some instances the client seemed more functional, together, and ready in the initial assessment than proved to be the

194 *Don W. Nance*

case as therapy unfolded. Thus, readiness needed to be reassessed. In other instances, new tasks emerged in the course of treatment. The problems were redefined. Blocks to the process needed to be identified and addressed. Many times that reassessment is a mutual process emerging out of treatment, e.g., uncovering previously repressed material. In other instances the reassessment is prompted by a lack of progress or satisfaction experienced by the therapist, client, or both. In general, don't just try more of the same if the treatment is not working. Adapt the form of treatment, adapt the tasks, adapt therapist style to gain information and move the process. Blaming the client or the therapist when treatment is not working only misdirects energy better spent on reassessment, redefinition, and renegotiation.

9. Therapist Readiness

The concept of therapist readiness is an important addition to the ACT model. As with much of the ACT model, the concept describes and explains already existing aspects of therapy. As the therapist (and the client) are determining the degree of willingness, ability, and confidence the client has toward a therapeutic task, so too is the therapist's readiness assessed.

The assessment may be intentional, overt, and systematic, or it may be unmentioned. The therapist and the client may conduct the assessment in concert with each other or in isolation. High therapist readiness as experienced by the client is likely to impact the client's own readiness. Therapy involves trust. When the client believes that the therapist is willing to help, able to help, and has confidence in the therapeutic value of the process and the client, willingness increases, confidences improves, and abilities are exercised. The circular, systemic elements of this process are important to remember.

The combination of willingness, ability, and confidence proposed for client readiness also exist for therapist readiness (TR). Each combination suggests a course of action for the therapist.

TR 4—Willing, able, and confident
   Highest probability for successful therapy
   Positive impact on client readiness

TR 3—Willing, newly or mostly able, unconfident
   Action option:
   Reinforce abilities and/or confidence via reading, peer consultation, expert
      consultation, or supervision (new area of competence).

Updating ACT **195**

TR 2—Willing, unable, unconfident
Action options:
Organize training experiences or observation.
Supervised practice with feedback (client feedback).
Balance it with current areas of expertise.
Refer to specialist.

TR 1—Unable, unwilling, unconfident
Lowest probability of success
Action options:
Tell client what you can and would do.
If frequent, transfer and refer yourself to a new position, a new therapist, a new career.

An overconfident combination in which confidence exceeds ability is conceivable if the therapist is not open to feedback and an examination of the result. If not corrected, then the therapist is at the least in over his or her head and at the most unethically incompetent. For the regressive cycle, which essentially involves reductions in willingness, the therapist can examine the sources of the unwillingness. Is counter-transference the issue? Has a disproportionate degree of responsibility been assumed or transferred to the therapist? Does the task need to be reassessed and redefined? These issues and options are likely to be relevant if the change is specific to one client. If the unwillingness is more general, then the issues are more likely to require a broader professional/personal inventory.

What is bothering me about clients?
My functioning as a therapist?
My professional responsibilities?
My work setting?
My balance of work-play, professional-personal, etc.?
What do I need to change?
How shall I go about accomplishing those changes?
What direction and support will I need in the process?
How will I get the necessary direction and support?

The concept of therapist readiness joins other ACT concepts that are applicable at the interactive level of a singular moment in therapy through individual case applications. Therapist readiness also applies to the level of professional identity and directions for professional growth. It is at these latter levels that I want to discuss the final item for this update on ACT.

196   *Don W. Nance*

10. Range in Style/Range in Content: Generalist vs. Specialist and Individual vs. Team

The ACT model suggests the necessity to operate from a range of styles as a therapist. All therapists have natural preferences—their comfort zones. All therapists have had more training, reinforcement, and opportunity for learning about particular content areas and/or client characteristics. Some of these content areas are identified by others and/or by practitioners as being specialities—alcohol, drugs, marriage and family, eating disorders. Other specialities are identified by methodology—biofeedback, hypnosis, and neuropsychological assessment. Some therapists have a strong theoretical allegiance to one theory and its methods. Others try to select the theories and the methods that seem to fit the situation. The therapist behaviors and clinical examples presented in this book illustrate that a range of approaches along these dimensions can be and are effective. Dr. Nickerson used an array of content expertise and therapist styles in her therapy. Dr. Robbins used a range of styles within a contained therapeutic process. Dr. Poland relied on his humanistic philosophy and Gestalt methods in working with Kevin. Both Robbins and Poland demonstrated expertise with the methods used. Dr. Deffenbacher operated from both content expertise about anger and an extensive knowledge of behavioral methods. Dr. Hart and Dr. Myers have specialized expertise with the issues presented and drew from a wide range of methods.

Every reader has his or her own comfort zones, preferred styles, theoretical orientations, content knowledge, and experience with various methods. With every client, you are therefore matching your content and process skills with the client's issues and readiness. What are your professional goals at this point in your career? Are you seeking out experiences that expand your range? Increasing your skills as a generalist? Are you focusing or specializing your efforts on particular methods, client types, and clinical issues? Do other professionals refer to you based on specialized expertise? Are such referrals your goal?

Mental health fields need both the generalist and the specialist, just as the broader health field needs primary care physicians and specialists. The traditional wisdom in most health professionals is to obtain the range required to be a competent generalist. In ACT terms, that translates into ranging from your preferred styles so that you can confront (S 1), or back off (S 4), as well as teach (S 2), and support (S 3).

The final aspect of this issue of range centers on the value of a team. If we all have strengths and gaps in our skills, our knowledge, our willingness, and our confidence, then a team approach has merit. Treatment teams frequently are utilized in inpatient and institutional settings. The ACT model would suggest that effective inpatient teams would have balance among not only the professional fields involved (M.D., Ph.D., R.N., L.C.S.W., CMHC, P.T., R.T., O.T., F.T.) but also cover the full range of ACT styles. Attention should be paid to utilizing the strengths of team members. Outpatient "teams" can be developed within an agency or setting. Even a solo private practitioner can utilize a team by developing a referral and consultation network.

Effective teams should not be a set of clones—all the same in orientation, skills, style, range, demographics, and preferences. Rather, the team brings expertise, skills, and support to assist the therapist and the client. With a team no one has to try to know it all or do it all. Rather, you know yourself and your therapist readiness elements. You utilize your abilities while developing your range and/or your specialization. You refer, consult, teach, learn, supervise, and receive supervision. In the process, you develop professionally and personally.

What an appropriate way to end this book, focusing on the concept of a team. I can say with certainty that this book would not have been possible without this team of contributing authors. I don't believe any one person could have written from the array of perspectives and in as many unique styles to illustrate the utility of the ACT model. I thank the team and trust at this point, in the process of assimilating this book, you join in that thanks.

INDEX

Ability, of client, 5, 23, 25–26
ACT:
  central tenet, 2
  as an organizing model, 189–190
  overview, 3–7
  role in specific therapeutic orientations, 3–4, 190
  use in team therapy, 196–197
ACT Therapist Style Inventory, 57
Adaptive Counseling and Therapy Model (*see* ACT)
Adjustment disorder, 88–89
Anger:
  case study, 26–47
  questionnaires, 32–33
  reduction as a therapeutic task, 44–45
Anger Inventory, 32
Anger Situation and Symptom (questionnaire), 32
Anxiety, of client, 89

Behavior in relationships, 170–172
Behavior, of therapist, 1–4, 115–116, 153, 154

dimensions, 3, *illus.* 4, *illus.* 6, *illus.* 8
  in psychodynamic counseling, 85, 87, 99, 101
  use in CBT case study, 31–32
flexibility, 126, 186
  in humanistic psychotherapy, 56, 59
  in psychodynamic counseling, 83–84, 99, 101
  range, 154
Behavioral family therapy, 109
Behavioral modification program, 4
Bracketing therapy, 65, 77, 80, 102

CBT:
  case study, 26–47
  characteristics of, 19–22
  integrated with ACT, 22–26, 48, 51–52
  use of teaching style, 191
Central issues (psychodynamic counseling), 83–87, 99, 101
  case study, 89, 90, 92

199

200 *Index*

Classical analysis, 102
Client anxiety, 84
Client awareness, 164, 169, 174
  goal of humanistic psychotherapy,
    57–59, 61, 79
    case study, 68, 80
Client-centered approach, 4, 79, 189
Client readiness:
  CBT and:
    assessment in case study, 29–31,
      35, 39–40, 45
    comparison with ACT, 23–24
    need for assessment, 25–26, 48
  concept in ACT, 4–7, *illus.* 6,
    illus. 8
  in eclectic counseling of men, 180
    case study, 166, 172–174
  in eclectic counseling of women,
    147–149, 153
    case study, 142, 143, 145
  humanistic psychotherapy and, 57
    case study, 65, 76–77
    Gestalt concept of polarities,
      59–60
  initial assessment, 186
  in psychodynamic counseling, 86,
    87, 99, 101
    case study, 89–90
  reassessment, 193–194
  sequence of therapeutic tasks and,
    51
  in systems theory, 107–108, 122
    case study, 110, 117, 121–122
Client resistance:
  to central issue, 85, 92, 99
  in eclectic counseling of men, 164
  in eclectic counseling of women,
    142
  from humanistic psychotherapy
    viewpoint, 58, 60
  (*See also* Willingness, of client)
Client, role of, 57, 89

Client selection, 83, 84, 101, 193
  criteria, 86
Cognitive Behavior Therapy (*see*
  CBT)
Cognitive behavioral methods, 4
Cognitive restructuring, 21
  case study, 38, 45
Communication skills training, 21,
  109, 127
Confidence, of client, 5, 23, 25–26
Conflict:
  as a central issue, 84–85, 98
    case study, 89
  goal of humanistic psychotherapy,
    79
Confrontation, 4, 25, 38
Coping capacity, 23
Counter-transference, 148, 195
Covert behavioral processes, 20

Delegating (style), 3, *illus.* 4, 57, 192
  in eclectic counseling of women,
    139
  in Gestalt therapy, 62
  in psychodynamic counseling, 87,
    95
Developmental approach to therapy,
    153, 157
  and ACT, 180, 181
Developmental cycle, 5, *illus.* 6, 7,
    23
Diary keeping, 143
Direction, dimension of behavior, 3,
    illus. 4
  in humanistic Gestalt therapy, 79,
    80
Dream/memory recall, 143
Dysfunctional cognition, 25, 37–39,
    51–52
Dysfunctional contingencies, 46–47

Eclectic approach to counseling, 87
   of men, 158
      developmental issues, 159–161,
         174
      integrated with ACT, 158, 161,
         172, 180–181
   of women, 127, 129–131
      case studies, 131–146
      developmental framework,
         130
      integrated with ACT, 137, 144,
         147–150
Ego resources, 83
Emotional conflict, 89
Empty chair technique, 75–76, 79,
   143
Experiential family therapy, 106,
   108
Experiments, 20–21, 59, 61, 68
Expert power of therapist, 173, 191

Family of origin, 108, 127, 130
   case study, 110–112, 115–117, 119,
      126
Family therapy (*see* Systems theory)
Feminist therapists, 130, 137, 153
Follow-up, 98
Free association, 3, 102, 143

Gender roles, 130, 146–147, 160,
   185
Gestalt age regression, 143
Guided fantasy, 143–144
Guilt, 112–114, 121, 176

Human development, 130, 131, 148
   (*See also* Developmental approach
      to therapy)
Human Potential Movement, 57

Humanistic psychotherapy:
   case study, 62–76
   initial phase of therapeutic process,
      58
   integrated with ACT, 57–60, 62,
      76–77, 79–81
   styles, of therapist behavior, 57
   underlying philosophy, 57–59
   use of teaching style, 191
Humor:
   use in therapy, 51–52, 181
   used in CBT case study, 38–40,
      43–44
Hypothesis formulation, 20, 89

Initial interview, 58–59, 84
Internal conflict (case study), 62–76
Internal Process Recall, 51
Intervention strategies, 172
   of CBT, 21–26
      case study, 34–35, 38–39, 45–47
      goals in case study, 30, 33, 44
      interface with ACT, 48
   in eclectic counseling of women,
      148–149
      case studies, 134, 137, 143,
         144
   in Gestalt approach, 61, 77
   in systems theory, 106, 107, 109–
      110, 122
      case study, 113
Intervention, timing of, 51
   in CBT, 25
      case study, 47, 48
Intimacy, men's search for, 160–161,
   177, 185

Learning model of CBT, 19–20, 23,
   29
Length of treatment, 87

202 *Index*

Limiting therapy (*see* Bracketing therapy)

Maintenance, 22, 23, 47–48
Mann, James (*see* Psychodynamic counseling)
Marital therapy (*see* Systems theory)
Match and move:
ACT concept, 6–7, *illus.* 8, 101, 158, 185
CBT applications, 23, 25, 30, 48
case study, 36–37, 40–44, 48
in eclectic counseling of men, 158, 185
Maturation crises, 86
Men, therapy of, 157–159
case study, 162–180
issues facing adult men, 159–161, 172
use of ACT, 181, 185
MMPI (Minnesota Multiphasic Personality Inventory), 21, 32
Mother-daughter relationships, 135–136
Motivation, 23, 25–26

Negative reinforcement, 3
Negative self-image, of client, 84
Negative transference, 85, 94

Overt behavioral processes, 20

Panic disorder, 88
Personal science, 20–21
(*See also* Self-exploration)
Phases of therapy:
in family therapy, 110

in psychodynamic counseling, 84, 89–97
use of ACT during different phases, 149, 181, 192
Phenomenological world, 57
Polarity struggle:
Gestalt concept, 59–60
case study, 71–73, 74
Positive reinforcement, 3
Power, men's search for, 159–161, 185
Psychoanalytical family therapy, 107
Psychodynamic counseling, 130, 189
case study, 87–98
first phase, 89–92
integration with ACT, 84–87, 98, 101–102
last phase, 95–97
Mann, James, model of, 84–87, 98–99
middle phase, 92–95
principles of, 83–86
time-limited models, 83

Reflective listening, 79
Regressive cycle:
of client readiness, 5, *illus.* 6, 7
of therapist readiness, 195
Rehearsal, 21–23
case study, 38, 39, 45–47
Relapse prevention, 22, 23, 47–48
Relaxation intervention, 21, 34–37, 45
Repressed emotional conflict, 83
Rogers, Carl, 56, 79, 189
Role, of therapist, 127

Scene visualization, 35
Self-concept, 130, 131

Self-dialogue, 74–76
Self-direction, by client, 23, 25, 95, 114–116
Self-efficacy, of client, 23, 25–26
Self-esteem, 117, 130
Self-exploration, 58, 59, 80
  CBT intervention strategy, 20, 21
Self-instructional training, 34, 39, 45, 47
Self-monitoring:
  as an assessment strategy, 21, 28, 30–32
  as intervention, 34, 38
Separation-individuation, 84, 86, 87, 92
Sequence of therapeutic tasks
  based on ACT concepts, 51
  in psychodynamic counseling, 85–86, 99, 101
  shifts in style, 192
Situational leadership theory, 22, 193
Socratic exploration:
  use in CBT, 20–21, 24, 25
    case study, 38
  use in eclectic counseling of men, 181
Strategic family therapy, 106, 109
Structural family therapy, 106, 108
Styles, of therapist's behavior:
  of ACT, 3, *illus.* 4, 6–7, 190–194
  in CBT, 23, 25,
    case study, 32, 35, 40, 45
  in eclectic counseling of men, 158, 180
    case study, 167–179
  in eclectic counseling of women, 147–149, 153
    case studies, 133–134, 139, 143–145
  in humanistic psychotherapy, 57, 59, 62

case study, 67–68, 70, 71, 73
  in psychodynamic counseling, 85, 87, 99
  range of styles, 196
  and schools of family therapy, 107–109, 122, 126
  shifts in style, 144, 181, 192
  in systems theory case study, 111–116, 118, 120, 121
Support, dimension of behavior, 3, *illus.* 4
Supporting (style), 3, *illus.* 4, 192
  in eclectic counseling of men, 158
  in humanistic psychotherapy, 57
    case study, 67, 71, 73
  in psychodynamic counseling, 85–87, 101
    case study, 90
Systems theory, 105–109, 122, 126–127, 185–186
  case study, 110–122
  family therapy, 105–107
    schools of thought, 106–109, 122, 126
  integration with ACT, 106–110, 122, 126

Teaching (style), 3, *illus.* 4, 191
  in CBT case study, 35
  in eclectic counseling of men, 158, 166, 186
  in family therapy, 109, 110
  in humanistic psychotherapy, 57, 62
    case study, 67
  in psychodynamic counseling, 85, 87, 89
Telling (style), 3, *illus.* 4, 24, 190–191
  in CBT case study, 35
  in psychodynamic counseling, 87

204 *Index*

Termination process, 110, 139
 during CBT, 22
 of psychodynamic counseling, 80, 87
  case study, 95–98
Therapeutic goals:
 in eclectic counseling of men, 158, 161, 185
  content goals, 172–174, 179
  process goals, 166–172
 in eclectic counseling of women, 148
 in family therapy, 107–108
 in humanistic psychotherapy, 58, 62, 79
 in psychodynamic counseling, 85, 89
Therapeutic impasses, 25–26, 149
Therapeutic mechanisms, 5–6
Therapeutic strategies:
 circular process, 127
 in eclectic counseling of women, 143, 145, 148
 in humanistic psychotherapy, 62
 readiness assessment in CBT, 24–26
 in systems theory, 105, 122
 of time-limited psychodynamic counseling, 83
 use of ACT in selection, 166
Therapeutic tasks:
 assessment, 21, 24–26
 and behavior of therapist, 3, 51
 of CBT, 19–22
  case study 28–30, 32–33
 and client readiness, *illus.* 6
 in eclectic counseling of men, 172
  case study, 164, 177

in eclectic counseling of women, 153
 case studies, 133–135, 142, 145
in humanistic psychotherapy, 58, 61, 74, 80
in psychodynamic counseling, 84, 90, 101
reassessment, 193–195
in systems theory, 106, 126
Therapist-client relationship:
 collaborative relationship of CBT, 20, 21, 24
  comparison with ACT, 24
  as task in case study, 30, 32
 in eclectic counseling of men, 166–167, 173
 in eclectic counseling of women, 130, 154
  case studies, 139, 143, 146
 in humanistic psychotherapy, 60–61
 in psychodynamic counseling, 85, 87, 93, 95
 in systems theory, 106–110
 use of supportive style, 192
Therapist readiness, 60–61, 79–80, 154, 186
 ACT concept, 194–195
 case study, 65, 76–77
Therapy content vs. process, 168, 172, 185, 191
 ACT and CBT, 24
 in humanist psychotherapy, 57, 79–81
Time-bound self-image, 85
Time-limited treatment, 83–85, 99
Time-out, 35, 39, 45
Trait Anger Scale and Anger Expression Scale, 32

Transfer, 22, 23, 45
Transference, 83, 99, 101
    analysis, 108
    case study, 93–94
    negative, 85, 94
Transgenerational family therapy,
    106–108

Vulnerability of client, 64–65, 68–70, 73

Willingness of client, 5, 23, 113
Women, therapy of, 129–131, 137,
    149–150, 153
    case studies, 131–146

ABOUT THE AUTHOR

Dr. Don W. Nance is Director of Counseling and Testing at Wichita State University, Wichita, Kansas. He received a B.A. degree from the University of Redlands in California, and his M.A. and Ph.D. from the University of Iowa in Counseling Psychology.

208 *About the Author*

After completing his doctoral degree, he accepted a position in the Counseling Center at Wichita State because it offered responsibility, freedom, and opportunities for varied involvements. He became director in 1974 and pioneered the fee for service model for counseling centers. He is responsible for the Center's involvement in the Wichita Collaborative Psychology Internship Program, one of the oldest collaborative internships with APA approval.

A commitment to training and supervision is one of the major themes of his professional career. Training involvements have taken many forms including teaching in counselor education, psychology, and administration programs; training faculty in the improvement of teaching, desegregation programs in schools, and family crisis intervention with police; training in communication skills for military supervisors; training of health care professionals; and providing consultation and training to business and industry. His teaching and presenting skills have been recognized through WSU's Excellence in Teaching Award.

Professional and personal collaboration with Dr. Pennie Myers, his colleague and spouse, has resulted in publications, *The Upset Book* and a series of field specific workbooks, that translate sound psychological concepts and methods into everyday language. As a presenting team, Nance and Myers have trained thousands of people across North America.

Active in both the American Counseling Association and the American Psychological Association, Don has been involved in the development and implementation of ethical codes, the development of ACES curriculum guide for supervision, plus numerous professional workshops and programs.

A practicing therapist for his entire career, Nance drew on his own clinical and supervisory experience to develop an organized framework to the diverse clinical situations encountered by counselors and therapists—hence, the ACT model.

The promise of varied opportunities that motivated Nance's original professional choices continues to be fulfilled by his ongoing development as a therapist, teacher, administrator, trainer, supervisor, consultant, presenter, and author.